HARVARD BUSINESS
SCHOOL

Career Guide

finance

Edited by
Christopher D. Wallis
Harvard Business School
Class of 1998

1998

In association with the
Harvard Business School
Finance Club

ISBN 0-87584-828-1
ISSN 0899-7098

Contents

Profiled Companies

Preface

Welcome to the sixth edition of the *Harvard Business School Finance Club Career Guide!* If you are new to this book, our hope is that you find it a comprehensive finance career research source. If you have used prior editions, you will find a more updated version here that includes profiles of new companies and locations of their Web pages related to finance. This book's most unique and most helpful feature for business school students and alumni heading into the job search is the company profile section. The profiles include investment and commercial banks, Fortune 500 companies, and other international and regional firms. They have been compiled in a standardized format so that information on each company is readily accessible and may be easily compared to that on its peers.

You will also find articles written specifically for this guide by distinguished Harvard Business School professors as well as interviews with HBS alumni concerning their careers in finance. A glossary of finance terms and, thanks to Carol Elsen and Sue Marsh at Baker Library, listings of additional finance career sources also await you.

In an effort to leverage the vast intellectual resources of the Harvard Business School, the guide provides insights from Professors Samuel L. Hayes III and Joshua Lerner. Their introduction has been updated for the sixth edition and reflects the latest thinking on careers in finance. To both Professor Hayes and Professor Lerner we offer many thanks. Additionally, HBS alumni Vikram Gandhi, Joel Peterson, and Girish Nadkarni devoted time to the guide in documenting each of their unique experiences in the field of finance. To them we are also grateful.

A debt of gratitude is also owed to Claudia Bruce of HBS Publishing for her continuing support and assistance to the Finance Club and to the publication of the sixth edition. Finally, we thank the many profiled firms for their time and energy in helping prepare this guide.

We hope that you will find this guide a useful tool while conducting your research of the world of finance. Best of luck in your job search!

CHRISTOPHER D. WALLIS, 1998

Introduction

Samuel L. Hayes III
Jacob H. Schiff Professor of Investment Banking
Harvard Business School

Joshua Lerner
Associate Professor
Harvard Business School

Business school faculty have many occasions to counsel students gearing up for the post-MBA job market. It is, to be sure, a time of high expectations. At the same time, the post-MBA job search can be daunting, even for those who have been through a search before.

Identifying and landing a job in the field of finance presents many of the same challenges of other functional areas: identifying promising potential employers, evaluating and discriminating among various job possibilities, assessing the long-term potential of a particular entry-level job, and so forth. At the same time, a finance job search raises some special considerations. This book will give you a head start in the investigatory "due diligence" effort we all go through in the course of a job campaign.

The word *financial* in a job description usually reveals very little about the work content. One business school student took a summer job between the first and second years of his MBA program that seemed to promise opportunities for financial analysis within a large corporation. He had in mind the sort of strategic decision-making process that had dominated his first-year finance course. The actual job content turned out to be bread-and-butter accounting. Thankfully, the job was only temporary; he gamely did the work as competently as possible and then gracefully withdrew at the end of the summer.

Although it is difficult to categorize financial jobs, they can be broken down into those that take place within a corporate organization and those whose setting is a particular financial institution. The structure of finance functions within a corporation is easier to articulate. Typically, there is a chief financial officer (CFO) under whom internal financial (controllership) and external financial (treasurer) activities are grouped. In many companies, strategic and long-range planning have considerable finance content and may also report to the CFO, if only on a dotted-line basis.

Jobs concerned with the collection, measurement, and evaluation of financial data generated from internal operations are typically placed under the controller's supervision. In these jobs, training in accounting (and possibly auditing) is very useful. An organization's relations with financial markets and institutions are often grouped under the supervision of the treasurer. These include management of bank lines and other credit facilities to ensure that the company can pay its bills in a timely fashion, communication with shareholders, and oversight of offshore financing arrangements. (The increasing frequency of foreign activities reflects the growing integration of national economies into a large, interdependent global market.) Evaluation of external acquisitions, or the sale of parts of the company's own operations, are often grouped under the treasurer's umbrella or within a separate office.

Most ambitious MBA graduates are eager to be at the heart of the real action in a company. In many ways, this is what you have been trained for. If you are of this disposition, it is important to determine the center of financial action within a prospective company.

Many graduating MBAs are immediately attracted to the treasury function and to strategic financial planning. These seem glamorous and represent activities that are closely related to the newly minted MBAs' training. In some companies, primarily those serving essentially as holding companies for a number of decentralized operating units, the financial focus may be on the company's relations with external capital markets. But despite the glitz associated with strategic planning and the treasurer's contacts with Wall Street and other external organizations, the real guts of the financial function for most firms—the site of the real action—is internal control.

Turning to financial vendors—commercial banks, investment banks, insurance companies, and money management firms—the array of job possibilities is extremely broad:

- Corporate finance
- Investment analysis
- Portfolio management
- Trading
- Private equity investing
- Institutional and retail sales
- "Financial engineering," or the application of quantitative methods to the construction of financial products
- General management

Corporate finance in the context of a financial vendor typically involves the basket of products, services, and counsel marketed to nonfinancial companies. This is an elastic definition. For investment banks, it encompasses the structuring and issuance of new securities to the public. For finance companies, such as GE Credit, corporate finance has a different meaning. GE Credit does not itself underwrite securities but does offer a broad variety of services to corporate customers, including secured financing and consulting on corporate financial strategy.

Investment analysis is usually associated with the role of the analyst of publicly traded securities. Typically focusing on only one category of securities (e.g., the auto industry, "junk" bonds), analysts are employed by many different vendors. These may be on either the buy side (investment management firms or other institutional investors such as insurance companies and pension managers) or the sell side (securities firms and commercial banks). Sell-side analysts typically focus on products that they and their institutional sales colleagues think can be sold to portfolio managers responsible for the investment of large pools of savings. Buy-side analysts generally play the role of thoughtful skeptics in evaluating ideas generated by vendor firms.

Portfolio managers are often veteran security analysts, although some vendors hire young people for direct assignment as assistants to portfolio managers. Some portfolio managers describe their field as the place "where the buck stops." While the analyst recommends actions on certain securities, the portfolio manager makes the ultimate decisions and is evaluated on the consequences.

If portfolio managers are under the gun to demonstrate quarter-by-quarter quality performance, traders of particular categories of stocks, bonds, and derivatives live minute-by-minute. The consequences of their judgments are usually priced out each day for everyone to see. This is an exciting, "white-knuckle" business that attracts certain types of personalities.

At the opposite extreme are private equity investors. Their investments in venture capital and leveraged buy-out deals can take years to mature to the point of being harvested, typically through the sale of stock to the public. Many MBAs are attracted to such private equity investing, which combines the satisfaction of building companies during their formative years with the potential for impressive capital gains. Unfortunately, the number of job openings each year in this area is modest, typically under 100 nationwide. Those interested in a career in private equity investing should bear in mind the stern odds against them and remember that many of the most successful investors first had experience as operating managers or in other financial sectors.

Institutional sales people work closely with traders and security analysts and create a bridge between them and the big institutions whose investment activities dominate modern public markets. They sell products that their firms have either developed or acquired for resale, and they must be conversant with the details of these products and how they serve the objectives of their institutional customers. The days of the "gentleman bond salesman" immortalized by F. Scott Fitzgerald are long gone. This is a demanding business—and the rewards for success are extraordinary.

Retail securities sales involves the marketing of stocks, bonds, and other financial products to individual investors. These investors are, on the average, likely to be less sophisticated than institutional investors and therefore are dependent on their brokers for more comprehensive counsel. Building a retail customer base takes time, but these customers tend to be loyal to their individual brokers and often follow them if they move from one brokerage house to another in search of a more lucrative deal or better support. Retail brokerage is one of the last bastions of relationship-based financial business.

Derivative securities—the disaggregation and reconstruction of securities with features specifically tailored to particular types of investors or issues—have become big business for many financial vendors and their clients. For vendors possessing the proprietary quantitative techniques used to construct and price out these hybrid securities, derivatives have been very profitable although fraught with risk.

Jobs focusing on the *management* of financial service firms have gotten much more attention in recent years. More than a decade of acquisitions, mergers, and internally generated growth has made these firms larger and more complex; they no longer lend themselves to the informal managerial oversight long characteristic of the business. Back-office jobs are a case in point. After a variety of securities vendors became overloaded by the trading volume in the late 1960s and 1970s, the firms' leadership realized that the fate of their organizations was tied to their ability to get their internal paperwork and controls better organized. This change has raised the stature of professionals opting for internal management careers. Similarly, commercial banks discovered that a secret to successful expansion and profitability in the contemporary marketplace lies in the management of their own information systems. John Reed, CEO of Citibank, owes his leadership post, at least in part, to his successful mastery of this area.

It should be cautioned, however, that many general managers of financial service organizations have come up through the ranks as specialists in a product or service rather than through an initial career entry into the vendor's internal management structure. Many of these organizations still hold the highest places of honor for top business getters and revenue producers. However, an appreciation for professional management skills is gradually developing.

Students seeking to enter the finance profession must grapple with several challenging decisions. A crucial issue is whether finance is the right occupation. A finance career almost invariably involves long hours, stress, and often great uncertainty. If the field itself does not genuinely excite you or stimulate your curiosity, it is unlikely to be a happy choice, no matter how generous the compensation.

The next question is the appropriate subfields of finance on which to focus the job search. The demands of various subfields vary considerably. Some areas, such as trading and selling complex derivative securities, place a premium on quantitative abilities. In others, such as retail brokerage, the ability to communicate clearly and persuasively is paramount. The time demands of these positions also vary considerably. For instance, while corporate finance demands a considerable amount of time—to the point of serious conflicts between family and work—trading positions have traditionally been less demanding from an hours-per-week perspective.

A third decision relates to the institutions on which to focus job-searching efforts. Each organization has a distinctive personality. Finding a good match between an employer's personality and your own is an important prerequisite to long-run success. The descriptions contained in this book and the promotional material you will receive during the interviewing process should provide some indication of these firm-by-firm differences. Important insights can also be gathered through conversations with peers who have worked or are currently working for these organizations. But ultimately it is very difficult for others to point you toward the best match; it is a personal choice and an issue to which you should be particularly sensitive during the interviewing process.

Concerning the job search itself, several thoughts may be helpful. One frequent source of concern of students relates to the résumé. What résumé features, students wonder, will pique the interest of a financial services vendor? How do you avoid either overselling or underselling your credentials? How should the "job objective" section be handled? Although there is no single answer to these questions, among the key things potential employers look for is evidence of your purpose and direction. Do you appreciate the demands of the position that you are seeking? Do you understand the characteristics of the firm that you are pursuing? Are you serious about a finance career, or is this just one more option along with consulting, marketing, and other industries? The importance of thorough preparation for the job search process cannot be overestimated. This same concern applies to the interview process, only more so.

The successful completion of a job search is just a beginning. To translate the promise of a new job into long-run success requires the same careful thought and planning that won the job. A sure prerequisite is unmistakable enthusiasm for the work, which manifests itself as energy and personal innovation.

As you take your first position, be aware of several pitfalls that have derailed promising careers. The first relates to workload. As already mentioned, finance jobs tend to be high pressure and demand long hours. Giving the job the best you have is essential. But it is also necessary to pace yourself and ensure that the office does not entirely dominate your life. Without outside interests and time to enjoy them, it will be only a question of when, not if, you burn out.

A second mistake can be to move too quickly toward specialization. One objective of your initial position should be to illuminate the variety of potential career opportunities. Limiting your early career experience to a narrow focus on a particular product or a single industry, for instance, may limit your ability to move on to other opportunities as they present themselves.

A final point concerns the very nature of "opportunities." Our natural tendency, when faced with an uncertain future, is to plan our way out of it. But developing too precise a plan, and sticking rigidly to it, is likely to be a mistake. Career opportunities have a way of surfacing when one least expects them. Be alert for new and unanticipated opportunities that will almost surely come along. As Disraeli warned, "What we anticipate seldom comes; what we least expected generally happens."

Good luck!

Jobs in Investment Banking

Seth A. Rosenblatt
Harvard Business School, Class of 1993

What Is Investment Banking?

Investment banking denotes and connotes a number of different ideas. For those who have not worked in the industry before and are considering a summer or full-time position in investment banking, the job search can bring confusion and frustration.

In a very general sense, the term *investment bank* is broadly used to describe any financial institution that provides services in the areas of security issuing and brokering, financial advisory, or asset management. From the smallest boutiques to the large full-service firms, the term *investment bank* is far too often used. Large investment banks such as the "bulge-bracket" firms engage in many arenas outside traditional commercial banking or insurance underwriting. However, the function of investment banking requires a narrower industry definition. Investment banking generally encompasses four functions, all interrelated. Some firms may engage in all of these functions, while some may specialize in one or more of these areas:

1. Corporate finance.
2. Mergers and acquisitions.
3. Merchant banking.
4. Advisory/financial consulting.

In addition, many firms may specialize in one or two industry groups. The largest firms tend to have many functional and/or industry groups to serve their client base fully. Although many of the terms used here are fairly universal, the terminology in different countries does vary. If you are looking for an investment banking job outside the United States, become familiar with specific terminology used there (exact translations do not necessarily apply).

Corporate Finance
Corporate finance is the process of raising money for corporate clients (or public institutions) in the form of equity, debt, convertible, or other derivative security. This process involves two steps: (1) determining the funding needs of the client (type, amount, and structure) and (2) finding investors to supply those funds. This second step can generally be accomplished through either of two methods: a public issue or a private placement. A public issuance of a security involves the investment bank's acting as an underwriter of the securities, purchasing the securities from the issuer and then reselling them on the public market. For larger investment banks, this process will involve other areas of the firm, such as sales and trading, research, and a syndicate function (sharing the underwriting responsibilities with other investment banks). A private placement, on the other hand, calls for the investment bank to act solely as an agent, matching the issuer of the security with one or a handful of potential investors in an offering not made available to the public.

Mergers and Acquisitions
For investment bankers the much publicized "M&A" business has the banker acting as an advisor to a company in transactions involving the sale of a whole company, a division, or just certain assets. The investment banker acts as an advisor to the client (on either the buy side or sell side), determines an appropriate valuation range, and negotiates terms most favorable to the client. The investment bank may also take a more active role by participating as a principal in the transaction. From an auction to a negotiated sale, from a stock swap to an LBO, the form and structure of an M&A transaction vary widely.

Merchant Banking
Merchant banking is the process whereby an investment bank acts as a principal in a transaction, either by purchasing newly issued securities of a firm or by purchasing (or selling) a stake in an M&A transaction. Some firms specialize only in merchant banking, while the largest investment banks tend to have a separate group to perform this function. Merchant banking is closely tied to the functions of corporate finance and M&A, and bankers from different industry or functional groups normally work on a merchant banking transaction together.

Advisory
Advisory work is linked to corporate finance, M&A, and merchant banking. It is generally performed as part of the overall service given to clients, or it may be tied to a specific transaction. Advisory or consulting work can take an infinite number of forms, including capital structure analysis, comparable analysis, and industry research. Much of the specific work is dependent on the particular client's industry. In addition, the past few years have seen a dramatic growth in advisory work related to corporate restructurings and reorganizations.

Looking for a Job in Investment Banking

For those who have not previously worked in the industry, a lot of anxiety arises in the investment banking job search. For first-year students who are seriously considering making a career switch into investment banking, I strongly recommend that you work in the field for the summer. Not only will this make it easier to find a job with an investment bank after your second year, but you will learn what the industry is all about. Investment banking is such a unique field that it is difficult to understand the work, the environment, and the culture without experiencing it.

When beginning your self-assessment and your job search, first speak to as many people as you can who are or have been in the industry. In your class, you will probably find at least a dozen people who worked in an investment bank for at least two years. Your peers will be your greatest resource. Ask a lot of questions; you will get a good cross-section of various experiences, good and bad.

Many of your business school classmates have been former "analysts." *Analyst* is the usual entry-level title for undergraduates. Understand, that if hired, you will probably enter at the associate level (or equivalent). Although the long hours may be similar, the responsibilities may be very different. Try to understand the general career path in investment banking and the specific one in each firm.

Your next stops should be at the placement center and the library. Try to research each firm in which you may be interested. Understand which firms are full-service broker-dealers and investment bankers, which are middle-market firms, and which are boutiques. What appears to be the corporate culture and reputation of each firm? Does a firm specialize in a particular industry, function, or geographic region? Does it match your interests? Try to discover, through speaking with peers and research, which firms are the leaders in each of the areas (industries or functions) in which you are interested. There are a number of specific places where you can look for information on each firm that you are researching. Your career resource center will have the following information:

- Annual reports, 10-Ks, 10-Qs, prospectuses (if it is a public company)
- Recruiting brochures
- Company files
- Industry file/packet
- Summer job reports
- Current and previous job descriptions
- Lotus One Source/Other on-line services
- Alumni career advisor list
- Book of job search and salary statistics

Additionally, check these sources:

- Company recruiting briefings and dinners
- *Wall Street Journal*
- Business magazines (*BusinessWeek*, *Forbes*, *Fortune*, *Economist*)
- LEXIS/NEXIS news searches (available on-line)
- Job Search Guide (available from your career center)
- Career fairs
- Friends, relatives, classmates, professors
- This book

Most of the larger investment banking firms, although they may have offices throughout the country and the rest of the world, tend to be based in New York City and do all recruiting from there. Regardless of which office you may be interested in, you may have to go through a general interviewing process based in New York. Be sure to understand each firm's policies and procedures for hiring outside the main office, particularly internationally. Many firms have a bias toward hiring nationals of a particular country to work in an office located there. If you are unsure, ask. During the correspondence and interviewing process, make your geographic preferences clear. If you can work only in city X, you will find it very frustrating to go through the entire process and be offered a job, only to find that the firm is not hiring this year in city X. Try to understand office placement policies before the interview.

Attend as many recruiting briefings as you can to get an idea of each firm's strategy, focus, and culture. Compare the people who have been successful in each firm to your own track record and where (or who) you would like to be in 5, 10, or 20 years. Finally, make it a practice to read the newspaper (the *Wall Street Journal* in particular) to get a good sense of what is going on in the industry and with specific firms.

If you have done sufficient researching and querying, the interview should be the easiest part of the process. These interviews are generally not like "stress" consulting interviews. You will probably not be asked the implications of an inverted yield curve or queried as to the number of restaurants in New York City. This, of course, varies by firm (and there are stories of difficult interviews), but in general investment banks are looking to see if you:

- Are a hard worker and detail oriented.
- Have leadership skills and enjoy working in groups.

- Have a genuine interest in the industry and are excited about it.
- Show good judgment and demonstrate responsibility.
- Are analytically inclined and comfortable with numbers and computers.
- Understand the lifestyle and are willing to make the sacrifices required.
- Are a fun person to be around. ("Would I like to go to dinner with you?")

Conclusion

You must determine what methods of research work best for you. Speak to people whose advice you value, and then draw your own conclusions. Two issues that need to be addressed are the money and the hours. Much time has been spent talking about both of these subjects.

All in all, I found investment banking to be a great experience. It was stimulating and challenging, and I got to work with some fascinating people. If you decide to make a career of it, do it for reasons like this. If you find, through talking to peers or through a summer job, that you do not expect to get the same kind of fun, challenge, or excitement that I did, do not go into the industry. You will be miserable. Investment banking is not for everybody. Where I worked, there were a few of my peers who thought that it was the greatest experience of their lives, while others, doing the exact same job, were miserable. In other words, the money should *not* be the deciding factor. There is little doubt that investment banking is one of the best-paying positions (in the short run) that you can take, and money is certainly not unimportant. Although compensation is always a consideration in any job decision, the people I knew who regretted the job the most were the ones who took it solely for the cash.

As for the hours, this is something also that has sparked quite a legend on Wall Street—and throughout the rest of the business world. Stories of all-nighters and ruined weekends plague the minds of former analysts. While it is true that investment bankers work very long hours, the variance within and among firms is so large that it defies most generalizations. Nevertheless, there usually is some lifestyle sacrifice that particularly a junior banker will have to make in investment banking. The only way to get an accurate sense of the hours is for you to talk to friends or classmates who worked for a particular firm. Even then, their information may not be accurate because different departments in the same firm may require much different hours. Additionally, changes in the business cycle and season can dramatically affect the workload in any firm.

Only through asking a lot of questions and through a little soul-searching can you determine if the investment banking lifestyle is indeed right for you.

Finance Careers in Manufacturing Companies

Brian M. Webber
Harvard Business School, Class of 1993

A variety of career opportunities are available to students interested in finance other than well-known financial services jobs. Manufacturing companies have positions in strategic planning, product development, and division controllers' offices. I worked as a financial analyst in product development at Ford Motor Company prior to attending HBS.

In the controller's office of product development, I worked on various product development teams associated with the development of new models of Taurus and Sable. Product development teams consist of engineers, marketing people, planning people, and a finance person. My main responsibility was to perform the financial analysis required by the team when making product decisions, but I was also exposed to a wide array of team decisions and problems and to the team strategies and solutions employed throughout the development process. I met daily with team members to review, update, and discuss the progress of the new product. The requirements of this assignment were to visit the plants of small suppliers, assist with cost control and financial projections, and work closely with development engineers and designers to report the financial status of the program to senior management. Since each team member is encouraged to contribute and to assume responsibility where feasible, I quickly gained a reasonable knowledge of the entire development process. Interaction with engineering, marketing, planning, and outside suppliers was extremely interesting and helped me to understand the engineering and marketing functions. Often the various functional areas are faced with conflicting goals, and compromises among team members are required. Frequently team meetings are held at supplier locations, where the team analyzes specific product proposals, or meetings are held in the prototype plant next to a prototype vehicle so that decisions can be implemented in real time. Finance positions in product development allow a finance person to work closely with the manufacturing process. Every member of the product development team provides input for decisions that affect the outcome of the product.

The environment in product development finance is intense, and the hours are demanding. The hours do not compare to investment banking hours but are considerably longer than other positions within the company. A great deal of responsibility is heaped on finance representatives with respect to reporting to senior management the financial status of the new product, preparing financial models to analyze the impact of various proposals, and assuming team leadership at times when financial analysis has a major impact on a product decision. Analysts may also evaluate future marketing programs and compare competitors' products from a financial perspective. Analysts perform business analyses for new programs that include profitability, return on capital, evaluation of alternatives, and presentations to senior management.

Product development is only one aspect of finance within a manufacturing company. Other areas requiring financial expertise are sales and marketing, capital markets, and manufacturing.

Sales and marketing finance positions require analysts to evaluate and develop appropriate strategies for retail pricing and various incentive programs. With recent developments in automobile pricing, such as cash back and low interest financing, a great deal of analysis is required to recommend appropriate pricing levels. Analysts also evaluate competitors' pricing strategies and form arguments for an appropriate counterresponse.

Capital markets finance positions exist both within credit areas, such as Ford Motor Credit, and in various treasury areas. Analysts provide financial support for issuance of commercial paper, long-term debt, common and preferred stock, and sale leaseback transactions. Analysts act as buyers of various investment banking services. Analysts recommend strategies for capital structure and dividend policies, manage daily cash flow, and perform analyses for acquisitions and divestitures.

Manufacturing finance positions involve developing capital budgets and analyzing specific capital spending projects. Analysts are involved with site analysis and evaluate new plant proposals. They also analyze financial and operating results of manufacturing plants.

A finance background can often open doors for international assignments depending on the size and needs of the company. Many of my colleagues planned to work internationally, and I saw doors open up for them to do so.

There are many things to consider when choosing a summer job or a career, including location and corporate environment. The best source of information is often individuals who have worked in the industry or have worked for the specific company you are considering. Do not hesitate to contact someone who has worked for a company or in an area you are considering.

Interviews: Three Harvard Business School Alumni Reflect on Careers in Finance

Vikram Gandhi
Harvard Business School, Class of 1989
Vice President, Mergers and Acquisitions
Morgan Stanley & Company

Describe the stages of your career path and changes in responsibility.

During the first couple of years, my career developed along a diversified set of experiences. I worked in Capital Markets, the Natural Resource Area, and the Merger and Acquisitions/Restructuring Area. These two years served as a time to build a network of relationships and access pockets of knowledge throughout the firm. In addition to being exposed to new functional and industry arenas, this stage enabled me to develop and refine my teamwork skills further. My role was primarily to complete modules of a large project and to contribute to the team's efforts in executing transactions.

The opportunity to move around in the first two years was a valuable experience for two reasons. First, given the nature of the investment banking industry and flux of the business, you should not expect to have a "home" for good, and so it is worthwhile to share in multiple experiences in case you need to shift specialties in the future. Second, given the importance of working with a variety of people, the more people you meet, the better you will be positioned later in your career.

My first two years emphasized agenda execution; my current career stage emphasizes agenda setting as a team manager in the M&A group. I now work more directly with the principals and managing directors, am responsible for ensuring the quality of the team's work, and manage analysts and new associates. A critical junction in my role as team manager is to manage upward and across specialty areas to ensure that the necessary expertise is brought to bear to solve client problems.

What have been the obstacles and challenges of your career progression?

Three challenges in my career have been managing up, coordinating resources, and motivating down. First, since I am now responsible for ensuring the quality of work yet lack many years of experience, it is imperative that I seek the perspective of senior people, and getting their time is not easy. Therefore, it is critical to get them to focus, and one must manage and communicate effectively to accomplish this feat.

Second, a key success factor in investment banking is bringing various resources of the firm to bear on a project. This requires a healthy dose of coordination, especially since I work on six to seven projects at a time. Achieving cooperation in a firm with many egos is a challenge. One must massage egos when coordinating to ensure that what colleagues and senior people say is intelligently articulated to the client.

A third challenge is motivating down. We work hard at Morgan Stanley, and it is vital to maintain a good experience for the analysts and new associates. I must position the work as a valuable and fun experience so that junior people do not mind being at work until 1 A.M. I need to motivate them so they feel involved and they have a high degree of job satisfaction.

Can you describe an experience that has significantly influenced your career?

I enjoy my job, but I cannot point to any one experience that has significantly influenced my career.

What strengths have helped you excel in your career?

A strength that has helped me in my career is being analytically oriented. This should come as no big surprise, but it is especially relevant to M&A given the abundance of valuation and creative structuring required. Another strength is being involved in many extracurricular activities while at school. This involvement was valuable for enabling me to obtain a better understanding of how people think and work. The key to success at Morgan Stanley is teamwork, and my extracurricular activities enhanced my ability to manage my time, to motivate, and to keep people interested in what they are doing while getting the most out of them.

Where do you see your career going over the next ten years? How will you prepare for such changes?

I'm happy in investment banking. I enjoy what I do because it builds on my strengths, and there is a fair degree of variety in the projects I work on. Yes, investment banking is tiring and difficult, but it's also fun. Hence, I'd like to continue for at least the next few years as I transition from a team manager to a team leader. Yet over the long haul, I can see myself getting involved on the principal side of the business.

To prepare for the future, I focus on my interactions with senior firm officials and senior client officials. Eventually, it will be important for me to secure clients if I hope to transition to a team leader. Therefore, I make sure I know current clients well and build those relationships while establishing others. Preparing for the future means that when a client has a problem, he or she will call on me.

To what extent did your HBS degree prepare you for the day-to-day life of Morgan Stanley?

HBS definitely prepares you for investment banking. One works on six to seven projects at a time in different industries, and the work requires creative problem solving. At Morgan Stanley, I might be considering a joint venture for a natural resource client, a buying opportunity for an auto client, and a selling opportunity for a telecommunications client. This might be only half of the projects on my plate at any given time. And like HBS, even though I had less time to think about the business situation, I would have to grasp key issues of three business situations each evening. So, similar to the requirements for being an exceptional investment banker, HBS prepares one to handle a lot of stuff in a short amount of time and effectively deal with the intensity of work.

The second way HBS prepared me was in the exercise of analytics. Every day I have to go through thick documents or consider complicated situations and come up with three key issues. The client describes a problem, and it's my job to figure out some options and decide which makes the most sense for the client. This type of work is not too different from discussions that occurred every day in Aldrich Hall.

Finally, a third way that HBS prepared me was with regard to people. The people at HBS are the same type that I work with at Morgan Stanley; they're smart and hard working, but they often have large egos. HBS prepared me well for those types of people.

Is there anything else you would recommend to future HBS graduates entering the finance industry?

First, teamwork is critical to success and should not be underestimated. HBS makes some people think they can be a solo star, but it just doesn't work that way.

Second, don't try to run before you can walk. Coming out of HBS, you may think there's not much more to learn. Nothing could be further from the truth. A place like Morgan Stanley can humble you. Consider your first couple of years as an opportunity where you are being paid to learn. I strongly recommend that you demonstrate an eagerness to learn.

Third, recognize that investment banking is a cyclical industry. You must anticipate that while today the equity product might be hot while M&A is slow, the situation could reverse itself very quickly. Given this industry nature, you should be flexible to change as it may become necessary to shift to different industry or function groups during your career. But the good thing to remember is that the HBS education enables you to be flexible because of the exposure to many industries, functions, people, and business situations.

Girish V. Nadkarni
Harvard Business School, Class of 1988
Vice President, Strategic Transactions
The Prudential Insurance Company of America

Describe the stages of your career path and changes in responsibility.

Before attending HBS, I practiced law on Wall Street: three years with Coudert Brothers and three years with Shearman & Sterling. Hence, my first job after HBS is not typical for MBAs straight out of school. After graduating from HBS, I was hired as Vice President and Assistant to the Vice Chairman of The Prudential Insurance Co. of America, responsible for handling a variety of special projects for the Vice Chairman. I also was "on loan" to the heads of several business units throughout The Prudential. The work I was assigned often pertained to strategic initiatives and gave me wide exposure to Prudential's businesses. For instance, one of the special projects required me to work on a task force to assess the sensitivity of Prudential's leveraged buyout (LBO) portfolio to recession.

Fourteen months later, I was promoted to Corporate Vice President in the Central Financial Services Group of Prudential Capital Corporation, responsible for new product development. One of the products I created was Pru-Shelf, a proprietary medium-term note program. Our first Pru-Shelf transaction was a $200 million financing with Toys R Us. To date, The Prudential has executed approximately 24 Pru-Shelf transactions totaling $1.6 billion. The product was featured in articles in *Corporate Finance*, *Investment Dealer's Digest,* and *Investors Daily* and was also included in a *Business Week* cover story on innovative financial instruments. I also led a team that helped Prudential Capital's 14 regional offices manage complex transactions, such as LBOs and cashouts.

In 1990, I transferred to the work-out area of Prudential Capital and assumed a portfolio of 16 troubled companies. No other job has stretched me so much physically, emotionally, and intellectually. Every day was a crisis. Extensive negotiating and posturing skills were critical in this job, and when I was reassigned to my current position 18 months later, I knew my strengths and weaknesses.

For a number of reasons that range from Hurricane Andrew to the new risk-based capital requirements imposed on insurance companies, The Prudential has embarked on a reassessment of its main lines of business. Consequently, in my current position as Vice President, Strategic Transactions with the Prudential Investment Corporation, I help with the strategic assessment of different businesses and carry out the decisions to eliminate or expand a business unit. If we decide to expand a business or acquire companies, then I might lead an effort to raise external capital. If, on the other hand, we decide to exit a business, then I will execute a sale of our operations in that business.

What have been the obstacles and challenges of your career progression?

I have faced three challenges: diversity, politics, and a line versus staff trade-off. I was born and raised in India and therefore am different from most of the other people at The Prudential. I have independent opinions, and I tend to state them. There is the natural challenge of being different from the status quo and the challenge of peers resisting someone like me who does not always agree with their decisions, analyses, and opinions.

Entering an organization at a high level has its own challenges. People often resent you for not having paid your dues. It therefore takes a lot of effort and time to establish your credibility.

I also have been challenged by my lack of roots to a home unit within The Prudential. This has come about because of my constant transfers from one area of the company to another—wherever the action is hot. I'm not really complaining, though, because putting out fires has been exciting. But movements between line and staff positions can be difficult. It's especially hard to move back into a line assignment after having been in a staff position. But, unfortunately, I am not considered part of the family by any group or senior person and there is no one other than myself who looks after my career.

Can you describe an experience that has significantly influenced your career?

Our business is fraught with legal issues; if we take the wrong step, we'll be sued. And though I am not trained in bankruptcy law, my legal background provides me with the ability to understand most of the intricacies of the work-out business. I also know how to make the most of our own lawyers. In fact, because of my legal experience, the synergy between our legal counsel and me is fantastic. Between us, we make one and one equal six.

A second significant experience is my assignment in the work-out area, where I honed my negotiating skills and learned and practiced the art of diplomacy, often facing people with diverging interests and constantly shifting alliances. I developed a better understanding of finance and strengthened my structuring skills. And I achieved better credit analysis as I saw what can and does go wrong in companies. I also learned that you cannot underestimate the critical need and value for good management and should not analyze a company without considering the probable significant changes imminent within the industry.

What strengths have helped you excel in your career?

My legal background has been a remarkable strength. Another strength is my generalist experience at The Prudential. Although it sometimes hurts not to have a home, transferring throughout the organization has given me wide exposure and a holistic view of Prudential's business. It also taught me to get up to speed quickly. The problems with diversity are synthesizing experiences that will make me an excellent senior manager in the long run. Other strengths include creative problem solving, structuring, and negotiating skills.

Where do you see your career going over the next ten years? How will you prepare for such changes?

I honestly have no clue where my career will be in ten years. The Prudential is experiencing a major transition. Its business is already very different than it was just five years ago. Uncertainty is a big problem. Like most other Harvard Business School alumni, I wouldn't mind being on my own one day, maybe with my own fund. And perhaps unlike most other HBS alumni, I have a strong interest in politics and am likely to run for some type of office one day. The future is definitely uncertain but exciting.

Preparing for uncertainty is a challenge. Often it's not what you know that is important but who you know. It is very important to know the right people—those who make the decisions and not those who make the most noise. It is valuable to adopt a mentor and build credibility.

To what extent did your HBS degree prepare you for the day-to-day life of The Prudential?

I loved my two years at HBS. They gave me tremendous analytical and problem-solving capabilities, as well as frameworks and paradigms to guide my thinking. The education forced me to understand the economics of a business. I graduated appreciating that there are times when the process of making decisions is more important than the substance; that achieving commitment, involvement, and organizational buy-in is not easy; that getting the rank and file to adopt and implement plans is about applying the right process; and that treating customers and employees well is critical to survival.

Nevertheless, HBS failed to prepare me for many of the soft issues that one deals with every day. Perhaps I wasn't listening, but it didn't teach me how to manage my career in a political organization. HBS taught me how to manage others but not how to be managed. It's like expecting one to be a parent before he or she has finished being a child. Furthermore, HBS fell short of enabling me to handle entering an organization at a high-profile level and to fight the stereotypes of an "HBS Baker Scholar type."

Is there anything else you would recommend to future HBS graduates entering the finance industry?

First, make sure you know why you want to be in finance. Too many people think it's a stepping-stone to bigger and better things. For instance, many people think investment banking or mergers and acquisitions is a stepping-stone to running your own business one day. Nothing in investment banking prepares you for running your own business. If you want to operate a business, then consider marketing. Investment banking teaches one only how to process transactions. Make sure you know what working life will be like on a day-to-day basis. Don't choose money management because you want your photograph in the newspaper as the next Peter Lynch. Make sure you understand what Peter Lynch did at Fidelity on a daily basis.

Know your strengths and play to them, and don't forget soft issues both inside and outside your company. Remember that judgment is more important than technical skills. It's critical to reach a judgment based on what the numbers say and not just crunch them. Don't hesitate to push the envelope. Too many people think they are pushing the envelope, but often they don't know where the envelope really is, or they define it too narrowly. Finally, to succeed at the top, it's helpful to be a generalist. Yet there's a trade-off, because to get to the top you need to be a specialist and the risk is obsolescence of your specialty; so be careful to follow industry dynamics constantly, and if they change, manage your career accordingly.

Joel W. Peterson
Harvard Business School, Class of 1983
Managing Director, Utilities
CIBC, a subsidiary of Canadian Imperial Bank of Commerce

Describe the stages of your career path and changes in responsibility.

I would describe my career in five stages: the Learning Stage, "Just Another Banker" Stage, "Not Just Another Banker" Stage, People Manager Stage, and "Not Just Another Manager" Stage.

The Learning Stage (about one year): This is the period right after business school, when I tried to absorb as much information as possible, figure out who's who, and simply do my best even though I was not sure what specific career benefit would accrue from a particular work matter.

"Just Another Banker" Stage (about two years): In this stage I sought valuable personal contacts and team-building opportunities. I knew enough to be dangerous yet not enough to be noticed or have too much impact.

"Not Just Another Banker" Stage (about three years): At this point in my career, I had real impact. This was manifested in specific transactions in which I could differentiate myself through personal excellence and organizational team-building skills.

People Manager Stage (about two years): Although I have always managed projects and people to some extent in my career (you have to manage people up, down, and sideways throughout a successful career), it was during this stage about three years ago that I had responsibility for ten direct reports.

"Not Just Another Manager" Stage: Finally, in the fifth stage, I now differentiate myself by fostering a culture of productivity and compatibility, hiring sincere and motivated people and setting high standards that are consistently met.

It's important to note that throughout the five stages it has been personal knowledge and abilities that enabled me to be successful. At the beginning of my career, technical, industry, and job knowledge were important, but my progression is rewarded and will continue to be rewarded due to personal knowledge and organizational abilities, which are competencies honed at HBS.

What have been the obstacles and challenges of your career progression?

The biggest challenge has been managing up. I didn't realize the critical importance of managing up, especially with respect to making sure my manager understands what I'm doing. I'm not promoting brown-nosing but rather the notion of effective communication of one's ideas. What good is the world's best idea if you can't effectively communicate it? Upward management through effective communication yields believability, credibility, and promotability. It is especially important and challenging to manage up when personal rapport with the manager is not ideal. I think that talking to unbiased parties and bouncing ideas off them— mentors or peers—is a great way to assess whether you're seeing the big picture and test how such should be communicated to your superiors.

Another challenge to keep in mind is that there are advantages and disadvantages to being in your company's corporate headquarters. In fact, I think there are better reasons for *not* being at headquarters, which is contrary to what many people usually believe. People often want to be located at headquarters because they feel they will reap benefits of greater visibility to the chairman. However, so much time at headquarters is spent gossiping and not enough on business. A satellite office operates as if it were running its own business. Being in a satellite office is liberating.

The other two challenges involve people. First, don't be surprised when the seemingly most neutral colleague backstabs you. The people who openly disagree are at least willing to talk about it; however, it's the people who are quiet who are plotting their actions against you and preparing for guerrilla warfare. Never expect to win every battle. Take the long-term view. Second, career advancement requires successful people management. It requires a lot of time and attention. Don't patronize and don't ignore your people because it may come back to haunt you. People management is more time intensive and critical than technical problems. Take care of people problems first.

Can you describe an experience that has significantly influenced your career?

The experience that significantly influenced my career is when I left First Chicago to pursue a long-term management opportunity at CIBC, where I would be more than just a banker. I took a long-term perspective regarding my career and took a risk in pursuit of this long-term opportunity because I was confident in my abilities to make another move if the CIBC opportunity did not materialize. As the saying goes, "No risk, no return."

What strengths have helped you excel in your career?

Three strengths that have enabled me to excel in my career are communicating persuasively, having a long-term perspective, and completing tasks I set out to perform. With regard to the first strength, anyone can run a computer or regression analysis, but those who excel can also communicate the analysis into a coherent strategy to follow. And to the strength of always completing tasks I set out to perform, I call this "consistent integrity"—doing what I promised. I will not make commitments I cannot keep; everyone is watching everything I do.

Where do you see your career going over the next ten years? How will you prepare for such changes?

Right now I'm at a juncture. I could continue my career per the status quo, but the limiting factor is the trend of flattening organizations, and hence increasing responsibility becoming limited. I like what I do, especially with respect to managing people, and I would not mind moving into more senior management levels, which suggests that I strongly consider broadening my horizons and perspective. But doing my own thing could be fun as well. I also think about working for a client.

Preparing for the future means continuing to develop and refine my skills, talking to a lot of people, and building a network of contacts and a broad knowledge base. It would be great to have a guardian angel, but it just doesn't work that way. In fact, mentor time is limited, and career development is usually nonexistent except for the first couple of years. Advice can be expected but is often unorganized and from many sources. In short, preparing for the future is difficult.

To what extent did your HBS degree prepare you for the day-to-day life of CIBC?

HBS attracts leaders and hones those skills. Personal values, knowledge, and abilities are extremely important, and I think HBS excels at developing and refining these personal attributes. Any smart person can learn technical, industry, and job knowledge, but it's the general, broad knowledge base and personal values that enable excellence, and HBS is distinguished at developing them. Because of my HBS education, I am well organized and see the big picture. These attributes are important in the day-to-day life at CIBC. Also, HBS made me sensitive to other cultures and international differences. This is especially important in the increasingly global world and has made a significant difference in my career.

Is there anything else you would recommend to future HBS graduates entering the finance industry?

I recommend that you set short-term, mid-term, and long-term goals. Evaluate these goals for yourself and your company. Ask yourself questions and ponder answers. Are you compatible with your job and the people around you at work? Do you enjoy your job? If not, then leave, because life is too short. But to a certain extent, you also have to put up with some things you don't like.

A helpful analogy is to think of your career as an investment. You would not put money in a stock and let it sit for 50 years. You would probably look at that investment every six months. Do the same for your career; HBS is an investment in yourself. Don't keep doing something you don't like. If you're unhappy, it will be obvious in your work and in your life.

About This Project

During the spring of 1996, a variety of firms that typically hire MBAs for positions in finance were contacted and asked to respond to the following questionnaire:

Company Description

Describe your firm's business and the types of clients served by your finance group(s).

Describe your ownership structure.

How does your approach to finance differ from that of other firms, and what do you consider to be your strengths and distinctive capabilities?

Discuss changes in your firm's revenues (both domestic and international) and professional staff over the past year; over the past five years.

The Finance MBA's Job Description

Describe the career path and corresponding responsibilities for an MBA at your firm.

Describe the opportunities for professional mobility between the various departments in your firm.

Discuss the lifestyle aspects of a career with your firm (i.e., average hours per week, amount of travel, flexibility to change offices, corporate culture, etc.).

The Recruiting Process

Describe your recruiting process and the criteria by which you select candidates. Is prior experience necessary?

How many permanent associates and analysts do you hire in a typical year? How many summer interns do you expect to hire? If you have a formal summer program, please describe it. Please be sure to indicate whether the summer program is in place for all offices or just some.

What international opportunities does your firm offer for U.S. citizens? For foreign nationals?

The firms contacted include investment banking firms, commercial banks, Fortune 500 firms, and regional companies. Responses from firms in this section are printed, for the most part, as received.

A.G. Edwards & Sons, Inc.

One North Jefferson
St. Louis, MO 63103
(314) 955-3000
Web site: www.agedwards.com

MBA Recruiting Contact(s):
Barbara H. Boyle, Vice President
(314) 955-3691

Company Description

Describe your firm's business and the types of clients served by your finance group(s).

Founded in 1887, A.G. Edwards is the largest securities firm headquartered off Wall Street; it is one of the few firms described as a "national full-line" firm by the Securities and Exchange Commission and the Securities Industry Association. For more than 100 years, the firm has played a major role in providing financial services to a variety of clients nationwide. From its headquarters in St. Louis, the firm and its subsidiaries provide securities and commodities brokerage, asset management, insurance, real estate, and investment banking services. Our department provides investment banking services in the areas of Corporate Finance, Mergers and Acquisitions, and Valuations.

Public and Structured Finance, a department that is separate and distinct from that discussed below, is also part of A.G. Edwards's investment banking services. While the Public and Structured Finance department does not currently recruit on college campuses, inquiries can be made to Jon Savage, (314) 955-3849, at the address listed above.

Describe your ownership structure.

A.G. Edwards, a publicly owned corporation for more than 20 years, is traded on the New York Stock Exchange under the symbol AGE.

How does your approach to finance differ from that of other firms, and what do you consider to be your strengths and distinctive capabilities?

Our success has been built in large part on our orientation toward relationship banking. Rather than emphasizing individual transactions, we provide a variety of services that meet our clients' needs and further our long-term relationships with them. Although our clients range from Fortune 500 corporations to small private companies, we consider our niche to be middle-market companies. We serve clients coast to coast and compete with other national, as well as regional, investment banks.

The close attention we provide our clients gives A.G. Edwards the distinction of being the nation's only retail brokerage firm to be included in both editions of *The Service Edge: 101 Companies That Profit from Customer Care* and both editions of *The 100 Best Companies to Work for in America.* We attribute the firm's success to our emphasis on consistently maintaining the customers' success as a primary focus, creating value with the services we deliver, and treating our employees "like members of the family."

According to *Institutional Investor,* at year-end 1995, A.G. Edwards was the second largest securities firm in the United States based on the number of offices (more than 500 in 48 states), and the sixth largest based on the number of registered representatives (more than 5,400). Well known within the industry for our national distribution network, our distribution of securities in small amounts to a large number of investors results in a large, geographically dispersed shareholder/bondholder base for the issuer.

Discuss changes in your firm's revenues (both domestic and international) and professional staff over the past year; over the past five years.

Although most of A.G. Edwards's revenues are derived from commissions generated by selling securities to individual investors, our department's revenues are derived from a diversified base of business that includes underwritings of equity and debt, mergers and acquisitions, valuations, and financial advisory projects. Our department has significantly expanded both the breadth and depth of our capability over the past decade. The rapid growth of our department affords a motivated individual the opportunity to make a meaningful contribution to A.G. Edwards. The number of professionals in the Corporate Finance, Mergers and Acquisitions, and Valuations departments has grown from 7 professionals in 1983 to more than 50 professionals in 1996. All associates are hired for our St. Louis headquarters, where over 2,700 of our more than 12,000 employees work.

The Finance MBA's Job Description

Describe the career path and corresponding responsibilities for an MBA at your firm.

A.G. Edwards's Corporate Finance and Mergers and Acquisitions department is a rapidly developing area of the company that affords talented, hard-working individuals recognition and responsibility early in their career development. A generalist program for an associate's development is strongly emphasized, and new associates in investment banking are given a wide variety of projects in corporate finance, mergers and acquisitions, and valuations.

A.G. Edwards emphasizes teamwork. Teams are small, and new associates can expect to work directly on client assignments with senior investment banking professionals, ensuring the associates' visibility and responsibility on projects. In addition, we have developed a system of semiannual and annual reviews, as well as specific project reviews, to provide individuals with feedback on their development.

Describe the opportunities for professional mobility between the various departments in your firm.

We expect associates to be generalists in corporate finance, mergers and acquisitions, and valuations in the early stage of their careers. Because there are no rigid boundaries separating these areas, new associates will be involved in projects in all of these areas. Associates are allowed to develop areas of expertise and specialization as they gain experience in investment banking.

Discuss the lifestyle aspects of a career with your firm (i.e., average hours per week, amount of travel, flexibility to change offices, corporate culture, etc.).

Demands and expectations at A.G. Edwards are very high. The firm, however, tries to maintain a reasonable balance between work and personal interests, which is reflected by a low turnover rate for our employees. St. Louis offers a very affordable and pleasant quality of life. The city consistently rates in the top ten of U.S. metropolitan areas in terms of quality of life. St. Louis provides an array of dance, theater, music, art, leisure activities, and sports and includes many nationally recognized landmarks. The city is also home to a significant number of Fortune 500 companies.

The Recruiting Process

Describe your recruiting process and the criteria by which you select candidates. Is prior experience necessary?

Our strategy for selecting new investment banking associates is to employ those whom we feel have the skills and compatibility to build long-term careers at A.G. Edwards. We have avoided the cutbacks common in our industry because we do not initially overhire. Instead, the number of new positions is commensurate with the firm's steady growth. Each new associate is carefully chosen to assume a role in which long-term dedication and a commitment to manage increasing responsibility are expected.

Leadership, personal integrity, academic success, and demonstrated success in other areas are some of the criteria we use to judge individual candidates. A commitment to investment banking, shown by summer internships or relevant experience prior to graduate school, is also an important criterion.

How many permanent associates and analysts do you hire in a typical year? How many summer interns do you expect to hire? If you have a formal summer program, please describe it. Please be sure to indicate whether the summer program is in place for all offices or just some.

We add new associates and analysts according to the quality of individual candidates and the compatibility of those candidates with A.G. Edwards. Therefore, we do not set yearly quotas for hiring. We have retained a very high percentage of the associates we have hired over the past ten years.

We currently do not offer a summer program.

What international opportunities does your firm offer for U.S. citizens? For foreign nationals?

While A.G. Edwards does participate in the international marketing of underwritings to a limited extent, all of our operations, including investment banking, are located in the United States.

Alex. Brown & Sons, Inc.

135 East Baltimore Street
Baltimore, MD 21202
(800) 638–2596
Web site: www.alexbrown.com

MBA Recruiting Contact(s):
Anne Ford

Company Description

Describe your firm's business and the type of clients served by your finance group(s).

Alex. Brown & Sons Incorporated is a national specialty investment bank based in Baltimore. It is also the nation's oldest investment banking firm, founded in 1800. The firm's main objective is to provide value-added financing and investment advice to its clients—corporate, institutional, municipal, and individual—regardless of the market environment. This commitment to client service and high ethical standards is fundamental to the firm's corporate culture.

The firm's services are based primarily on industry knowledge, and its resources are concentrated on six dynamic industry sectors with attractive long-term fundamentals. These sectors are consumer, financial services, industrial, health care, media/communications, and technology.

Alex. Brown operates in two general business areas which capitalize on our industry knowledge and technical competence: Capital Markets and Private Investor Services. Capital Markets includes Research, Investment Banking, Equity Sales and Trading, and High Yield Sales and Trading. Private Investor Services includes Private Client Services, Asset Management, and Fixed Income.

The firm has significant global capabilities, yet remains highly focused on the areas in which it can leverage its industry knowledge and technical competence. Today, Alex. Brown has more than 2200 employees in 22 offices in the United States, Europe, and Asia.

Describe your ownership structure.

Alex. Brown Inc. is a public company. Its common stock trades on the New York Stock Exchange under the symbol "AB."

How does your approach to finance differ from that of other firms, and what do you consider to be your strengths and distinctive capabilities?

We believe that industry knowledge and technical competence, more than any other factors, distinguish our ability to provide differentiated, value-added, and superior advice and service. The dynamic nature of the investment world requires knowledge of many areas, including markets, individual securities, types of transactions, and economic and societal trends. Because of the focused nature of our business and the consequent accumulation of experience, we feel that our technical competence in each of these areas is substantial. We believe, however, that our most valuable and distinctive competence is industry knowledge.

By concentrating our resources on a limited number of industries and encouraging a teamwork approach to communicate our collective knowledge efficiently throughout the firm, we are able to develop valuable insights and bring them to bear in each client relationship. Over the years, we have invested heavily in the human and technological resources necessary to build this knowledge base into a substantial corporate asset. The cumulative effect of this investment provides us with the "intellectual capital" to compete favorably with other entities, some of whose overall resources are much greater than our own. Most important, it is our commitment to long-term relationships and our constantly expanding resources that serve our clients well, even as the markets change.

Discuss changes in your firm's revenues (both domestic and international) and professional staff over the past year; over the past five years.

Over the past five years, the firm's revenues have grown 122% from $272 million in 1990 to $605 million in 1994. The growth in revenues is attributable, in part, to equity and fixed income market conditions conducive to the firm's particular mix of business. The firm has also succeeded in leveraging its industry knowledge and technical competence to expand its services and its global presence.

The Finance MBA's Job Description

Describe the career path and corresponding responsibilities for an MBA at your firm.

Investment Banking
Associates in the Investment Banking Division work in either industry groups or product groups where they are

usually part of small project teams consisting of a managing director or principal, a vice president, and one or more analysts. An associate may work on several assignments simultaneously. In one of our six industry groups, this may include working on public offerings, mergers and acquisitions, or private placements. In product groups, such as mergers and acquisitions, high yield, or private equity placements, an associate may work simultaneously on several assignments with different industry groups. By the end of the first year, associates are expected to assume a high degree of responsibility for project management and client maintenance.

Public Finance
Associates initially rotate through product groups within the division and are then placed in a group depending on where the associates are needed and on individual interest. During the first year, an associate is exposed to all aspects of a transaction, from getting the business to selling and closing a bond issue. Working closely with senior bankers on each project, the associate will write proposals and organize presentations. As the public finance associate develops, he or she will become more involved in various phases of client contact and presentations.

Equity Research
The associate analyst is teamed with a senior analyst to cover a specific industry sector. The position entails development of specialized industry and analytical skills, frequent interviews with senior corporate management, company visits, primary research, and ultimately intensive interpersonal marketing to the investment community and companies. Analysts are expected to build a franchise with the institutional investment community and companies through published research and client interaction.

Institutional Sales
Sales professionals are responsible for marketing research recommendations and investment banking products to buy-side analysts and portfolio managers at institutional investment firms. Sales associates are teamed with senior institutional salespeople to cover specific institutional accounts. An associate will have daily contact with research analysts and clients, frequent client visits, and interaction with corporate management teams. By the end of the first year, associates are expected to assume a high degree of responsibility for client relationships.

Trading
Trading professionals are responsible for trading securities, with a focus on industries that are covered by the firm's research analysts. The firm is one of the leading OTC market makers and has significantly increased its listed securities trading activity over the last five years. Trading associates are teamed with senior traders and work with institutional and retail sales, research, and other traders within the firm.

Describe the opportunities for professional mobility between various departments in your firm.

Alex. Brown recruits associates and analysts directly into the various departments described above. Professional mobility between departments is handled on a case-by-case basis.

Discuss the lifestyle aspects of a career with your firm (i.e., average hours per week, amount of travel, flexibility to change offices, corporate culture, etc.).

A career at Alex. Brown is challenging and rewarding and requires a significant commitment of time and energy. The firm's emphasis on teamwork creates a very positive working environment, particularly for new professionals who want to benefit from the firm's distinctive industry and technical competence. The lifestyle aspects of a career with Alex. Brown vary from department to department, particularly when market conditions are conducive to a department's particular industry or product expertise. Associates are encouraged to make their lifestyle decisions within the context of doing the best job possible for the firm and its clients.

The Recruiting Process

Describe your recruiting process and the criteria by which you select candidates. Is prior experience necessary?

The recruiting process involves a series of interviews, initially on campus and ultimately in one of the firm's offices. We strongly believe in building consensus within the firm regarding any new hire and, as a consequence, try to have each candidate meet as many people as possible. Alex. Brown has no predetermined criteria in evaluating candidates. We look for individuals whose work experience and academic record emphasizes initiative, excellence, and creativity in a team-oriented environment.

How many permanent associates and analysts do you hire in a typical year? How many summer interns do you expect to hire? If you have a formal summer program, please describe it. Please be sure to indicate whether the summer program is in place for all offices or just some.

Alex. Brown's philosophy is to concentrate hiring at the entry level, seeking each year to attract a small number of MBA candidates to fill openings on an as needed basis. We have no immediate plans to initiate a summer intern program.

What international opportunities does your firm offer for U.S. citizens? For foreign nationals?

Alex. Brown has offices in Europe and Asia which support investment banking and institutional sales efforts. The typical career path for a new associate or analyst with an interest in international opportunities is to start with Alex. Brown in the United States and transfer to one of the foreign offices after a suitable indoctrination period within the firm.

Banco Pactual S.A.

Av. Rep. do Chile, 230/29° andar
Rio de Janeiro-RJ, 20.031-170
Brazil
55 21 272-1300
Fax: 55 21 533-1661

MBA Recruiting Contact(s):
Rachel Goldgrob

Company Description

Describe your firm's business and the types of clients served by your finance group(s).

Banco Pactual S.A. is an investment banking firm based in Rio de Janeiro, Brazil, that specializes in proprietary trading, of Brazilian and another Latin American securities, portfolio management, and corporate finance activities.

The firm has an office in São Paulo, a broker-dealer in New York, subsidiary companies in Uruguay and Cayman Islands, as well as affiliates in England, Chile, and Argentina.

Pactual has consistently produced high returns on investment, both for its own account and for its clients. The firm is managed in an entrepreneurial spirit, with a lean and flat organizational structure focusing on opportunities that will offer potentially significant margins while seeking to reduce downside risk.

Describe your ownership structure.

Pactual is a limited partnership, currently with twenty-one partners. Furthermore, it is a requirement that all partners must be active executives of the bank. All professionals at Pactual work in a highly entrepreneurial environment and everyone is encouraged to become a partner of the firm.

How does your approach to finance differ from that of other firms, and what do you consider to be your strengths and distinctive capabilities?

If there is one key factor for Pactual's success over the past fourteen years it is the firm's ability to remain flexible and adapted to Brazil's volatile financial market and increasing competitiveness. Pactual believes Brazil is undergoing a transformation toward a more open, competitive, and internationally integrated economy, although many political obstacles still remain to be overcome. A truly international perspective and understanding of events not only in Brazil but in other countries and markets is imperative. Pactual is firmly committed to ensuring that both our professionals and the structure of the firm enable it to stay at the forefront of these changes.

Discuss changes in your firm's revenues (both domestic and international) and professional staff over the past year; over the past five years.

Pactual was founded in 1983 as a securities dealer with US$600,000 of capital, focusing principally on proprietary trading and financial intermediation. Since then, Pactual has grown at an impressive rate to become one of the most successful investment banks in Brazil. Over the last five-year period, the number of employees has increased 186% and, more specifically, from 305 in 1995 to 350 in 1996.

The Finance MBA's job description

Describe the career path and corresponding responsibilities for an MBA at your firm.

Hired candidates start at the associate level. Candidates may start at any of the bank's main business divisions (Proprietary Trading, Sales & Trading, Corporate Finance, Research, Portfolio Management and Risk Management) and will work under the supervision of one of the firm's partners. We tend to emphasize performance in determining compensation. The semiannual bonus is usually a substantial part of overall compensation.

Discuss the lifestyle aspects of a career with your firm (i.e., average hours per week, amount of travel, flexibility to change offices, corporate culture, etc.).

Lifestyle varies from one business division to another, being in line with typical investment banking conditions. Pactual's corporate culture—also comparable with that of other successful investment banks—is entrepreneurial, aggressive, intense, fast changing, and demand driven.

The Recruiting Process

Describe your recruiting process and the criteria by which you select candidates. Is prior experience necessary?

We have a strong commitment to recruiting the best people, with emphasis given to individuals with independent thinking, drive, aptitude for numbers, and initiative to work without constant supervision. No prior banking experience is needed. We are strongly committed to promoting a working environment that places a premium on internal cooperation.

Selected candidates will be interviewed in New York, Miami, or Brazil. Interviews are expected to start in late November (Miami) and December (Brazil and New York).

How many permanent associates and analysts do you hire in a typical year? How many summer interns do you expect to hire? If you have a formal summer program, please describe it. Please be sure to indicate whether the summer program is in place for all offices or just some.

Pactual actively recruits students graduating from prestigious foreign institutions. In 1995 and 1996, Pactual hired, on average, thirteen graduates from top American and European Schools. Typically, two summer interns are hired per year and are normally taken on by the Rio de Janeiro and São Paulo offices.

What international opportunities does your firm offer for U.S. citizens? For foreign students?

We offer full time and summer positions in Rio de Janeiro, São Paulo, and eventually in London and New York.

Bankers Trust

130 Liberty Street
New York, NY 10006
Web site: www.bankerstrust.com

MBA Recruiting Coordinator:
Debbie Barry (New York)
Global Investment Management
12th Floor

MBA Recruiting Contact(s):
Susan Markell (New York and Chicago)
Corporate Finance, Latin America, Real Estate
12th Floor

Colette Gardner (New York)
Global Markets Proprietary, Derivatives,
Global Risk Management and Policy
31st Floor

Jennifer B. Lemaigre (New York)
Technology
31st Floor

Karen McCartney (New York)
Management Consulting Group
15th Floor

Elizabeth Wood-Snell (Los Angeles)
Global Investment Bank
300 South Grand Avenue, 41st Floor
Los Angeles, CA 90071

Liz Lieberman (Asia)
New York, 12th Floor

Anne Peach (London)
One Appold Street
Broadgate
London EC2A HE England

Company Description

Describe your firm's business and the type of clients served by your finance group(s).

Bankers Trust New York Corporation, with headquarters in New York City, is a registered bank holding company incorporated in 1965. Its principal banking subsidiary, Bankers Trust Company, began business in 1903 as a trust company and became a commercial bank in 1917. In the early 1980s it sold its retail branch network and redirected its resources toward investment banking, focusing its businesses on major corporations, financial institutions, governments, and high net worth individuals worldwide.

Today, Bankers Trust is a global financial services company that operates in the world's financial markets to deliver tailored financial solutions to its clients and to provide superior returns to its shareholders. All of the human and financial resources of Bankers Trust are committed to preeminence in the strategic management of risk for its clients and for the firm.

Consistent with this business strategy, the firm is organized globally into five major business units. The Global Investment Bank combines the firm's financing, derivative, and advisory capabilities. Global Emerging Markets delivers a full range of financial services to clients in the Pacific Rim and Latin America. The firm's funds management activities are performed by Global Investment Management. Global Assets consists of the trust, securities processing, cash management, and private banking businesses. And finally, proprietary trading and positioning activities are undertaken by Global Markets Proprietary.

Within and across these businesses there are five business functions that represent the fundamental roles that are performed in the marketplace: Client Finance, Client Advisory, Client Financial Risk Management, Client Transaction Processing, and Trading & Positioning. These functions provide earnings diversity during all phases of the market cycle.

The success of Bankers Trust's business strategy has been demonstrated by its strong financial performance. Since 1979, our return on average common equity has increased from 13% to an average of 22% since 1990, making Bankers Trust one of the most profitable major financial services companies in the world.

Describe the opportunities for MBAs interested in finance.

Global Investment Bank
Bankers Trust Investment Banking Division combines the firm's capital markets and finance business with the strategic risk management products and strategic advisory capabilities. Bankers Trust is able to provide underwriting, distribution, and trading services to its corporate, institutional, and investor clients. Bankers Trust combines global expertise and local finance presence in over 30 countries making BT a recognized leader in international investment banking. Associates joining the Global Investment Bank may work in the **Derivatives, Corporate Finance,** or **Advisory businesses.**

The **Derivatives** group at Bankers Trust is responsible for medium and long-term financing, investments, and hedging transactions for the bank's customers. At Bankers Trust the Derivatives Group is not product oriented; rather we make a fundamental distinction between origination/marketing and risk management. The marketing function is structured parallel to the different customer groups. The risk management function is organized around five key market risks: interest rate, foreign exchange, equity, commodity, and securities (bonds and mortgage backed).

Interested students should contact Colette Gardner, Liz Lieberman, or Anne Peach.

Bankers Trust's **Corporate Finance Group** is one of the leading underwriting/investment banking groups serving global corporate, institutional, and investor clients. BT is a leader in the non-investment grade companies serving top-tier leveraged buyout firms and non-investment grade companies. Bankers Trust is the only firm with a major presence in both the high yield bond market and the leveraged loan market. We've been consistently rated in the top two in the High Yield Finance lead tables. BT ranks as the top issuer of B-rated issues and is the largest underwriter of zero coupon securities.

Associates begin as generalists, gaining both diverse product, industry and relationship management expertise. Associates take on a high level of responsibility early on in both transactions and business development. Positions are available in New York, Chicago, Los Angeles, Europe, and Asia.

Bankers Trust's **Advisory** groups are collectively known as The Risk Merchant Bank and include Mergers and Acquisitions, Asset Finance, Risk Management Advisory, and the Transactional Development Group. Bankers Trust offers a full range of advisory services including divestitures and corporate sales, recapitalizations, defense advisory, restructuring and reorganizations, and privatizations. The Mergers and Acquisitions Group ranked 12th in advisory deal rankings for the first half of 1995 with over $7.1 billion in completed deal volume. The Transaction Development Group provides expertise in M&A, equity risk management, dollar and non-dollar interest rate hedging, structured notes, and capital raising. Associates are hired into one of the specific advisory groups.

Interested students should contact Susan Markell, Elizabeth Wood-Snell, Liz Lieberman, or Anne Peach.

Real Estate Investment Bank

The Real Estate Investment Bank provides client financial advisory services, performs debt placements and syndications, structures innovative real estate securities and real estate investment trusts, and completes equity investments and placements. With a real estate debt and equity position valued at more than $1 billion, Bankers Trust has extensive hands-on experience with real estate investment and asset management. Associates rotate through three main departments: Finance and Origination, Direct Investment, and Positioning and Distribution.

Interested students should contact Susan Markell.

Latin America Merchant Bank

The Latin America Merchant Bank (LAMB) is comprised of several functional specializations, including Client Advisory (country-specific), Capital Markets (Debt/Equity/Hybrids), Derivative Products, M&A, Structured Finance, Real Estate, and Trading and Distribution. Associates work on a variety of projects simultaneously, including writing proposals, analyzing companies, monitoring capital markets pricing and trends, and meeting with clients. The majority of the positions are available in New York; select positions are available in Latin America.

Interested students should contact Susan Markell.

Global Risk Management and Policy Business

The Global Risk Management department is responsible for overseeing the worldwide market risks of Bankers Trust's proprietary and client-driven businesses. The department defines risk management policy, sets and approves market risk limits, and sets uniform standards for market risk assessment. This is accomplished by determining market risk limits, using a uniform standard for market risk assessment (RAROC), identifying, evaluating, and reporting market risk in all business lines and performing strategic planning. The GRM&P Group also conducts fee-based market risk consulting for external clients.

During the first year, MBA associates can expect to generate models, participate in new product development, create market strategies, execute trades, and prepare client presentations. MBA associates in Global Trading's Funds Management Group have helped determine that the Portuguese Escudo represented excellent value, enabling BT to accumulate sizable positions in the currency before its EMR entry and subsequent appreciation. MBA associates in the Global Portfolio Group worked on fixed-rate cross currency swaps to help extend the maturity of the firm's foreign exchange hedges during a period of divergent yield curves in the United States (steeply positive) versus Europe (slightly inverted).

Interested students should contact Colette Gardner.

Global Markets Proprietary Business

The Global Markets Proprietary business is comprised of the Global Trading and Global Portfolio groups as well as the trading, capital markets, funds management, and merchant banking businesses in the Australia/New Zealand markets.

The Global Trading Group trades liquid instruments including U.S. Treasury and Federal Agency Securities, Foreign Government Securities, Foreign Exchange, and Currency Options. Global Trading also manages a fund for a performance-based fee and foreign exchange funds for institutional clients.

The Global Portfolio Group is responsible for the funding of the corporation worldwide, capital and liquidity management, the management of the corporation's investment portfolio, and the intermediate and longer term proprietary trading of liquid securities, foreign exchange, and derivative products.

The traditional trading businesses consist of foreign exchange, sovereign bonds, and U.S. government securities. The Foreign Exchange Group is responsible for capturing risk and market opportunities through spot trading, cross currency trading, interest rate differentials, and currency options. The Sovereign Bond Group is responsible for capturing risk and market opportunities through liquid trading, arbitrage activity, and intermediate-term risk taking. The U.S. Government Securities Group is responsible for capturing risk through primary market participation and secondary market trading. The proprietary business is responsible for maintaining and enhancing the financial structure of the corporation. The group focuses on managing the bank's balance sheet, maintaining liquidity and low-cost funding for all bank transactions.

During the first year, MBA associates can expect to generate models, participate in new product development, create market strategies, execute trades, and prepare client presentations. Officer trainees in Global Trading's Funds Management Group have helped determine that the Portuguese Escudo represented excellent value, enabling BT to accumulate sizable positions in the currency before its EMR entry and subsequent appreciation. Officer trainees in the Global Portfolio Group worked on fixed-rate cross currency swaps to help extend the maturity of the firm's foreign exchange hedges during a period of divergent yield curves in the United States (steeply positive) versus Europe (slightly inverted).

Interested students should contact Colette Gardner, Liz Lieberman, or Anne Peach.

Global Investment Management Business

The Global Investment Management (GIM) business brings together all of the resources dedicated to asset management at Bankers Trust. With a network of global investment offices, more than $180 billion in assets under management, and over 50 years of investment management experience, Bankers Trust's GIM business offers institutions and individuals a range of products that span the investment spectrum. GIM employs over 400 individuals in New York, London, Tokyo, and Hong Kong.

In contrast to the Global Markets Proprietary business at Bankers Trust which operates as a principal in markets and advises client origination of securities (the "sell" side), GIM is a fiduciary asset manager, investing client assets (the "buy" side). GIM portfolio managers also invest proprietary capital in high-performing strategies in separate accounts from client funds.

The GIM business has integrated the Bank's risk management and investment management talent and is leading the way in introducing new forms of specialization and dynamic asset allocation methods to the industry. By working regularly with our customers on identifying, asset allocating, and thoughtfully executing a client-driven investment strategy, GIM is able to deliver superior performance-driven products that precisely fit the needs of our clients.

The scope of GIM's capabilities is unique, covering advanced trading and derivative strategies as well as traditional active and indexed products. GIM manages over 66 investment strategies, roughly equal amounts in equities and fixed income, and equal amounts in active and quantitative strategies. Although GIM is large in terms of assets under management, it is an organization comprised of small teams of talented specialists who focus on a particular market niche. This type of organization structure fosters entrepreneurial initiative within a large organization.

GIM's proven traditional investment management capabilities include active equity management, active fixed income management, cash management, and equity index management. In addition to our traditional investment management capabilities, GIM also has a dedicated Hedge Funds and Derivative Products team. This team has been continuously engaged in structuring derivatives for asset managers in world securities, commodities, and foreign exchange markets, providing unique advantages in altering return and risk exposures and lowering overall transaction costs. The Hedge Funds and Derivative Product team uses advanced analytical models developed in our Proprietary Trading Group to measure and manage diversified portfolios to achieve the highest return per unit of risk for our clients.

GIM's extensive investment capabilities are sold by GIM product specialists and Private Advisory Services relationship managers. While historically our clients have been primarily U.S. corporate pension funds, GIM has established a solid presence in managing assets for governments, central banks, insurance companies, and high net worth individuals. Bankers Trust's goal is to become the global leader in asset management and is aggressively expanding its domestic and international base significantly by focusing on performance and risk management. We intend to achieve this goal by continuing to attract and retain talented individuals, encouraging an entrepreneurial business environment, and developing innovative investment solutions for our clients.

During the first year an associate with the group can expect to participate in and contribute to all aspects of the business, from generating models, marketing the group's capabilities and products, tailoring and structuring investment vehicles for clients, to selecting and trading for the group's portfolios.

Interested students should contact Debbie Barry.

Technology

Bankers Trust views technology as key to its competitive success. The Bank relies on a combination of application development units embedded in each business and a central technology organization. Developers are part of their respective businesses, participating in the creation of new products and responding quickly to shifts in the market. The central organization provides architectural strategy and standards as well as "economies of scale" functions like telecommunications and systems engineering. This approach is uniquely successful for Bankers Trust in large part due to the understanding and commitment it receives from all levels of management.

The result is a technology function that is responsive to the business, yet consistent in architecture and direction. This powerful combination has been cited by industry analysts and regulators as giving us a position of true leadership in the effective leveraging of information technology.

As Technology associates, MBAs work in partnership with their respective businesses or with the technologists who provide engineering and infrastructure support throughout the firm. The specific role associates play depends on their experience and interests, not just their position in the organization. Bankers Trust Technology encourages employees to take initiative and to work as a team to help the business evolve and improve.

Typical technology assignments include:

- designing and implementing a new interest rate swap processing system;
- building a fully object-oriented trading support system;
- conceptualizing and implementing "groupware" for the front-office professionals of a business on a worldwide basis, including PC-based market data feeds, filtered news feeds, document management capabilities, and retrieval engines with links to a variety of internal and external databases;
- rebuilding Bankers Trust's worldwide telecommunications infrastructure with next-generation technology; and
- marketing and then delivering an integrated customer workstation for a large new fiduciary and trust services customer.

Interested students should contact Jennifer Lemaigre.

Management Consulting Group

The Management Consulting Group can be your introduction to Bankers Trust. Here you will be immediately exposed to many of the key issues facing the bank today. As an MCG consultant, you will work closely with the senior managers who lead Bankers Trust's businesses. Our clients and project work span the entire spectrum of BT's business portfolio: Global Investment Management, Global Investment Banking, Global Emerging Markets, Global Institutional Services, the Private Advisory Services Group (our Private Bank), the Risk Merchant Bank, Global Markets Proprietary, and the Office of the Chief Financial Officer.

The MCG is a unique, respected, and truly innovative consulting practice. Our senior professionals have joined us from the world's leading consulting firms. We offer something no other external organization can match—after learning about BT's products, culture and major initiatives, and raising the value of key businesses, you will rotate into a key line or staff position and assume significant management responsibilities.

As a professional with the MCG, you will deliver a diverse range of advisory services. Your client activities will include projects focused on new product introduction, core business process re-design, competitive bench marking, systems and MIS enhancement initiatives, and market/financial analysis. Working on these projects requires you to negotiate initial proposals with prospective clients, structure the problem solving effort, complete a comprehensive analysis, and present our final recommendations. In addition, MCG professionals participate directly in the execution and implementation of our recommendations, further preparing you for a line position.

Considering BT's flat organizational structure, performance-based management style, and distinct institutional culture, you will be able to direct your own career into areas where your talents are continually enhanced and your interests are matched to the bank's most important challenges.

Interested students should contact Karen McCartney.

The Finance MBA's Job Description

Describe the career path and corresponding responsibilities for an MBA at your firm.

Global Investment Bank/Real Estate Investment Bank/Latin America Merchant Bank/Global Risk Management and Policy/Global Markets Proprietary/Global Investment Management

All MBA associates in the Global Investment Bank, Real Estate Investment Bank, Latin America Merchant Bank, Global Risk Management and Policy, Global Market Proprietary, and Global Investment Management groups attend a two-month Financial Services Training Program.

The objective of the program is to provide an overview of each group's fast-paced, ever-changing environment. The program includes presentations on foreign exchange, trading, long- and short-term origination, trading and distribution, mortgage-backed securities sales and trading, liabilities/positioning, derivative products, client advisory, as well as financial strategies and arbitrage. All course work is developed and taught by our internal line managers.

Upon completion of the training program:

Global Investment Bank trainees are placed in one of the GIB businesses based upon their individual interests, aptitude, and current needs of the business groups.

Real Estate Investment Bank associates receive on-the-job training in essential real estate concepts and practices.

Latin America associates participate in a two-week Latin America training program addressing more regionally specific issues such as inflationary accounting, bond math, and valuation techniques.

Global Risk Management and Policy trainees are placed in one of the businesses based upon their individual interests, aptitude, and current needs of the business groups.

Global Markets Proprietary trainees are placed in one of the businesses based upon their individual interests, aptitude, and current needs of the business groups.

Global Investment Management training also includes an introduction to various areas within GIM, including High Yield Fixed Income, Derivative Products, Hedge Funds, and Passive and Active Equity funds.

Technology

Bankers Trust believes in staying flexible with a solid technical architecture as a foundation. Therefore, the firm does not pre-program your assignments, ongoing skills development, or career. Instead, associates are allowed to progress at their own pace, quickly assuming responsibility for increasingly demanding assignments.

Management Consulting Group

MBA's entering the MCG receive a combination of formal and informal training on a wide range of disciplines including analytical and conceptual problem solving, influence management, core process re-design, derivatives, and communications and presentation skills. The emphasis is on skills development through direct client interaction, project work, and immediate responsibility.

The Recruiting Process

Describe your recruiting process and the criteria by which you select candidates. Is prior experience necessary?

Global Investment Bank/Global Risk Management/Global Markets Proprietary

The successful candidate will be an MBA with outstanding academic achievement, proven leadership ability, drive, and motivation to succeed. We are seeking individuals who possess flexibility, a strong analytic and quantitative background, and demonstrate a risk orientation. The successful candidate is bright, outgoing, creative, flexible, and aggressive, possessing the ability to perform optimally in a high-pressure environment.

Real Estate Investment Bank

The ideal candidate has an MBA in finance and/or real estate. We are seeking MBAs who possess strong analytical and communication skills, along with the ability to prioritize tasks and work as part of a team. Successful candidates will have a strong command of accounting and financial modeling using a PC. Prior professional experience in finance or real estate is preferred.

Latin America Merchant Bank

The successful candidate is an MBA with strong analytic and quantitative ability and excellent communication skills both in English and the relevant foreign languages (Spanish and/or Portuguese, Hebrew, Arabic and Asian dialects).

Global Investment Management

The successful candidate will be an MBA with outstanding academic achievement, proven leadership ability, drive, and motivation to succeed. We are looking for individuals who possess strong analytical and quantitative skills. The successful candidate is creative, aggressive, and performs optimally in a dynamic and constantly changing environment.

Technology

A successful candidate's qualifications will include technical depth and breadth, well-developed interpersonal and communicative skills, and the ability to manage several projects simultaneously. Experience in the financial services industry is valuable but not required.

Management Consulting Group

We hire individuals who are challenged by the project-oriented, rapidly changing environment of a professional consulting firm and who, at the same time, express a longer-term interest in moving into line positions in one of BT's businesses. Successful candidates will demonstrate very strong problem solving skills—at both the pure analytical and more conceptual levels—and will be able to develop, recommend, and execute insightful solutions with confidence. We require self-starters with high energy and motivation who can come up the learning curve quickly across a broad range of business issues.

We look forward to meeting many of you.

Bear, Stearns & Co. Inc.

245 Park Avenue
New York, NY 10167
(212) 272-2000

MBA Recruiting Contact(s):
Jennifer Rolnick,
MBA Recruiting Manager
Investment Banking
(212) 272-7749

MBA Recruiting Coordinator:
Amy Rosen
Debt and Equity Markets
(212) 272-3586

Company Description

Describe your firm's business and the types of clients served by your finance group(s).

Bear, Stearns & Co. Inc. ("Bear Stearns") is a leading global investment banking and securities firm with over $8.9 billion in total capital and more than 7,800 employees worldwide. The firm's primary businesses are the Investment Banking Department and the Debt and Equity Markets groups. In addition, Bear Stearns provides professional and correspondent clearing services to over 1,989 securities firms.

Over the past ten years, Bear Stearns has grown rapidly in size and capital base. Bear Stearns has built its reputation as an aggressive and innovative investment banking and trading firm by carefully matching its capital and underwriting commitments with disciplined and sustained growth, and since its founding over 70 years ago, Bear Stearns has never had an unprofitable year. The combination of rapid growth, disciplined management, and an entrepreneurial culture creates tremendous opportunities for those people with the talent and desire to excel in investment banking.

Bear Stearns is headquartered in New York City. In addition to nine domestic offices, Bear Stearns maintains offices in Beijing, Geneva, Hong Kong, London, Madrid, Manila, Paris, São Paulo, Shanghai, and Tokyo.

Investment Banking Department

Bear Stearns' Investment Banking Department offers a full range of advisory and underwriting services to a broad array of public and private sector clients. These services include:

- Mergers and Acquisitions
- Corporate Finance
- Emerging Markets Finance
- Debt and Equity Capital Markets
- High Yield Finance
- Financial Restructuring
- Project Finance
- Asset-Backed Finance
- Public Finance
- Principal Investments

Bear Stearns' investment banking capabilities are enhanced by a focus on certain specialized industries. Bear Stearns' industry specializations include retailing, media and entertainment telecommunications, technology, energy, forest products, financial institutions, health care, aerospace/defense, chemicals, utilities, and gaming.

1996 was another record year in the mergers and acquisitions advisory services, with 97 announced or completed transactions with a value of over $95 billion. The firm's accomplishments in mergers and acquisitions exemplify the progress and success of Bear Stearns' investment banking effort. In 1996, Securities Data Company, Inc. ranked Bear Stearns ninth as top advisor on all announced global transactions and fifth as advisor to targets on domestic announced transactions. Recently the firm has advised clients including: Cablevision Systems, Corp., HFS, Inc., Hoechst AG, Honeywell, Inc., ITT Corp., Libbey Inc., Lockheed Martin Corp., Maidenform Worldwide, Inc., Nynex Corp., Nynex CableComms plc., Paul G. Allen, Raytheon Company, Rhone-Poulenc Rorer, Time-Warner, Inc., The Walt Disney Company, and Warner-Lambert Company.

Bear Stearns' Capital Markets Departments ensure efficient and appropriate funding for clients through the origination, underwriting, trading and distribution of corporate equity and debt securities. Significant equity offerings in recent months include Planet Hollywood International, Vail Resorts, Guangshen Railway, and Donna Karan International. Moreover, Bear Stearns managed transactions for Lucent Technologies and Associates First Capital, which were the largest two initial public offerings by U.S. issuers in history.

In 1996, Bear Stearns managed 69 high yield transactions, raising over $15 billion in proceeds. The firm ranked second among underwriters of public and 144A high yield transactions and first in 144As. Transactions completed in 1996 included a number of innovative structures and "firsts in the market, such as the introduction of a revenue participation structure for ORBCOMM Global, L.P. Other notable transactions include a $1.6 billion PIK Preferred issue for Time Warner Inc., $875 million of Senior Notes for Unisys Corporation in two separate transactions and a $650 million PIK Preferred issue for Cablevision Systems Corporation.

Fixed Income & Equity Markets

Fixed Income

Bear Stearns is a leader in the Fixed Income Markets; these markets include mortgages, derivatives, high yield, corporations, governments and municipal securities. The firm's recognized position in these markets is enhanced by product innovation, unique systems technology and fixed income research. Our goal is to add value to our customers by leveraging our research, trading and distribution capabilities.

Bear Stearns is recognized by the Federal Reserve Bank of New York as the primary dealer of U.S. government securities. The firm has consistently ranked within the top three for the lead manager of mortgage-backed issues for the past seven years and offers a full line of mortgages as asset-related products in the U.S. and Euromarkets. Domestically, Bear Stearns accounted for 27% of the public issuance of asset-backed securities in 1996, which is an 80% increase from the previous year.

Underpinning the firm's success in the fixed income markets is the Financial Analytics and Structured Transactions (F.A.S.T.) Group, a firmwide resource providing financial engineering and securitization capabilities, investment research, fixed income portfolio management and analytical systems, trading technology, and general financial expertise. This group has developed one of the most advanced fixed income analytical capabilities in the securities industry, and serves as a primary tool in facilitating the trading and sales of all the firm's fixed income products.

Equities

Bear Stearns is a leader in the trading and distribution of equity securities for institutional customers. The firm consistently represents about 10% of the volume on the NYSE, which is more than any other firm on Wall Street. Our significant floor operations and order flow result in superior execution capabilities.

Through the combined efforts of the equity sales force, trading professionals and equity research, the institutional equity department offers premier sales and trading services to its clients. The Equity Research Department provides value-added ideas to Bear Stearns' client base by focusing on over 65 specific industries and categories of stocks representing 800 companies.

Bear Stearns is acknowledged as a leader in over-the-counter ("OTC") equity trading. By limiting the number of stocks in which the Firm makes markets to 400, we are able to maintain standards of depth and trading-service quality. Bear Stearns has developed a major presence in the secondary trading of NASDAQ-listed stocks.

The Finance MBA's Job Description

Describe the career path and corresponding responsibilities for an MBA at your firm.

Investment Banking

Associates work on a wide variety of corporate finance and merger and acquisition transactions in a variety of different industries. Often, an Associate will be working on three to five different transactions in project teams that typically consist of three to four people.

Job responsibilities include detailed financial analysis and modeling; due diligence with respect to a client's business, industry, financial results, and projects; creation of new business proposals/presentations; and preparation of internal memoranda for the various committees that review and approve transactions.

After a three week training program, Associates begin working either as generalists or in a product or industry specialty group. Associates are typically eligible for promotion to Vice President after three years. The timing of future promotions is based entirely on performance.

MBA Job Description

Sales & Trading Associates are hired by either the Fixed Income or Equity divisions. The Associates will participate in a classroom training program for a period of eight weeks and then they will rotate among the various products areas within the division they have been hired by. After a period of three months of rotations the Associates will be placed on a desk based on the preference of the Associates and the needs of the firm. The timing and frequency of promotions are based entirely on an individual's performance.

The Recruiting Process

Describe your recruiting process and the criteria by which you select candidates. Is prior experience necessary?

Bear Stearns endeavors to hire individuals who have demonstrated outstanding academic achievement and a proven track record of performance excellence. In addition, a candidate should possess strong oral and written communications skills, attention to detail and concern for accuracy, the ability to work well with others under pressure, and a willingness to work long hours. No specific academic major is a prerequisite; however, a strong finance and accounting background is desired and candidates must be proficient with financial and mathematical concepts.

Do you have a summer program for associates or analysts? If so, please describe.

Bear Stearns has a Summer Associate program in which MBA candidates are hired as generalists in Investment Banking and Debt and Equity Markets. Over the course of the summer, Investment Banking Summer Associates will have the opportunity to work on a variety of projects in the mergers and acquisitions, capital markets, and corporate finance areas. Debt and Equity Markets Summer Associates have the opportunity to work with the firm's sales and trading professionals in variety of different product areas. Bear Stearns views the Summer Associate program as an important part of its overall hiring process and recruits Summer Associates to aid in providing the firm with the best possible assessment of an individual's long-term potential.

Bowles Hollowell Conner & Co.

227 West Trade Street
Charlotte, NC 28202
(704) 348-1000
Fax: (704) 348-1099

MBA Recruiting Contact(s):
Matthew B. Salisbury
(704) 348-1015

Mike Peters
(704) 348-1052

Company Description

Describe your firm's business and the types of clients served by your finance group(s).

Bowles Hollowell Conner & Co. is a national investment banking firm specializing in corporate finance services for middle-market companies. From its Charlotte headquarters, the firm assists corporations, private investment firms, and middle-market companies with mergers and acquisitions; divestitures; structured financing, including private placements of senior and mezzanine debt and equity securities; and valuations. Transaction values typically range from $15 million to $200 million.

Describe your ownership structure.

Bowles Hollowell Conner & Co. is a private corporation owned by its employees.

How does your approach to finance differ from that of other firms, and what do you consider to be your strengths and distinctive capabilities?

Bowles Hollowell Conner & Co. was founded in 1975 to provide middle-market companies with a level of corporate finance expertise generally not available to them. Although the nation's largest corporations have long had the benefit of expert consultation and assistance with complex corporate finance matters, this same expertise has not been readily available to smaller companies.

Our firm has been successful in helping to fill this void. A professional staff of approximately 60 employees provides clients with the high level of knowledge and experience in business, finance, accounting, law, and taxation needed for success with corporate finance transactions.

Bowles Hollowell Conner & Co. has demonstrated capability in a wide range of transactions in many different industries, from basic manufacturing to high technology and from consumer products to industrial commodities. In all of its services, the firm emphasizes thoroughness of preparation, professionalism in execution, and effectiveness in assisting clients in meeting business objectives.

A specialty of Bowles Hollowell Conner & Co. is in the area of mergers, acquisitions, and divestitures involving companies with values less than $200 million. Clients include large corporations, private investment firms, and public and private middle-market companies. The firm represents either the buyer or the seller in a typical transaction. In addition, Bowles Hollowell Conner & Co. provides valuation services to public and private companies for purposes such as fairness opinions, employee stock ownership plans, or individual estate and gift tax planning.

During the 1990s, Bowles Hollowell Conner & Co. has increased its emphasis on assisting clients in the capital raising process. The Corporate Finance Group is focused on raising capital for organizations for a variety of purposes, including financings, leveraged recapitalizations, and restructurings.

Discuss changes in your firm's revenues (both domestic and international) and professional staff over the past year; over the past five years.

Bowles Hollowell Conner & Co. has enjoyed tremendous growth over the past five years, and 1996 was a record year for the firm in terms of transactions completed, revenue, and profits. As such, Bowles Hollowell Conner & Co. offers a new associate the opportunity to develop corporate finance skills in a dynamic environment.

The Finance MBA's Job Description

Describe the career path and corresponding responsibilities for an MBA at your firm.

Bowles Hollowell Conner & Co. expects each MBA whom it hires as an associate to become a managing director and owner of the firm. The responsibilities of an associate revolve around working in a team environment on a variety of transactions and generally on several transactions at the same time. As a critical member of the team, the associate is responsible for managing the work of one or more analysts on the team, overseeing the preparation of qualitative and quantitative analyses, writing comprehensive business descriptions and other documents, ensuring the accuracy and quality of all the analytical work supporting the transaction, and relating the ideas of the firm to the client. The firm offers a flexible environment that rewards initiative and allows the associate to develop as quickly as he or she is capable.

Describe the opportunities for professional mobility between the various departments in your firm.

Because the firm is devoted exclusively to the corporate finance needs of middle-market companies, each new professional is developed as a generalist working on a variety of assignments and teams within the firm.

Discuss the lifestyle aspects of a career with your firm (i.e., average hours per week, amount of travel, flexibility to change offices, corporate culture, etc.).

The business of the firm requires a great deal of hard work, dedication, and sacrifice. A high level of commitment is necessary to deliver financial expertise of the highest quality in the timeliest manner. Because approximately seventy-five percent of our assignments are outside the southeastern United States, an associate will be required to travel regularly throughout the country on firm business. Nevertheless, the firm respects the requirement of each individual for personal time away from the office and the importance of developing interests outside the firm.

In addition, involvement in outside activities within the community is viewed as an important aspect of an associate's development, and members of the firm participate in a variety of external community activities.

The Recruiting Process

Describe your recruiting process and the criteria by which you select candidates. Is prior experience necessary?

The firm is looking for MBAs who have demonstrated the potential to analyze financial problems quickly and effectively. We look for academic achievement, intellectual ability, demonstrated leadership abilities, personal integrity, and the ability to communicate ideas and recommendations effectively, orally and in writing. Although not a strict requirement, we look for individuals with two to four years of meaningful work experience.

How many permanent associates and analysts do you hire in a typical year? How many summer interns do you expect to hire? If you have a formal summer program, please describe it. Please be sure to indicate whether the summer program is in place for all offices or just some.

Bowles Hollowell Conner & Co. expects to hire five to seven associates and ten to twelve analysts in the coming year. The firm has brief, formal training programs for both associates and analysts but strongly favors on-the-job training. Associates and analysts are expected to become productive members of the firm quickly.

The firm currently has no summer program for MBAs, but the initiation of such a program is under consideration.

What international opportunities does your firm offer for U.S. citizens? For foreign nationals?

Bowles Hollowell Conner & Co.'s Charlotte headquarters is currently the company's only office. However, since roughly one-quarter of its sell-side engagements are completed with foreign buyers, Bowles Hollowell Conner & Co. relies upon its professionals' knowledge of foreign languages and their ability to conduct business in an international arena. A good portion of an associate's international work is in the form of phone calls, conversations, and visits with parties who are candidates to purchase or finance a transaction for which Bowles Hollowell Conner & Co. has been engaged.

Broadview Associates, LLC

One Bridge Plaza
Fort Lee, NJ 07024
(201) 346-9000
Fax: (201) 346-9191
Web site: www.broadview.com

MBA Recruiting Contact(s):
James Calver, Senior Associate and Harvard Team Captain

Bonnie Frankel, Recruiting Coordinator

Company Description

Describe your firm's business and the types of clients served by your finance group(s).

Broadview Associates, LLC is the leading merger and acquisition (M&A) firm serving companies in the global information technology (IT) industry or seeking initial participation in the industry. Founded in 1973, Broadview dominates M&A within the principal sectors of the IT industry, which encompasses software, hardware, internetworking, telecommunications, media, marketing/processing services, and database publishing businesses. Broadview completed eighty-eight transactions in 1996 with a total value approaching $5 billion. In addition to M&A, Broadview services include minority investments, private placements, and strategic alliances. The firm is also a general partner to Geocaptal, a venture capital firm formed to make private equity investments in the IT industry.

Broadview represents both buyer and seller clients. Buyer clients include large IT suppliers as well as smaller, specialized IT companies. IT companies seek to secure a sustainable competitive advantage and boost shareholder value by adding technologies, products, operations, and access to markets. Frequently, their objectives can be satisfied by acquiring part or all of a niche player. On the other side, seller clients that want to manage the passage between early growth stages and sustainable, superior equity value seek to leverage the resources of a larger, more established enterprise. Typically, companies wishing to sell have developed new technologies and products, gained unique market positions, or marshaled unique human resource capabilities that they cannot fully exploit alone. An appropriate partner for a seller client can telescope market-product development cycles, provide required capital, shrink the associated risks, and gain an innovative and focused management team.

The interaction of these corporate supply and demand forces has made IT the most M&A-prone industry in the world. Given the complexity and rapid change in this industry, finding the right strategic fit can be a difficult task. As a result, buyers and sellers utilize Broadview to grasp the industry's strategic underpinnings, as well as to leverage our track record of transaction experience. Broadview has over 175 employees located in offices in Fort Lee (NJ), Foster City (CA), and London. Opportunities exist for career growth and development throughout the firm.

Describe your ownership structure.

Broadview Associates is structured as a limited liability corporation. Each of the firm's eighteen managing directors is recognized by the IT industry as an expert and spokesperson in M&A.

How does your approach to finance differ from that of other firms, and what do you consider to be your strengths and distinctive capabilities?

Developed and seasoned for twenty-four years, Broadview's unique set of qualifications includes the following:

- *Transaction experience.* The managing directors and associates of Broadview know the IT M&A environment because of their strong roots in the IT industry. They have been founders of privately held IT companies, as well as corporate officers of public companies. Their hands-on knowledge and experience assure clients that highly informed analysis and judgment concerning the multiple aspects of an acquisition will be readily available throughout the acquisition process.
- *Concentration.* Through its experience and industry focus, Broadview offers its clients an exceptionally high degree of expertise in a dynamic and complex environment.
- *Commitment.* Broadview's deal activities mirror those of the overall IT industry. Broadview has participated in the industry's largest, most highly visible transactions, including Softbank's $1.5 billion majority investment in Kingston Technology and IBM's purchase of Data Sciences. However, given that the average deal in the IT industry has a value of under $20 million, Broadview also participates in many transactions whose size is typically outside the focus of the M&A departments of traditional investment banking firms. One of Broad-

view's strengths is its depth of experience in these middle-market transactions.

- *Contacts.* Broadview enjoys relationships with managers and directors throughout the IT industry, as well as with other players seeking to participate in this segment. In addition, Broadview maintains close working relationships with the venture capital community, given the predominance of venture-backed IT companies. This network provides unparalleled insight into the external development needs and strategies of IT companies.
- *Proprietary information.* Broadview's research department maintains the industry's most comprehensive databases in support of the firm's M&A and minority investment activity. The firm maintains active files on over 40,000 companies, as well as a proprietary database of IT industry acquisitions. Since 1980, Broadview has published the semiannual *Broadview Merger Report,* which tracks and analyzes M&A activity and valuation benchmarks within the industry. This report is well recognized throughout the industry and serves a valuable tool for both marketing to prospective clients and valuing companies engaged in transactions.

The Finance MBA's Job Description

Describe the career path and corresponding responsibilities for an MBA at your firm.

Associates are quickly given client management responsibility. The associate assists in the development of acquisition and divestiture strategies, identifies companies in relevant IT segments that represent potential partners, handles approaches to target companies, and ultimately helps to structure and negotiate deals between client and target companies. In managing the client relationship, the associate usually serves as part of a three-person team, joined by a managing director and an analyst. Each team member has unique responsibility and interacts daily. The associate manages daily client contact and leads in coordinating activities among the team members.

Discuss the lifestyle aspect of a career with your firm (i.e., average hours per week, amount of travel, flexibility to change offices, corporate culture, etc.)

Broadview attracts and seeks dedicated, self-motivated professionals who can generate a superior quality of work without sacrificing their lifestyles. Travel is required, but the extent varies by specific assignment.

The Recruiting Process

Describe your recruiting process and the criteria by which you select candidates. Is prior experience necessary?

Broadview seeks individuals with excellent written and oral communication skills, transaction experience, and demonstrated interest or experience in the IT industry. The ideal candidate must also be a highly motivated self-starter and possess strong interpersonal skills.

If you have a formal summer program, please describe it.

A summer associate at Broadview will work with the firm's senior management team on one of a number of projects to advance Broadview's position in the market. The projects are likely to include analysis of:

1. Opportunities in Asia for IT M&A.
2. Emerging niche markets and companies in software, hardware, digital media and/or wireless telecommunications services.
3. New management practices that can advance Broadview's franchise.

What international opportunities does your firm offer for U.S. citizens? For foreign nationals?

Broadview's London office is staffed by U.S. citizens and foreign nationals from France, Germany, the United Kingdom, and other European countries. Candidates for the London office typically have foreign language fluency.

BT Wolfensohn
Division of BT Securities Corporation

599 Lexington Avenue
New York, NY 10022
(212) 909-0878
Fax: (212) 909-0831

MBA Recruiting Contact(s):
Donna Freet, Recruiting Coordinator

Company Description

Describe your firm's business and the types of clients served by your finance group(s).

BT Wolfensohn provides personalized financial advisory and investment banking services on a global basis to international industrial corporations and financial institutions in the following areas:

- Mergers, acquisitions, divestitures, and strategic alliances;
- Corporate share value and asset optimization; and
- Corporation reorganizations, workouts and bankruptcy.

BT Wolfensohn ranks among the top investment banks as measured by the value of the transactions in which it has acted as financial advisor to its clients. These transactions have included several highly visible, important transactions such as the acquisition of Capital Cities/ABC by The Walt Disney company; the merger of Chase Manhattan Corporation and Chemical Banking Corporation; the acquisition of AIM Management by Invesco PLC; the sale of U.S. Shoe Corporation to Luxottica; the sale of Labatt to Interbrew; the buyback of Seagram's stake in Du Pont; the purchase by NCNB, now NationsBank, of C&S Sovran and MNC Financial Inc.; the purchase of the Boston Globe by The New York Times Company; the merger of Cyprus Minerals and Amax Inc.; and significant corporate spin-offs by American Express, Marriott Corporation, and Amax Inc.

BT Wolfensohn provides its services in the context of broad, long-term relationships with its clients. BT Wolfensohn believes that it can be much more effective on behalf of its clients when it works on a long-term strategic basis rather than on a transaction-by-transaction basis. The firm often participates in the development of its clients' financial strategy, providing transaction-related advisory services in the context of these strategic objectives.

In August 1996, Wolfensohn & Co. and Bankers Trust merged to form BT Wolfensohn, which will constitute the M&A and corporate advisory practice of the bank. Its charter will be to continue the Wolfensohn approach on the broader Bankers Trust platform. The merger with Bankers Trust gives recognition to the hard-earned prominence and reputation of Wolfensohn through retention of its valued name, maintenance of its existing management structure, strict adherence to its core culture, and integration of Bankers Trust's merger and acquisition operations under the BT Wolfensohn structure. The merger combined Wolfensohn's proven abilities in senior strategic advisory and M&A activities with Bankers Trust's leading abilities to create and execute innovative financial structures and transactions.

James D. Wolfensohn founded the firm in 1981 and served as the firm's President and Chief Executive Officer until his appointment as President of the World Bank in June 1995. Paul A. Volcker, the former Chairman of the Federal Reserve Board, served as CEO of Wolfensohn & Co., Inc. until the merger, at which time he joined the Board of Directors of Bankers Trust.

BT Wolfensohn is committed to the M&A and corporate advisory business on a global basis. Through our London office, Latin America effort and international joint venture with Fuji Bank, we service many clients headquartered in Europe, Latin America, and Asia/Pacific. We also leverage our international business presence and capability in order to service better our U.S.-based clients, many of whom are facing decisions which are becoming increasingly global in nature.

The Latin American Group at BT Wolfensohn, New York
BT Wolfensohn has a group of professionals dedicated to Latin America advisory business. The breadth of this group was significantly enhanced by the merger with Bankers Trust. The group has completed a series of Latin American transactions, including the acquisitions by Cemex, S.A. of Tolmex, S.A. de C.V., Cementos Nacionales, S.A., and a controlling interest in Vencemos, S.A.C.A., the acquisition of Asgrow Seed Company (a subsidiary of the Upjohn Company) by Empresas La Moderna, and the acquisition of a 22% stake in FEMSA Cerveza by John Labatt Ltd.

Fuji Wolfensohn
Fuji Wolfensohn International (FWI) advises retainer clients on strategic and transaction matters, focusing exclusively on Japan-U.S. transactions. FWI calls upon the full range of expertise provided by both the BT Wolfensohn

group and Fuji Bank, the world's second largest bank. Fuji Bank and BT Wolfensohn have also established an International Advisory Board for FWI in order to further the group's global strategies and the international interests of our clients.

How does your approach to finance differ from that of other firms, and what do you consider to be your strengths and distinctive capabilities?

To accomplish its mission, BT Wolfensohn advisory practice was oriented such that the client would always come first:

- **Advisory excellence:** BT Wolfensohn hires a limited number of high-quality professionals each year to provide thoughtful advice and judgment based on an analytical, research-based approach, taking into account long-term strategic and operating considerations, as well as near-term market trends.
- **Personalized approach:** BT Wolfensohn insists on senior-level participation throughout the duration of all projects and not merely during the selling phase. Each client receives rigorous attention from all team members, permitting bankers, at all levels, to develop long-term relationships with their counterparts within the client organization.
- **Long-term relationships:** BT Wolfensohn establishes long-term relationships with our clients which are generally defined by annual retainer arrangements. Such arrangements allow us to participate in the development of each client's long-term financial strategy and to identify and execute transactions consistent with this strategy.
- **Client comes first:** BT Wolfensohn adheres to a "client-comes-first" approach. This principle premeates the firm and is paramount to our hiring, the firm's work ethic, its professionalism, its integrity, and its strict adherence to insuring against any perceived or actual conflicts of interest.

The Finance MBA's Job Description

Describe the career path and corresponding responsibilities for an MBA at your firm.

Given BT Wolfensohn's size and structure, associates can assume significant levels of responsibility early in their careers. During the first years, an associate works as a member of several client teams engaged in specific transactions or analyses. Each client team typically consists of the managing director responsible for the client, a vice president (typically with over four years' experience), an associate (typically with one to four years' experience), and an analyst. As associates gain experience, they take on additional client responsibilities. BT Wolfensohn's philosophy is to develop its bankers as generalists. Associates are therefore given the opportunity to work on assignments across a range of clients and industries in order to gain experience on the strategic and financial issues facing corporations.

Successful associates at BT Wolfensohn possess a balance of sound analytical abilities and the potential to develop strong client and transaction skills. Due to the size and culture of BT Wolfensohn, its bankers work closely with each other. It is therefore critical for new associates to enjoy working in an extremely interactive and tightly knit environment.

BT Wolfensohn's basic approach is on-the-job training for associates. However, new associates are also provided with a three-week orientation and training program upon joining the firm.

The Recruiting Process

Describe your recruiting process and the criteria by which you select candidates. Is prior experience necessary?

BT Wolfensohn's philosophy is to concentrate hiring at the entry level, seeking each year to attract a small number of MBA candidates with the highest academic standing and greatest potential to become outstanding professionals. New associates come from a variety of educational, cultural, and geographical backgrounds. However, given our focus on investment banking and advisory services, most entering associates typically have some previous experience in corporate finance or M&A.

How many permanent associates and analysts do you hire in a typical year? How many summer interns do you expect to hire? If you have a formal summer program, please describe it. Please be sure to indicate whether the summer program is in place for all offices or just some.

BT Wolfensohn's advisory business has grown at a significant rate over the past several years, and the firm plans to recruit 8–10 new associates in total each year for its New York and London offices, as well as for the Latin American practice. BT Wolfensohn plans to hire 4–6 summer associates each year and considers the summer program a critical component of its full-time recruiting process.

BZW

5 The North Colonnade
Canary Wharf
London E14 4BB
(44) 171 623-2323

MBA Recruiting Contact(s):
Jessica Dwerryhouse, Director, Campus Recruiting
Darrin Moy, Director, Campus Recruiting

Company Description

Describe your firm's business and the types of clients served by your finance group(s).

BZW is the investment banking arm of Barclays PLC, one of the world's leading financial services groups. With headquarters in London, BZW acts internationally as intermediary and adviser to major corporations, financial institutions, and governments and has the global reach and distribution power to meet the needs of issuers and investors world-wide.

With substantial operations in New York, Hong Kong, and Tokyo, and offices in thirty-five other cities world-wide, BZW employs 7,500 staff, over half of which are based outside the UK. The firm seeks to distinguish itself by the skill and excellence of its strategic and market advisory services supported by the Barclays Bank balance sheet—one of the strongest in the global banking industry.

BZW's business is organised into three principal divisions: Equities; Investment Banking, comprising corporate finance and structured finance with dedicated resources in project, structured lending and acquisition financing; and Markets, which includes the firm's fixed income, derivatives, foreign exchange, treasury, futures and metals operations.

These three divisions are underpinned by a Capital Markets Group which seeks out and creates product opportunities which involve any or all of Equities, Investment Banking and Markets. At its core is the integration of product structuring with derivatives, credit products and equities.

BZW's strengths can be attributed to four key features:

- Innovative skills applied to problem solving. BZW's willingness to understand the complexities of the needs of its clients is fundamental to the way the firm delivers the appropriate solutions.
- The commitment and support of a strongly capitalised banking group is increasingly seen as essential for a successful investment bank. Such support permits investment in technology and people and allows BZW to mobilise capital on behalf of clients. Barclays has an AA credit rating, assets of £186 billion and capital of £11 billion.
- The ability to nurture and develop its people determines the level of BZW's success. So too does the development of a global technology platform, allowing the firm to manage the complex information flows which are the essence of its business.
- BZW is located in every major financial centre. The reputation the firm enjoys with international investors through its commitment to research and its sales and trading capacity enables the firm to advise, structure, and distribute new issues in a way which meets the needs of both issuers and investors.

The Finance MBS's Job Description

Describe the career path and corresponding responsibilities for an MBA at your firm.

BZW offers outstanding opportunities for MBAs across the firm. Considered as strategic hires the expectation is that they will quickly develop on a fast tracked career. Initial off the desk training, provided in London, is designed to give all hires an overview of the firm and the investment banking sector.

Total access will be provided to senior members of the firm. MBA associates will work closely with a full range of colleagues and will be expected to develop the technical capabilities applied across a whole range of services and products to provide clients with solutions to their needs.

The Recruiting Process

Describe your recruiting process and the criteria by which you select candidates. Is prior experience necessary?

We are looking for outstanding professionals considered to be at the top of their peer group and profession. Diversity is the key to success and you may come from a range of disciplines or backgrounds. Successful applicants will have outstanding interpersonal and communication skills, be commercially focused, and capable of thriving in a dynamic and fast moving environment. The capacity to respond positively to and manipulate change is essential.

How many permanent associates and analysts do you hire in a typical year? How many summer interns do you expect to hire ? If you have a formal summer program, please describe it. Please be sure to indicate whether the summer program is in place for all offices or just some.

We have a significant need for outstanding MBAs throughout our business. We offer international opportunities for permanent and summer internship associates across all geographical locations and divisions.

The Chase Manhattan Corporation

270 Park Avenue
New York, NY 10017

MBA Recruiting Contact(s):
Annette Cuffley, Vice President
(212) 270-7072

Company Description

Describe your firm's business and the types of clients served by your finance group(s).

The Chase Manhattan Corporation is the largest bank holding company in the United States. We are creating a new kind of competitor in the global financial marketplace that combines the best of investment and commercial banking with an ever present focus on the client. Chase's global industry and market focus extends to aerospace & shipping, automotive, trucking and railroads, chemicals, financial institutions and financial sponsors, global natural resources & commodities, healthcare, insurance, media & telecommunications, multinationals, oil & gas, power & environmental, real estate, retail, as well as institutional investors and private clients.

Chase has world class financial advisory, structuring, research, and execution capability across a wide range of investment banking and capital markets products including mergers & acquisitions, syndicated and leveraged finance, high yield corporate finance and sales, trading & research, asset backed securities, derivatives, private placements, project finance, corporate bond origination, trading and research, foreign exchange, global emerging markets and US securities.

Chase is a global leader with a strong presence in the major global financial centers that provide around-the-clock access to a substantial range of capabilities including financing and advisory, sales and trading, trade finance, asset management, private banking and operating services.

Chase has established a critical franchise that extends to more than fifty countries throughout the world as well as locations across the United States. Chase is uniquely positioned to deliver value-added solutions to clients by leveraging its substantial resources of capital, product expertise, industry knowledge, and geographic reach. These resources are fully leveraged for the benefit of clients' local and cross-border financial service needs.

Describe your ownership structure.

The Chase Manhattan Corporation is a publicly owned corporation. As of December 31, 1996, Chase had total stockholders' equity of nearly $21 billion with approximately 441 million common shares outstanding. The corporation conducts its domestic and international financial services businesses through various bank and nonbank subsidiaries. The principal bank subsidiaries of the Corporation are The Chase Manhattan Bank, a New York State bank headquartered in New York City, Texas Commerce Bank National Association, a national bank headquartered in Texas, and Chase Manhattan Bank USA National Association, a national bank headquartered in Delaware. The principal nonbank subsidiary of the corporation is Chase Securities Inc.

How does your approach to finance differ from that of other firms, and what do you consider to be your strengths and distinctive capabilities?

Relationships are the hallmark of Chase. Our global relationship approach allows us to look at a client holistically and more fully understand their broad-based needs. As a result Chase is better positioned to deliver the integrated financing or investment solutions clients need to meet their own corporate objectives.

Chase is among a small group of institutions leading the convergence of traditional commercial and investment banking. At the heart of this effort is a commitment to providing clients with access to a complete range of advisory, financing, and capital markets capabilities. The list of Chase's wholesale clients includes the largest and most dynamic multinational corporations, institutions, government entities, and wealthy individuals throughout the world.

The comprehensive approach we are emphasizing requires superior understanding of our clients and their needs, coupled with product excellence and a management culture that assures the seamless integration of our capabilities globally. Based on our success thus far in forging this new model, we will continue to invest for growth in our investment banking and securities underwriting activities.

Discuss changes in your firm's revenues (both domestic and international) and professional staff over the past year; over the past five years.

(NOTE: On March 31, 1996, The Chase Manhattan Corporation merged with and into Chemical Banking Corporation. Upon consummation of the merger, Chemical changed its name to The Chase Manhattan Corporation. The merger was accounted for as a pooling-of-interests and, accordingly, the information included in this release reports the combined results of Chase and Chemical as though the merger had been in effect for all periods presented.)

1996 was a terrific year for Chase. The corporation met or exceeded all its key financial targets and achieved significant growth across its major business lines while carrying out, on or ahead of schedule, the most complex merger in the history of banking. We did this amid the sweeping change that is so evident within the financial services industry and, most importantly, without compromising the high standards of service that Chase customers rightly expect. This performance was recognized and rewarded by the marketplace with a fifty-two percent appreciation in our share price.

Financial highlights of the past year included:

- A 23 percent increase in fully diluted operating earnings per share to $7.27
- An 18.4 percent return on common equity
- A decline of two percent in operating expenses
- A six point improvement in the efficiency ratio to 57 percent, from 63 percent in 1995
- The return of more than $3 billion in capital to shareholders through stock buybacks and common dividend payout of 29 percent

Chase's financial performance reflected the strength of our two primary business franchises, an attractive economic and market environment and the exceptional dedication and talent of more than 65,000 Chase employees around the world.

Looking ahead, we are confident that we can consistently achieve our baseline financial goals of double digit earnings per share growth, an efficiency ratio in the low 50s and an 18 percent return on equity. To the extent that market or business conditions in a given year are particularly attractive, we would expect to attain even higher levels of profitability.

These are rigorous objectives, but they are in keeping with our conviction that the potential of the new Chase is far greater than we first anticipated and that we are only just beginning to realize the organization's full capacity.

The Finance MBA's Job Description

Describe the career path and corresponding responsibilities for an MBA at your firm.

New associates join Chase in early August, and complete an intensive nine-week training program. In addition to the academic portion, which includes case studies, team assignments, and trading modules, the program also provides extensive introduction to the business units within the Global Bank through presentations from senior practitioners.

The career path for a new associate at Chase will vary depending upon the group the MBA joins. Following successful completion of the training program, Corporate Finance associates will be placed on a series of rotations in both industry and product groups, providing significant exposure to a variety of business units in the Global Bank. These rotations may include an overseas assignment.

Sales & Trading associates have the opportunity to join Chase's Global Markets Group as either generalists or specialists. Generalists are exposed to a variety of product groups within Global Markets prior to permanent assignment. Specialists are hired directly into a product group, typically based on previous experience.

Describe the opportunities for professional mobility between the various departments in your firm.

New associates are encouraged to build relationships throughout Chase. The success of the Global Bank across industries, global markets and products is built upon teamwork and partnership. Movement among business units is supported, based upon business needs, interests and individual development plans.

Discuss the lifestyle aspects of a career with your firm (i.e., average hours per week, amount of travel, flexibility to change offices, corporate culture, etc.).

Lifestyles and requirements vary depending upon which business unit an MBA joins but are typical for the investment banking and sales and trading industries.

The Recruiting Process

Describe your recruiting process and the criteria by which you select candidates. Is prior experience necessary?

Chase invests substantial resources in identifying and recruiting high-quality candidates. Chase hosts on-campus presentations and conducts on-campus interviews. Successful candidates are invited to New York for "Day in Bank" interviews. Selected candidates then participate in "Final Round" interviews at which point an offer decision is made. Chase observes individual school policies in its recruiting process.

The qualifications for a Chase associate include superior quantitative and analytical abilities, excellent interpersonal and marketing skills, maturity, initiative, and a team approach. Strong academic performance is important. Previous work experience, while preferred, is not required.

How many permanent associates and analysts do you hire in a typical year? How many summer interns do you expect to hire? If you have a formal summer program, please describe it. Please be sure to indicate whether the summer program is in place for all offices or just some.

Recruiting goals are set early in the fall for the coming recruiting season based on the staffing needs of each business unit. In 1996, the Global Bank hired fifty-seven MBAs for permanent associate positions and thirty-eight MBA summer associates.

The MBA Summer Associate Program offers candidates an opportunity to work in Global Investment Banking and Client Management or Global Markets Sales & Trading. For corporate finance candidates, Chase offers a unique two rotation program, exposing summer associates to both Client Management and Investment Banking Product units. Summer associates have significant responsibilities and participate directly as part of deal teams during their assignments. Sales & Trading candidates are assigned to a specific group for the summer and participate in a rotation program which introduces them to several capital markets and trading units.

In addition to the MBA Associate and Summer Associate Programs, the Global Bank recruits a significant number of undergraduates each year for its two-year analyst program, which includes formal credit and corporate finance training.

Chevron Corporation

575 Market Street
Suite 3438
San Francisco, CA 94105
(415) 894-2752
Web site: www.chevron.com

MBA Recruiting Contact(s):
Donald Paiva, Coordinator
Finance MBA Development Program

Company Description

Describe your firm's business and the types of clients served by your finance group(s).

Chevron Corporation is an international, integrated petroleum company consistently ranked among the leaders of the Fortune 500. Approximately 41,000 employees generate $43 billion in annual revenues and are responsible for nearly $35 billion in assets.

Headquartered in San Francisco, we are one of the largest producers of petroleum products and natural gas in the United States. Chevron has operations in over 90 countries and is pursuing worldwide ventures in petroleum exploration, production, refining, and marketing. Chevron is an industry leader that is positioned for international growth, building on a rich history of innovation and making the investments needed to provide the world with clean, safe, and economical energy.

In an age of accelerating globalization of the world's national economies, the petroleum industry was one of the first and remains one of the largest, truly global enterprises. The products of this industry can truly be said to drive the engine of our global economy, providing the energy to run our factories, fuel our transportation networks, and heat our homes. This industry vividly defines the risk/reward trade-off: not all multimillion-dollar wells drilled will result in commercially viable finds, and capital-intensive developments often require investments of billions of dollars over time horizons of 10–50 years.

The Finance MBA's Job Description

Describe the career path and corresponding responsibilities for an MBA at your firm.

We are always seeking highly motivated individuals to help us achieve our goals. Chevron recruits MBAs to bring bright, highly talented, and ambitious individuals with leadership and management potential into the finance function. Our goal is to develop senior financial management, including such positions as vice president of finance, comptroller, and treasurer, both at the corporate level and at any of our worldwide operating companies (predominantly headquartered in the Bay Area). Chevron pursues a deliberate policy to give top performers experience in many financial arenas in preparation for senior management.

In order to launch MBAs into this environment, Chevron maintains the Finance MBA Development Program, designed to give MBAs rapid exposure to the company and the finance function. This is a select, entry-level program that has been successfully developing financial and general managers for nearly 50 years. The program provides its members with four six-month assignments over a two-year period and is designed to give them broad exposure to financial and operating activities throughout the corporation. In addition, it provides MBAs with opportunities to apply the financial skills they acquired in business school to activities that contribute directly to the achievement of Chevron's business goals. These assignments are generally greater in responsibility than entry-level positions offered to graduating MBAs by other companies.

The assignments available to program members are located typically in organizations where financial skills are at a premium—corporate units such as the Comptroller's and Treasurer's Departments, plus finance, planning, and other functional positions at major operating companies such as Chevron Production, Chevron Products, Chevron Chemical, Chevron Shipping, and Chevron Overseas Petroleum. There is no preestablished sequence of assignments. Instead, a balanced program is tailored to fit each individual's evolving needs and preferences while meeting the company's changing business requirements.

Having rapidly acquired expertise in many of Chevron's business areas and a wide range of company contacts, program members are placed in challenging positions at the program's conclusion. Many MBAs return to a group in which they had program assignments, while others undertake positions in areas new to them. An individual's personal preferences are considered in conjunction with company needs. By virtue of the high caliber of the participants and the broad experience they have gained in the program, MBAs are in great demand and are well positioned to pursue careers leading to senior financial and, often, general managerial positions. For example, Chevron's CFO, Comptroller, and Treasurer as well as CEO, President-Chevron Production, and President-Chevron Research and Technology are all program alumni.

The Recruiting Process

Describe your recruiting process and the criteria by which you select candidates. Is prior experience necessary?

Applicants must have authorization to work on a full-time basis in the United States (does not include practical training authorization). Although Chevron does not restrict candidates to specific majors or levels of work experience, the Finance MBA Development Program is considered to be most attractive to MBAs with a strong interest in finance who welcome the opportunity to gain rapid exposure to a wide variety of financial activities at Chevron. On average, program members have two to four years of work experience before obtaining their MBA.

How many permanent associates and analysts do you hire in a typical year? How many summer interns do you expect to hire? If you have a formal summer program, please describe it. Please be sure to indicate whether the summer program is in place for all offices or just some.

We hire four to six MBAs into the Finance MBA Development Program each year.

The Finance MBA Development Program sponsors an ongoing summer internship program. Similar to full-time Development Program members, summer interns are challenged by hands-on, meaningful work that provides an opportunity to experience the issues and actions of one of the world's leading corporations. Interns are placed within corporate groups (e.g., Treasury, Comptroller's, Planning) and operating companies (e.g., Chevron Products, Shipping, Chemical).

Internships are typically project oriented, utilizing strong analytical, organizational, and communication skills. Application of financial theory to actual business problem solving is encouraged. All positions are in the San Francisco Bay Area. Exposure to the company and managers outside each intern's particular work group is enhanced by a series of communications meetings, organizational presentations, and other activities. Interns usually have the opportunity to present their accomplishments and conclusions to finance managers at the end of the summer.

In recruiting summer interns, we look for individuals with strong interpersonal and analytical skills, leadership potential, and knowledge of a broad range of financial theory, from financial accounting to capital markets. Prospective interns should have long-term interests in careers in financial management. Again, applicants must have authorization to work on a full-time basis in the United States (does not include practical training authorization).

What international opportunities does your firm offer for U.S. citizens? For foreign nationals?

Although the domestic petroleum industry is often characterized as mature, Chevron continues to pursue growth opportunities around the globe. We are aggressively expanding our activities in Kazakhstan, Australia, West Africa, and Indonesia.

MBAs can almost immediately gain exposure to our international operations with Bay Area assignments working in the worldwide headquarters of our international subsidiaries. Limited opportunities to work overseas are generally not available to our new hires until they have gained several years of domestic experience, largely a reflection of the complexities and scope of our business. We historically have not hired foreign national MBAs into our Development Program.

Credit Suisse First Boston

11 Madison Avenue
New York, NY 10010
(212) 325-2000
Web site: www.csfb.com

MBA Recruiting Contact(s):
Sheila Cull, Assistant Vice-President, Equity Recruiting
(212) 325-7758

Joanne Fagioli, Manager, Fixed Income Recruiting
(212) 325-4458

Elaine Schneider, Director, Credit Suisse Financial Products
(212) 325-7703

Lori Todd, Manager, Corporate & Investment Banking Recruiting
(212) 325-4703

Company Description

Describe your firm's business and the types of clients served by your finance group(s).

Credit Suisse First Boston is a leading global corporate and investment banking firm, providing comprehensive financial advisory, capital raising, sales and trading, and financial products for users and suppliers of capital around the world. The formation of Credit Suisse First Boston integrated the resources of Credit Suisse, CS First Boston, Bank Leu and Credit Suisse Financial Products under a united management and merchant banking team. As of January 1, 1997, the firm had over $8.5 billion of equity capital, over 10,000 employees, and operated out of fifty-one offices across thirty-two countries and six continents. The firm is based in Zurich and wholly owned by the financial services organization Credit Suisse Group.

1996 Accomplishments
In 1996, Credit Suisse and CS First Boston, two of the components of the new Credit Suisse First Boston, enjoyed a year of tremendous accomplishments.

- In **investment banking** we continued to assist our clients with some of the best capital raising and advisory work in the industry: from the largest ever non-US corporate debt issue (Petronas, $1.9 billion), to only the second German stock listing on the New York Stock Exchange (SGL Carbon which, at $1.06 billion, also happened to be one of the largest ever European corporate secondary issues), to complex, high value-added advisory assignments like the privatization of the Victorian electricity industry at $6.4 billion and Boeing's $13.3 billion purchase of McDonnell Douglas.
- Our agility and intelligence in **fixed income** business once again proved decisive. We were particularly successful in the emerging market sector and leveraged finance (with record earnings), as well as in foreign exchange. Mold-breaking transactions for issuers included the $2.6 billion of senior notes for The Walt Disney Company, and the $1 billion issue that represented China's first successful global bond offering. Credit Suisse was once again the number one lead-manager in the Swiss franc capital markets with a market share of over 30%.
- In **equities** we saw outstanding results in the equity derivatives and convertibles sectors and continued to expand our research and trading capabilities. The capital markets group maintained its position as one of the best in banking, as evidenced by, amongst other prestigious deals, the $5.85 billion ENI issue—the largest secondary equity offering of all time.
- Our 80% owned subsidiary Credit Suisse Financial Products (CSFP) consolidated its position as one of the world's best **derivatives** houses. High earnings were achieved once again by means of a two-pronged strategy: on the one hand sales and trading of standard products, on the other, provision of customized risk management, financing and investment strategies for a global clientele.
- 1996 was also an extremely good year for Credit Suisse's **corporate banking** business. Strong relationships with multinational companies, intensified efforts within structured finance, and one-stop banking in cooperation with CS First Boston all contributed to the success. Landmark deals included the $3 billion revolving credit facility for JC Penney's acquisition of the Eckerd Corporation (with CS First Boston), and the funding of the PT Jawa power plant in Indonesia—one of the largest and most prestigious infrastructure project financings ever seen in Asia.

In 1997 and beyond, Credit Suisse First Boston will have the resources, the geographical presence, the expertise, and the strategy to keep us at the forefront of our industry.

The Finance MBA's Job Description

Associate: Corporate & Investment Banking
The position: Employment opportunities exist in all major geographic regions. Incoming associates are hired either

into specific product or industry groups. Within groups, each associate works as an important part of various client and transaction teams. Career opportunities for corporate and investment banking associates include specialization in mergers and acquisitions, leveraged finance or global power and project finance; working in one of our U.S. regional or overseas offices; or specializing in an industry sector such as media and telecommunications, retail, or financial institutions.

What we look for: Associate candidates typically have earned graduate degrees in business or law, or have significant relevant prior experience. Credit Suisse First Boston is noted for the diversity of its staff, but does look for certain characteristics in all of its candidates—highly motivated individuals who have demonstrated academic achievement, quantitative skills, and strength in verbal and written communication. Computer literacy is essential to all that we do.

What you can expect: As an associate, you might typically be asked to review a spreadsheet model of a client company, examine the impact of a transaction on your client's capital structure, initiate acquisition deals for your client, or participate in a client presentation. Key success drivers include strong interpersonal skills and problem-solving abilities, the ability to balance a multitude of tasks, and a high degree of dedication. As your career progresses and your objectives change, we encourage you to broaden your product, industry, and cultural knowledge.

Associate: Sales & Trading

The position: Employment opportunities exist in the Americas, Europe and the Pacific. Incoming associates are hired into specific product groups in either fixed income or equity sales & trading.

What we look for: Credit Suisse First Boston is noted for the diversity of its staff, but seeks candidates with a common set of abilities—highly motivated individuals who have demonstrated academic achievement and strength in verbal and written communication. The dynamic, information-intensive environment of the trading floor requires candidates to be able to master new concepts quickly, with a high degree of creativity and interpersonal skills. Candidates must be able to lead and to work on a team and must be geographically mobile. Foreign language fluency is required for European and Pacific offices, and computer literacy is essential to all that we do.

What you can expect: Working in a fast-moving, team-oriented environment, you will be expected to react to changing market conditions, elicit Credit Suisse First Boston research opinions, formulate a trade strategy, communicate with accounts and execute trades. As your career progresses, you will be encouraged to continue developing your professional and technical skills to meet the challenges of evolving global financial markets.

Associate: Credit Suisse Financial Products—marketing, trading, product development

The position: CSFP recruits MBAs and Ph.Ds for associate positions in either marketing, trading, or product development teams located in London or in one of CSFP's regional offices. Over time, these employees will have significant opportunity for career flexibility, in terms of product focus, group and location.

What we look for: Candidates for all positions must be capable of achieving excellence in our fast paced and dynamic culture. Strong analytical skills and the ability to think intuitively and creatively are prerequisites. Our experience shows that candidates with math, physics, and engineering backgrounds often have the quantitative skills necessary to work in derivatives. Additionally, because associates interact closely with clients and other professionals, demonstrable team skills as well as strong interpersonal and presentation abilities are essential. CSFP's diverse product and client base makes the job well suited for students with international interests and skills.
Note: In order to be considered for CSFP, candidates must specify an interest in one of the three positions (marketing, trading or product development).

What you can expect: As a CSFP associate you will be educated in the pricing, hedging, and risk management aspects of derivative products as well as the applications and structures created to address our client-driven, problem-solving approach to the business. You will gain responsibility quickly within your respective area, with the expectation that you will soon begin making significant contributions to your team. You can be assured that your career at CSFP will offer you continued challenge and the broadest possible range of opportunities.

Analyst: Equity Research

The position: The firm's equity research analyst position is a fast-track career opportunity to join a respected team of research analysts covering U.S., European, Latin American and Asian stocks. Our research is noted for its creative, value-added focus.

What we look for: Credit Suisse First Boston is noted for the diversity of its staff, but seeks candidates with a common set of abilities—highly motivated individuals who have demonstrated academic achievement including finance and accounting courses and strength in verbal and written communication. The equity research analyst position requires candidates who are self-directed and entrepreneurial; independent, creative thinkers who can identify patterns and trends within complex data; and the ability to operate under time pressure. Foreign language fluency is required for European and Pacific offices, and computer literacy is essential to all that we do.

What you can expect: As an equity research analyst you will gain expertise and recognition within your industry in the shortest possible time. There is no apprenticeship; you are immediately awarded an industry, and the firm's support program helps build needed skills on the job. You can also expect a stimulating work environment that allows for rapid individual development and professional growth.

Associate: Asset Finance

The position: Opportunities exist in the firm's highly rated Asset Finance Group which is responsible for the marketing, structuring and origination of asset-backed securities and for M&A activity related to consumer loan portfolios. The group generally focuses on the securitization of consumer loans including automobile loans, credit card receivables, home equity loans, student loans and similar U.S. assets. It also provides financing for assets in Latin America, Europe, and Asia such as remittances, and revenue streams created from exports such as petroleum and grain.

What we look for: Credit Suisse First Boston is noted for the diversity of its staff, but seeks candidates with a common set of abilities—highly motivated individuals who have demonstrated academic achievement, quantitative skills, and strength in verbal and written communication. Candidates for this position should be bright, enthusiastic MBA graduates. Computer literacy is essential to all that we do.

What you can expect: As an asset finance associate you will perform financial modeling and mathematical analysis and portfolio valuation. You will interact significantly with the fixed income trading floor, clients, attorneys, rating agencies, and others in executing transactions. You will have primary responsibility for executing new securities offerings, and will draft and participate in client marketing presentations. As an associate you can expect to work on ten to fifteen lead-managed transactions per year. The position will provide an opportunity for you to apply your computer and technical skills in a dynamic, growing environment.

Summer Associates:

The position: The firm offers challenging and educational summer associate positions to candidates from a wide variety of backgrounds—prior experience in the investment banking industry is not required. The Summer Associate Program lasts ten to twelve weeks. In sales & trading, rotational assignments permit exposure to both fixed income and equity products. In investment banking, roles and responsibilities are the same as that for first-year associates. All of our summer associates have the opportunity to spend time with senior management and department heads as part of a broad exposure to the investment banking industry.

What we look for: Summer associate candidates are typically preparing to enter their final year of business or law school. We seek individuals with a proven record of leadership, strong interpersonal skills, willingness to participate in team- and goal-oriented tasks, and a fundamental grasp of the principles of finance.

What you can expect: As a summer associate, you will participate in orientation to the firm, with exposure to all aspects of both investment banking and sales & trading. You will gain direct experience with a wide variety of products and markets, and will develop marketing and communication skills. Your training will also include weekly seminars and monthly presentations by senior management.

Credit Suisse First Boston is an Equal Opportunity/ Affirmative Action Employer.

Dain Bosworth Incorporated

60 South Sixth Street
Minneapolis, MN 55402
(612) 371-2711
Fax: (612) 371-2763

MBA Recruiting Contacts:
Charles A. Kennedy
(612) 371-2863

Hugh J. Hoffman
(612) 371–7700

Company Description

Describe your firm's business and the types of clients served by your finance group(s).

Dain Bosworth Incorporated is a full-service investment banking firm, based in Minneapolis. Founded in 1909, Dain Bosworth has approximately 1,100 professionals in 65 offices in 18 states and is one of the nation's largest regional investment banks.

Dain Bosworth corporate finance group consists of 34 professionals in Minneapolis and Seattle and provides a full range of investment banking services including public offerings, mergers and acquisitions, private capital, strategic alliances and corporate partnering, and valuations. Twenty equity research analysts follow over 200 public companies while 32 equity traders in Minneapolis, Seattle, and Boston make a market for over 350 public companies. The firm's 59 fixed income underwriters/traders provide taxable and tax-exempt bond sales, trading, underwriting, and research services, in addition to public finance services. The institutional sales staff is comprised of 19 equity and 56 fixed income investment executives in Minneapolis and Boston and maintains and develops long-term established relationships with mutual funds, pension funds, insurance companies, and other investment groups in the United States, Europe, and the Pacific Rim. The Private Client Group is comprised of over 800 professionals who provide a solid retail sales foundation throughout the Midwest and Western states.

Dain Bosworth's corporate clients can be characterized as rapidly emerging companies whose management teams rely heavily on the financial advice provided by Dain Bosworth bankers. Because of the firm's emerging market client base, Associates at Dain Bosworth have the opportunity for increased responsibility and extensive client contact. The key industry groups served by Dain Bosworth include Technology, Healthcare, Financial Services, Consumer (Food and Agribusiness, Leisure and Entertainment, and Retailing), Business & Information Services, and Emerging Growth.

Among mid-sized investment banks, Dain Bosworth is a consistent leader in mergers, acquisitions, and restructurings. This is primarily due to the firm's people, relationships, and well-established track record. Dain Bosworth's knowledgeable and experienced professionals devote themselves full-time to M&A and restructuring work and have built a nationally recognized M&A group through a commitment to and focus on these deals over the past several years. The firm's expertise in this area has solidified its ability to serve its clients over time, and complements its expertise in public offerings. As the record shows, every deal Dain has taken to market in the last three years has resulted in a completed transaction.

Describe your ownership structure.

Dain Bosworth is a wholly owned subsidiary of the Interra Financial, Inc. (IFI). IFI is publicly traded on the New York Stock Exchange. Rauscher Pierce Refsnes, Inc. is also a wholly owned subsidiary of IFI and is a full-service investment bank focused regionally in the Southwestern United States. IFI is the 10th-largest securities firm in the United States, based on the size of its combined sales force. Approximately 40% of IFI's 12 million outstanding shares are held by employees, assuring a commitment to superior client and shareholder value.

How does your approach to finance differ from that of other firms, and what do you consider to be your strengths and distinctive capabilities?

The firm's investment banking department is one of the largest groups outside New York, with over 30 corporate finance professionals focusing on six industry groups. Over the past two years, it has raised approximately $3.0 billion for its clients, including over 45 equity offerings totaling $2.0 billion. Dain Bosworth's entrepreneurial attitude combined with its seasoned Wall Street professionals enable the firm to reach for creative solutions for clients and to promote excellence, reward high performance and share a common vision to be the premier investment bank for the industries it serves. The firm's focus on middle market companies also allows it to provide superior service and a comprehensive understanding of its clients' problems, needs, and opportunities.

Of particular significance is the firm's strong trading and research departments. Dain Bosworth believes that its clients are best served by focusing its resources on a select number of companies and backing these clients with superior trading and research in the aftermarket.

Dain Bosworth maintains a strong retail distribution force that is premier among regional investment banks. This capability allows for distribution into markets which are not available to many of its peers. As a result, this provides for opportunities for the firm's clients which further increase both service quality and value to them.

Discuss changes in your firm's revenues (both domestic and international) and professional staff over the past year; over the past five years.

For the fiscal year ended December 31, 1996, Dain Bosworth's revenues were $409 million, up 16% from 1995 while earnings before taxes were $65 million, up 49% from 1995. This growth was largely driven by the Corporate Capital Group (Corporate Finance, Institutional Sales, Equity Research, etc.) generating a 39% revenue increase through higher underwriting and M&A activity. Over the past five years, Dain Bosworth has shown strong positive trends in revenues and earnings, with compound growth rates of 15% and 20%, respectively.

The Finance MBA's Job Description

Describe the career path and corresponding responsibilities for an MBA at your firm.

Dain Bosworth seeks candidates with a proven record of success, both work related and academic, and strong written, oral, and interpersonal communication skills. The firm's entrepreneurial environment requires individuals who are self-motivated and demonstrate the ability to take initiative and proceed independently. These persons must be willing to operate in its highly collegial setting where an open door policy is the norm. Projects and tasks are performed by employees who maintain the requisite skill sets and/or the desire to learn and grow in a particular industry or functional area.

Dain Bosworth recruits MBAs for positions within its Corporate Finance, Research, Public Finance, and Institutional Equity Sales business lines. Although specific responsibilities vary by business line, they may include new business development, financial modeling, company research, industry analysis, preparation of research reports, and marketing materials as well as valuations of client organizations and financial consulting services to corporate clients.

Discuss lifestyle aspects of a career with your firm (i.e., average hours per week, amount of travel, flexibility to change offices, corporate culture, etc.).

Dain Bosworth's employees are an entrepreneurial group of experienced Wall Street professionals who promote excellence, reward high performance, and share a common vision to be the premier investment bank for the industries it serves. It provides for a true meritocracy where reward is based on performance with no pre-determined time requirements for advancement. An immediate opportunity to learn is provided through lean deal teams while the chance to work with senior bankers is the norm rather than the exception.

A career with Dain Bosworth provides for many exciting opportunities which require dedication and a strong commitment. Travel is typically frequent and the average hours per week varies depending on the individual and the workload encountered. A quality life outside the firm is highly encouraged and is influenced by the tremendous cultural and outdoor recreational activities provided for in the Twin Cities.

The Recruiting Process

Describe your recruiting process and the criteria by which you select candidates. Is prior experience necessary?

Dain Bosworth recruits MBAs from the top business schools in the nation. At select schools, on campus recruiting is scheduled as well as attendance at finance club fairs and other recruiting functions. Final hiring decisions are made after a series of interviews with several persons within the respective department. Dain Bosworth seeks individuals who will work well in its entrepreneurial and collegial environment and who can demonstrate the ability to make a significant contribution to the firm. Although prior investment banking experience may be considered a plus, it is not a requirement for potential hires. Historically, however, many of Dain Bosworth's hires have held positions of a financial nature or with significant relevant industry experience.

How many permanent associates and analysts do you hire in a typical year? How many summer interns do you expect to hire? If you have a formal summer program, please describe it.

Dain Bosworth typically hires recruits based on the needs of each department so from year to year the number of new hires may fluctuate. Although the firm does not maintain a formal summer associate program, qualified MBA students who have completed their first year may be considered for a summer internship.

Deutsche Morgan Grenfell

C. J. Lawrence Inc.

31 West 52nd Street
New York, NY 10019
(212) 469-8000
Web site: www.deutsche-bank.de

MBA Recruiting Contact(s):
Sarah Seaman, Vice President
Campus Recruiting
(212) 469-8459

Alan Krouk, Senior Recruiter
Corporate Finance
(212) 469-8450

Heather Loughlin, Senior Recruiter
Global Markets
(212) 469-6671

Company Description

Describe your firm's business and the types of clients served by your finance group(s).

Deutsche Bank, with its 125 years of successful experience, and Morgan Grenfell, with its 85 years of history, have combined their diverse investment banking capabilities in order to become one of the world's top flight investment banks. With a staff of over 7,000 and offices in over 30 countries, Deutsche Morgan Grenfell has a significant presence in global investment banking. Our worldwide reach is matched by our expertise across a full range of investment banking products and our readiness to use these skills, frequently in complex and sophisticated combinations, to respond to our client's needs. Our activities are organized into seven core areas: Global Markets, Corporate Finance, Equities, Structured Finance, Emerging Markets, Assets Management, and Development Capital.

The Finance MBA's Job Description

Discuss changes in your firm's revenues (both domestic and international) and professional staff over the past year; over the past five years.

Global Markets
With activities in the foreign exchange, debt, commodity, and related derivatives markets, Global Markets offers recent MBA graduates a dynamic career opportunity in one of the world's premier financial institutions. Through 38 dealing rooms in 28 countries, we provide an integrated service to governments, supernationals, corporate and other investors, and corporations. We are a primary dealer in 14 government bond markets and a major lead manager in the Eurobond markets. We offer borrowers and investors a comprehensive coverage of the debt derivatives market, a complete liquidity management service in the short-term money market, and a service in repo instruments—all across a wide range of currencies.

Equities
With some 1500 professional staff in 35 locations, the Equity division is responsible for the research, distribution, and trading of equity and equity related securities on a worldwide basis for our institutional and corporate clients. To provide the highest standard of service to our clients, research is the heart of our equity business. Our Global Equity Derivatives business, operating from New York, Frankfurt, London, and Tokyo, offers clients inventive, derivative-based solutions to their investment problems.

Global Markets and Equities Associate Program
Newly placed Associates will work closely with our sales, trading, research, and origination professionals located in London, Frankfurt, New York, Asia, and other international locations. Associates will enter our prestigious training program which includes two separate classroom training components, one in New York and one in London. Classroom training features an orientation to Deutsche Morgan Grenfell, meetings with senior management, product and market training, sales and trading simulations, and Series 7 and 63 exam training. Classroom training culminates in a comprehensive case study presentation, viewed and critiqued by senior management. Subsequently, Associates will complete rotational assignments throughout Global Markets/Equities' domestic and international offices. In addition, all new Associates are assigned a mentor to help provide a smooth transition into the Global Markets and Equities culture and businesses.

Corporate Finance
Corporate Finance (including Equity Capital Markets) is responsible for advising companies on key strategic issues such as mergers and acquisitions, disposals and restructuring, and for arranging domestic and international equity and equity-linked issues, including underwriting and syndication. We provide the same services to governments in privatizations worldwide. We have a leading position in corporate finance in Europe, based on our two home markets in the United Kingdom and Germany, and strong representation in all other key markets worldwide. Our geographical strengths, complemented by interna-

tional expertise in key global sectors, facilitate the active and idea-driven approach that our clients expect. We place considerable emphasis on building long-term relationships with companies to enhance our overall understanding of their needs.

Corporate Finance Associate Program

Associates joining Corporate Finance will serve on teams with our Investment Managers, Relationship Managers, and/or Product Specialists in one of 15 industry groups providing financing and advisory services to our corporate clients. Associates will participate in a training program designed to prepare them to meet the challenges and responsibilities they will face on the job. Program highlights include an orientation to Deutsche Morgan Grenfell and its philosophy, ethics, and culture, modules on computer applications, fixed income analytics, accounting, financial strategies, capital markets, and derivatives products as well as Series 7 and 63 exam training. Specialized training will be provided in valuation, modeling, and corporate taxation. Newly placed Associates will be directly exposed to senior professionals working with our Firm's clients from the initial meeting to the final execution of a transaction or closing. In addition, all new Associates will be assigned a mentor to help provide a smooth transition into the Corporate Finance/Equity Capital Markets culture.

The Recruiting Process

Describe your recruiting process and the criteria by which you select candidates. Is prior experience necessary?

Deutsche Morgan Grenfell/C. J. Lawrence seeks individuals who possess superior analytical skills, creative problem solving abilities, excellent communication skills, and demonstrated leadership potential. The candidate must have a distinguished academic record as well as significant work experience in the financial arena. Proficiency in a foreign language is a plus, but is not required. U.S. and foreign nationals will be considered.

If you have a formal summer program, please describe it.

Deutsche Morgan Grenfell's Summer Associate program is a diverse, eight- to twelve-week learning experience designed to give first-year MBAs an overview of our firm's culture, products, and approach to doing business. It also offers an opportunity to interact with some of the key professionals in the business.

Global Markets and Equities Summer Associates are assigned a mentor, attend one day a week classroom presentations, complete two rotations through sales and trading desks, and interact with senior management in weekly briefing sessions. They will be assigned a project to be completed by the end of the program that will be critiqued by Global Markets and Equities professionals.

Corporate Finance Summer Associates are assigned an in-depth project in one of our industry groups, supervised and critiqued by a senior manager. Project work includes providing financial advice to companies on mergers and acquisitions, the origination and execution of traditional institutional banking transactions, and the arrangement of domestic and international equity and debt issues.

D.H. Blair Investment Banking Corp.

44 Wall Street
New York, NY 10005
(212) 495-4000
Web site: www.dhblair.com

MBA Recruiting Contact(s):
J. Morton Davis, Chairman
(212) 495-5000

Company Description

Describe your firm's business and the types of clients served by your finance group(s).

D.H. Blair is an independent investment bank based in New York City. The firm has a capital base of over $150 million. Blair specializes in financings of small- and medium-size growth companies, as well as early-stage venture financings. Established in 1904, D.H. Blair has a strong and growing track record of providing financing for these types of companies. Equity financings include initial public offerings, private placements, venture capital, merchant banking, and mergers and acquisitions. Leveraged buyout (LBO) debt financings are growing in number and size at Blair. As a result of our long-standing relationships built up over many years with these companies, Blair has the opportunity to provide many investment banking services to its clients.

Describe your ownership structure.

D.H. Blair is an independent, privately held investment bank.

How does your approach to finance differ from that of other firms, and what do you consider to be your strengths and distinctive capabilities?

D.H. Blair is a focused, well-capitalized investment bank. It does not attempt to provide services outside its specific niche. The firm provides private and public equity and debt financing for small- and medium-size emerging-growth and high-technology companies. D.H. Blair has purposely remained an agile, niche organization with a strong capital base and retail client base. This gives us the flexibility and strength to act very quickly on finding and funding significant investment opportunities. Due to the numerous client and portfolio companies served over many years, D.H. Blair has developed relationships with several of the largest industrial and service companies in the United States as well as overseas. These relationships have led to many acquisitions, joint ventures, and other forms of investment in these D.H. Blair companies.

Discuss changes in your firm's revenues (both domestic and international) and professional staff over the past year; over the past five years.

D.H. Blair is located in New York City. The Investment Banking Group includes approximately 25 individuals. The firm has grown rapidly over the past decade and is committed to maintaining this growth. Because D.H. Blair is an entrepreneurial firm serving this nation's entrepreneurs, the current national trend toward increased levels of this activity provides even greater demands for our services.

The Finance MBA's Job Description

Describe the career path and corresponding responsibilities for an MBA at your firm.

The Corporate Finance Department of D.H. Blair considers highly motivated and aggressive MBAs who have a great deal of initiative and desire to work in various areas of investment banking. Public and private placements of equity and debt securities, as well as merchant banking, venture capital, and LBOs, are areas of opportunity at D.H. Blair. Due to the firm's entrepreneurial flair and structure, there is a great deal of opportunity for the aggressive individual to assume primary responsibility at an early stage. Thinly staffed teams allow us to recruit people looking to take on responsibility quickly. The investment banker should be able to handle all aspects of a deal, as opposed to being a transaction specialist. The banker should be able to understand all areas of a client's business, including knowledge of product, market, financial, and other nonfinancial analyses. The banker should be able to assist in management presentation, negotiation, and sales. Also, the investment banker will be responsible for solicitation of new business opportunities. The speed at which the banker will grow in importance at the firm will depend on the banker's ability to assume responsibility and develop business opportunities.

Describe the opportunities for professional mobility between the various departments in your firm.

Career paths vary greatly depending on an individual's abilities and goals. There is not the rigid structure found in larger investment banks. D.H. Blair encourages individuals to experiment in new areas in order to seek out the best opportunities and further their career goals. Due to the thin staffing structure, there is plenty of opportunity for the banker to be observed by and interact with the staff in order to determine which areas are the most appropriate for career growth.

Discuss the lifestyle aspects of a career with your firm (i.e., average hours per week, amount of travel, flexibility to change offices, corporate culture, etc.).

A career at D.H. Blair is challenging and requires dedication, hard work, and flexibility. Lifestyles vary depending on the individual's own goals as well as those of the group in which the banker works.

The Recruiting Process

Describe your recruiting process and the criteria by which you select candidates. Is prior experience necessary?

We seek people with a history of achievement and success. These candidates show a great deal of initiative and aggressiveness, as well as the requisite analytical skills and strong interpersonal skills. Many successful candidates have had previous work experience, although it is not required. Although grades are a meaningful criterion, each candidate is considered as a combination of many abilities, and no single one is dominant.

How many permanent associates and analysts do you hire in a typical year? How many summer interns do you expect to hire? If you have a formal summer program, please describe it. Please be sure to indicate whether the summer program is in place for all offices or just some.

D.H. Blair hires between two and four associates each year. Although D.H. Blair offers no formal training, there is very thorough on-the-job training.

D.H. Blair has no formal summer program. We hire summer associates, depending on availability and need, in investment banking and brokerage.

Donaldson, Lufkin & Jenrette

277 Park Avenue
New York, NY 10172
(212) 892-3000

MBA Recruiting Contact(s):
Elizabeth Derby, Investment Banking
(212) 892-7217

Marguerite Haran, ISG, Fixed Income, Equities and Asset Management
(212) 892-3073

Company Description

Describe your firm's business and the types of clients served by your finance group(s).

Donaldson, Lufkin & Jenrette (DLJ) is a top-ranked, full service investment and merchant bank. Founded in 1959 by three entrepreneurial Harvard MBAs as a research boutique specializing in institutional equity analysis, DLJ has developed premier franchises in research, sales, trading, and underwriting of equity and fixed income securities. These franchises extend to all major sectors of the capital markets and complement the firm's expertise in merchant banking, high yield financings, initial public offerings, and mergers and acquisitions. Furthermore, DLJ has expanded its emerging markets presence, particularly in Latin America and Asia.

DLJ services a wide variety of clients, ranging from small start-ups to Fortune 500 companies. DLJ has successfully grown its businesses by focusing on transactions in which the quality of ideas and execution skills can make a difference in our clients' performance.

Describe your ownership structure.

In 1985, DLJ was acquired by The Equitable Life Assurance Society of the United States. In turn, the AXA Group, one of France's largest insurance concerns, owns 60% of The Equitable. Through our October 1995 public offering, The Equitable reduced their ownership interest to approximately 80%.

How does your approach to finance differ from that of other firms, and what do you consider to be your strengths and distinctive capabilities?

DLJ's approach to capital raising, merchant banking, and venture capital investing has yielded superior results for our clients and portfolio companies. We believe that no transaction is easy or routine; each requires the personal attention and commitment of senior professionals. DLJ encourages teamwork to leverage the diverse talents of our various departments. DLJ values close client relationships, innovative solutions, and high quality transactions and utilizes the intelligent employment of capital, our distinctive research strength, and strong institutional distribution capabilities.

Discuss changes in your firm's revenues (both domestic and international) and professional staff over the past year; over the past five years.

Total revenues were a record 3.5 billion in 1996, compared to 2.8 billion in 1995. With the exception of the slight revenue decline in 1994, DLJ's revenues have been growing steadily over the past five years as have the number of employees.

As of January of 1997, DLJ employed 5,885 people in thirteen cities in the U.S. and twelve cities abroad.

The Finance MBA's Job Description

Describe the career path and corresponding responsibilities for an MBA at your firm.

Investment Banking
Each associate's career path is largely a function of his/her unique strengths and talents. There is no predetermined, limiting time frame for advancement. Compensation and advancement are based solely on merit and achievement.

The majority of associates are generalists and receive broad exposure across industry and product lines. Associates naturally gravitate to specialized areas after two years. A limited number of groups require dedicated associates from the start. Associates assume immediate responsibility working with DLJ's senior professionals and our clients' senior management. DLJ is committed to providing exposure to a wide range of transactions.

Project teams are relatively small, offering the associate high visibility, impact, and recognition on each transaction. An associate may work on four or five assignments simultaneously. By the end of the first year, associates are expected to assume a high degree of responsibility for both project management and client maintenance.

Institutional Equity Research
The entry-level analyst (MBA) is given immediate responsibility for coverage of a mutually agreed upon industry. The position entails development of specialized

analytical skills, frequent interviews with senior corporate managers, company visits, secondary research, and ultimately intensive interpersonal marketing. A group of senior analysts will be fully accessible to, and will assist in the development of, the new analyst. Ultimately it is the individual's responsibility to build a franchise of authority and expertise within the investment community through his or her written product and client interaction.

Institutional Equity Sales
Sales professionals are responsible for transmitting research recommendations generated by analysts and banking products generated by the Investment Banking Division to analysts and portfolio managers at institutional firms. Sales associates will spend the first six months in an Equities Division training program that incorporates rotation on various desks; meetings with research analysts; a research department project; and weekly meetings with senior sales professionals. Following training, a new associate takes on direct account responsibility.

Investment Services Group (ISG)
Sales professionals work directly with high-net-worth individuals, family groups, and small to mid-sized institutions in developing and executing customized investment portfolios. Sales associates will spend the first six months in New York in a rigorous and thorough training program. The program will include a rotation through several key areas of the firm, classroom presentations, sales skills seminars, and technology training. Following the training program, sales associates will return to their respective offices for additional training. The ideal candidate will possess a keen entrepreneurial spirit, an interest in and broad knowledge of the investment markets, and the ability to operate in an unstructured environment.

Fixed Income
The Fixed Income Division recruits MBAs for its sales and research areas. In the sales area, new MBAs are assigned to work closely with experienced professionals for the first six months to obtain product knowledge. They then assume responsibility for smaller accounts in order to build their own book. In research, new MBAs work directly with senior professionals in a specific product group (high yield, quantitative research, investment grade or real estate). DLJ has the most respected fixed income research on Wall Street and earned more first place citations than any other Wall Street firm in *Institutional Investor* magazine's "All-America Fixed-Income Research Team" survey.

Describe the opportunities for professional mobility between the various departments in your firm.

DLJ hires associates directly into the various departments described above. There is no preplanned mobility among departments, but if interest is expressed and the individual has demonstrated competence, there is some opportunity to move to a different area of specialization.

Discuss the lifestyle aspects of a career with your firm (i.e., average hours per week, amount of travel, flexibility to change offices, corporate culture, etc.).

The lifestyle aspects of a career with DLJ vary from department to department. Nevertheless, some career choices place large demands on an individual's time and require much travel. DLJ's corporate culture emphasizes excellence, informality, and independent initiative. We want our associates to take pride in personal and corporate accomplishments, assuming early responsibility without losing sight of our traditional final corporate objective: to **have fun!**

The Recruiting Process

Describe your recruiting process and the criteria by which you select candidates. Is prior experience necessary?

The recruiting process is centrally managed from New York with the participation of our regional offices. Students must submit a resume to the appropriate contact previously listed. DLJ has a three-round interview process in most cases.

New MBAs are hired principally into the Investment Banking Division, with additional opportunities in Equity and Fixed Income Research, and Equity and Fixed Income Sales and Trading.

DLJ has no predetermined formula for selecting candidates. Prior experience in finance, while helpful, is not required. More importantly, we look for individuals with demonstrated intelligence, initiative, excellence, and creativity.

How many permanent associates and analysts do you hire in a typical year? How many summer interns do you expect to hire? If you have a formal summer program, please describe it. Please be sure to indicate whether the summer program is in place for all offices or just some.

In 1996, the Investment Banking Division hired approximately thirty-eight associates and seventy-five analysts. Equities hired 6 MBAs and anticipates hiring 10–13 undergraduates. ISG will hire 20–25 associates, and Fixed Income hired 4 associates. We conduct a formal training program when people start, but most of the training is on-the-job experience.

Investment Banking is the only department with a formal

summer intern program. This year we hired twenty-eight summer associates and have opportunities in New York, Los Angeles, and Chicago. For the most part, summer interns are generalists and work on a broad array of transactions. DLJ considers its summer associates to be integral and active members of the professional staff and strives to provide each with a summer experience truly reflective of full-time employment. Summer interns are exposed to banking's specialty product and industry groups through a weekly lunch series and to other departments through weekly breakfast meetings with senior executives.

What international opportunities does your firm offer for U.S. citizens? For foreign nationals?

There are growing international opportunities at DLJ. We have opportunities for Investment Banking associates in both our Asian and Latin American efforts and require that associates spend time in New York first. DLJ's work authorization is as follows: U.S. citizens, green card recipients, persons eligible for legal visa status or foreign nationals for appropriate openings.

DLJ took important steps in 1995, 1996 and 1997 to build its presence in international markets, most notably in Asia and Latin America. In early 1997, DLJ acquired the Phoenix Group Limited, a leading financial advisory based in London, to bolster our European presence. Investment Banking expanded its Asian regional headquarters in Hong Kong. In 1996 we opened Latin American offices in Argentina, Mexico and Brazil. In late 1995, DLJ joined forces with Pleiade, a South African merchant banking firm that is affiliated with South Africa's largest publicly traded black-controlled company.

Our Equities and Fixed Income Departments have leading international franchises in Geneva, Hong Kong, London, Lugano, Paris, and Tokyo.

Enron

1400 Smith Street
Houston, Texas 77002
(713) 853-6402
Fax: (713) 646-3441
Web site: www.ect.enron.com

MBA Recruiting Contact(s):
Cindy Shiffler, MBA Recruiting Coordinator

Locations of Main Offices:
Houston, London, Calgary

Total Number of Professionals
7,500

Company Description

Describe your firm's business and the types of clients served by your finance group(s).

Enron is one of the world's largest integrated energy companies with approximately $16 billion in assets. In addition to its merchant business within Enron Capital & Trade Resources (ECT), Enron operates one of the largest natural gas transmission systems in the world. The company is also one of the largest independent developers and producers of electricity in the world, and owns a majority interest in Enron Oil & Gas (EOG), one of the largest exploration and production companies in the United States.

Describe your ownership structure.

Enron is a publicly traded company on the New York Stock Exchange under the ticker ENE.

How does your approach to finance differ from that of other firms, and what do you consider to be your strengths and distinctive capabilities?

Enron is a leader in the natural gas and electricity industry in developing innovative physical and financial products for producers and end users.

There are four specific groups within Enron that rely heavily on finance skills and abilities.

First, **ECT,** the merchant arm of Enron, was formed in 1989 to provide a multitude of financial services to the parent and to the domestic and international energy industries. During its short existence, ECT has grown to be one of the largest buyers and sellers of natural gas in North America, one of the largest traders of natural gas on the NYMEX and the Over-the-Counter Market, and the largest electricity marketer. ECT's aggressive and entrepreneurial staff has achieved this level of market presence through focusing on creating customized solutions to complex, energy-related problems.

ECT's success has been achieved through its focus on its key core businesses: cash and physical transactions (sales and trading), risk management products (derivatives), and innovative financing activities in natural gas, crude oil, liquids, and electricity. These businesses are described below:

Cash and Physical:

- Day-to-day buying, selling, and transporting of commodities using cash and the NYMEX
- Supported by ownership or access to physical assets including major pipelines, storage facilities, and power generation facilities

Risk Management:

- Activities include long-term contracting (> 1 year), commodity risk solutions, and contract restructuring
- Manage books in crude oil, natural gas, liquids, crude products, clean fuels, electric power, interest rates, and currencies
- Extensive portfolio in each area allows ECT to provide its customers with a wide array of physical and financial hedging products

Enron Risk Management Services (ERMS) provides structured risk management products that are physical and/or financial in nature to producers, consumers, investors, and lenders in the energy industry. ERMS acts as principal in a wide variety of structured product transactions, such as swaps, caps, floors, collars, swaptions, participating swaps, product spreads, and the product spread options. These products are an integral part of the long-term contracts offered to a wide range of ECT customers. For the third consecutive year, *Risk Magazine,* a leading trade publication, ranked ERMS first among worldwide commodity traders in natural gas, crude, and gasoline swaps, options, and exotic products.

Finance:

- Arranges debt and equity capital for the energy industry and develops capital funding vehicles that support its financial product offerings

- Since 1991, ECT's funding activity has arranged more than $3.0 billion of capital

Enron Finance Corp. (EFC) arranges for funding of reserves that provide ECT with long-term supply commitments both domestically and internationally. EFC has developed unique programs to provide acquisition capital and price hedging to independent gas producers. One product offered is the volumetric production payments (VPP). With the VPP, ECT receives a stated volume of the producer's oil and gas production over time. The producer, in exchange, receives cash up front as a purchase price for the production. With more than $950 million in production payments originated as of July 1995, EFC has solidified its position as one of the largest independent entities arranging for capital to the independent oil and gas sector in North America. The debt and equity raised to fund these products does not affect Enron's balance sheet. EFC forms special companies to fund asset acquisitions. Through these companies, EFC packages collaterized natural gas reserves and sells them to banks and institutional investors, much like a bank packages home loans and resells them. EFC continues to search for financing opportunities within the United States and abroad. In 1994, EFC created a funding vehicle to augment the growing need for producer capital in the Canadian market.

These three core businesses support a wide array of domestic and international energy users and producers. ECT's businesses stress internal product and skill integration so that optimal and customized physical and financial solutions can be developed for our customers. ECT sources energy from gas, oil, and electricity producers and suppliers through a variety of financial techniques including long-term contracting, acquisition financing, and price hedging. ECT, using similar financial techniques, supplies energy to local gas distribution companies, cogeneration facilities, electric utilities, and industrials. ECT's upstream and downstream customers find the company's tailor-made products provide critical value in managing their purchase and sale of energy in a market of significant risk and volatility.

ECT's success and industry advantage has been due, in large part, to its clear vision and ability to anticipate coming regulatory change and market developments. ECT has been aggressive in capitalizing on developing opportunities and is extremely well-positioned in nearly all segments of the worldwide natural gas industry and in the developing electricity markets.

Second, **Enron International (EI),** identifies and maximizes opportunities worldwide. EI's competitive advantage is its integrated market-led approach to infrastructure development. The Enron subsidiary ties together various components such as fuel supply, construction supervision and financing, and effectively manages risk management from project conception to completion.

Third, **Enron Capital Management (ECM),** includes funding, capital pricing and capital management activities, as well as corporate treasury and corporate risk management functions. ECM is responsible for pricing of capital and funding for all of Enron's businesses.

Finally, the **Corporate Development** group is involved in merger, acquisition, and divestiture activities. This group analyzes companies from a financial perspective to determine strategic fits between Enron and other businesses.

Discuss changes in your firm's revenues (both domestic and international) and professional staff over the past year; over the past six years.

Six years ago, Enron Corp. had the vision of becoming the world's first natural gas major—the most innovative and reliable provider of clean energy worldwide for a better environment. In 1994, Enron reached that objective and has now set its five-year sights on becoming the World's Leading Energy Company—creating innovative and efficient energy solutions for growing economies and a better environment worldwide.

To receive these accolades requires significant growth in market presence and earnings. Enron's growth over the last five years has been substantial and has clearly outpaced our competitors. Over this period, Enron's earnings per share have grown at a compound growth rate of 20% and a return to shareholders of 135%.

ECT is a significant contributor to the parent having provided 20% of operating income in just seven years. ECT's EBIT reached $280 million in 1996, 20% increase over 1995.

Enron has committed to a growth of 15% per year in earnings per share for 1996 and beyond. Growth is primarily targeted in three areas: the international marketplace, the domestic retail energy marketplace, and the domestic electric power industry.

Staff at Enron has increased in the last year to 7,500 today. This number also represents the growth over the last twelve years since Enron was formed in 1985, with the merger of Houston Natural Gas (HNG) and Internorth Natural Gas Company.

The Finance MBA's Job Description

Describe the career path and corresponding responsibilities for an MBA at your firm.

MBAs are hired into Enron's Associate Program where

they work for 18 to 24 months. At the completion of the program, the associate transitions into a commercial role with direct and specific customer responsibility.

The Associate Program is designed to give the MBA extensive exposure to all facets of Enron's innovative approach to marketing physical and financial products for the natural gas and electricity industries. While in the program, the associates will provide commercial and analytical support to different Enron profit centers during three to four, six-month rotations. As contributing members of deal teams, associates' efforts will directly affect the company's financial success and future growth. Projects and deals could include structured finance, trading and risk management, and marketing for the natural gas and power industries. Opportunities exist for associates to work on international development and merchant projects while based domestically or in one of our international offices.

Describe the opportunities for professional mobility between the various departments in your firm.

As described above, an associate will typically make three to four rotations between the different commercial groups within Enron. These rotations give the associate a robust understanding of the way that Enron works and how best to create integrated solutions. The associate has a great deal of input in deciding where these rotations will be and how best to craft a career path that takes advantage of individual skills and capabilities as well as company needs. As the associate graduates into the commercial ranks, it is not uncommon for people to move between groups as new opportunities arise.

Discuss the lifestyle aspects of a career with your firm (i.e., average hours per week, amount of travel, flexibility to change offices, corporate culture, etc.).

Individuals that are attracted to Enron are ones that thrive in a fast-paced, intellectual, and entrepreneurial environment. Furthermore, Enron employees are self-motivated, deal-oriented, and biased for action. The company accommodates these types of individuals through a flat, nonbureaucratic organization that gives individual employees a great deal of latitude in setting their own schedule and monitoring their own work.

While it is difficult to precisely categorize the average hours per week and the amount of travel that would be required of an associate, most find that they are able to achieve a diverse and quality lifestyle that combines challenging and stimulating work with substantial time for leisure activities.

The Recruiting Process

Describe your recruiting process and the criteria by which you select candidates. Is prior experience necessary?

Enron is seeking candidates for its associate program who have received an MBA degree and have at least two years of work experience. As has been previously discussed, Enron is looking for candidates who are self-motivated and have well-developed quantitative and interpersonal skills. These candidates must be creative thinkers and able to work in unstructured surroundings. Candidates are not required to have an energy background, although prior knowledge or work experience in this industry is helpful.

Enron conducts interviews for associates during the late winter and early spring of each year. The interviews are conducted first at the university and then a final round is held at the home office in Houston. Most associates begin work in middle to late summer.

How many permanent associates and analysts do you hire in a typical year? How many summer interns do you expect to hire? If you have a formal summer program, please describe it. Please be sure to indicate whether the summer program is in place for all offices or just some.

As Enron continues to grow domestically and internationally, the need for associates will continue to grow as well. Enron is committed to staff its commercial positions from the associate program. Enron plans to hire 30 to 35 associates a year for the next several years.

Enron also maintains a formal summer associate program for first-year MBAs. Enron typically hires 15 to 20 summer associates. The summer associates are assigned to specific profit centers where they are fully integrated into deal teams. Summer associates are expected to be fully contributing team members and able to apply newly learned business skills to real life situations. The summer associate program is run out of the home office in Houston.

What international opportunities does your firm offer for U.S. citizens? For foreign nationals?

Enron has targeted numerous international opportunities that are well-suited to the risk management and commercial skill set that Enron has so well utilized in the United States. Enron currently has international opportunities in Calgary, Colombia, Buenos Aires, Dubai, Ontario, Oslo, Singapore and London. International opportunities exist for U.S. citizens and foreign nationals alike.

First Marathon Securities Limited

The Exchange Tower
2 First Canadian Place
Suite 3200, Box 21
Toronto, Ontario M5X 1J9
CANADA
(416) 869-3707
Web site: www.fmarathon.com

MBA Recruiting Contact(s):
Mark Knakowski, Vice-President, Investment Banking

Company Description

Describe your firm's business and the types of clients served by your finance group(s).

First Marathon Inc. (FMS.A - TSE) is a Canadian company that provides a broad range of financial services to corporations, financial institutions and individual investors. Its principal subsidiary, First Marathon Securities Limited, is the leading independent Canadian investment bank with additional capabilities and offices in Europe and the United States.

First Marathon's businesses include securities underwriting, distribution and trading; merger and acquisition and other financial advisory services; investing as principal; securities and mortgage banking; and securities execution and clearing services for third parties.

Through its various subsidiaries, the company is a member of the Investment Dealers Association of Canada and all Canadian stock exchanges, as well as the London Stock Exchange and the National Association of Securities Dealers in the United States.

Investment Banking Division. The investment banking division provides to Canadian corporations both public and private financing services, as well as merger and acquisition, restructuring and other financial advisory services, primarily through its offices in Toronto, Montreal, Calgary, and Vancouver.

Although the success and growth of our investment banking division has resulted in many strong client relationships with senior, blue chip Canadian corporations, First Marathon continues to be highly successful in working with rapidly growing, younger companies in all industry sectors which are in the first or early stages of raising public funds, or who are growing their businesses through acquisi-tion. Entrepreneurially-led companies often find that First Marathon's own entrepreneurial history and approach to conducting its business helps to understand the opportunities they are seeking to realise and the operational challenges they must overcome.

First Marathon is also active in U.S.-Canada cross-border financings, which have become more frequent in recent years.

As well as raising capital for our clients, First Marathon has acted as a financial advisor in a number of assignments, in most cases providing merger advice, fairness opinions and/or valuations.

When advising on mergers and acquisitions, First Marathon's industry expertise, independence from lenders, ability to add value through the creative structuring of transactions and marketing capability to place the difficult and complex financings which sometimes arise from such transactions have all assisted its growing client base.

We expect the growing globalisation of capital markets to continue. An increasing percentage of the equity offerings of Canadian companies are U.S.-Canada cross-border financings. In order to fully assist our Canadian issuer clients to complete such offerings, we will continue to develop our working relationships with investment banking firms in the United States and Europe. The Company's status as a leading independent Canadian investment bank provides a strong foundation for building mutually beneficial working partnerships with such firms. In addition, First Marathon's exceptional strength in the resources sector, where Canada is emerging as a leading market for financing mining companies on a world-wide basis, gives it a superb opportunity to develop such international relationships.

In order to capitalise on existing and future investment banking opportunities, First Marathon intends to continue its efforts to expand activity in all areas of corporate finance and advisory work. First Marathon intends to continue to broaden its areas of expertise and, as a result, its corporate coverage, in the expectation that providing corporate finance and advisory services will account for a significant part of its growth in the coming decade.

Institutional Equity Division. This division is comprised of professionals who engage in trading, research, and sales of equity securities.

First Marathon's investment banking success has been based upon developing specialised market niches where its substantial experience, close knowledge of the industries involved and in-depth research and trading coverage allow for superior responsiveness to client needs. A major source of value for issuing and investor clients is the company's commitment to providing research coverage and liquidity to its issuers and investors after it has completed financings. In this regard, the company's exceptional trading capability and strength with leading institutional investors has been of great benefit to issuer clients, both in setting new issue prices and in ensuring liquid after-market trading conditions. Furthermore, First Marathon's ability to quickly deploy its capital resources has been a feature of many underwritings and will grow in importance in future years.

Institutional and other clients demand quality investment advice which must be based on superior investment research and timely recommendations. First Marathon has made a major investment towards the ongoing development of its research capability by substantially increasing the number of our research analysts. Successful industry/investor conferences have been sponsored in both the wireless communications and biotechnology areas.

While the research department's breadth of industry coverage has increased significantly in order to serve the needs of our investor clients, we continue to place the primary focus on the quality of our research, which is chiefly directed at selecting superior individual investments. First Marathon's analysts focus on identifying industries and companies that promise outstanding relative investment returns as a result of growing earnings or cash flow, the superiority of a competitive franchisee or assets and/or the quality of management. In this way, we try to help investors achieve a return, which, while not wholly independent of the overall market result, will invariably be superior to it.

As institutional investors become more global in their outlook, international sales and trading have grown in importance to First Marathon. European and U.S. institutions increasingly look at Canada as a part of an emerging single North American market. In many industries, our companies are recognised as current or emerging world leaders. In anticipation of this new reality, First Marathon has made it a major goal to bring Canadian equities to a world market. In this process, international, like domestic, institutional clients have been attracted to First Marathon for Canadian investment products, not only because of the quality of our research, sales and trading, but also because of the company's stable management, independence and financial strength. Such characteristics provide a firm foundation on which to build long-term mutually beneficial client relationships.

FM Financial Products (FMFP). FM Financial Products is perhaps the best example of First Marathon's emphasis on pursuing growth in knowledge-based and/or proprietary business niches. The operations of FMFP include proprietary secondary market trading, institutional securities lending and structured transactions for investor clients. By staying at the leading edge of new financial technologies while insisting upon careful risk assessment and hedging of transactions, FMFP has grown substantially while operating profitably for each of the last thirty-six quarters. One of the reasons for the consistent profitability of FMFP's transactions is that they generally involve hedged strategies that are constructed so as to earn an attractive return while minimising risks. Indeed, minimising market risks through careful prior assessment of trading strategies and frequent monitoring of outstanding positions is the primary operational imperative.

Many of FMFP's investment strategies involve the creation of synthetic positions in stocks, bonds or indexes that promise a preferential rate of return and risk profile relative to that of the underlying securities that they replicate. State-of-the-art, proprietary models have been developed which enable FMFP to evaluate different strategies in order to minimise risks while enhancing rates of return. These models are also used to adjust hedge ratios for each strategy as prices change over time, thereby allowing the Company and its clients to further improve the rate of return profile on investments. In addition, FMFP has developed proprietary trading systems which allow First Marathon to quickly and efficiently execute the often highly complex trades required to implement investment strategies. First Marathon's derivatives activities are almost always fully hedged and FMFP does not make investments where return is primarily dependent upon directional market movements.

First Marathon has been, and believes that it will continue to be, highly successful in utilising derivatives securities to achieve superior risk-adjusted investment returns. In the future, we expect to build upon the knowledge and experience we have obtained while acting as a principal in these markets to develop attractive investment products for other corporations and substantial investors. We are confident that the use of derivatives will grow and that First Marathon is well positioned to benefit further from this increase in activity.

Other Divisions. First Marathon also is active in the sales and trading of fixed income securities, mutual fund management, individual investor services and principal investments. Also, First Marathon enjoys access to significant retail distribution capabilities through its correspondent network.

Describe your ownership structure.

Founded in 1979, First Marathon went public in 1984. The common shares of the company are traded on The

Toronto Stock Exchange and Montreal Exchange and have a market capitalisation of approximately $450 million. Management and employees have voting control of the company.

The shares of First Marathon Inc. are listed on The Toronto Stock Exchange and Montreal Exchange.

How does your approach to finance differ from that of other firms, and what do you consider to be your strengths and distinctive capabilities?

As Canada's leading independent investment bank, First Marathon is able to offer its clients a blend of top-notch talent, entrepreneurship, an independent ownership structure versus our primary Canadian competitors, and solid financial backing. The company has historically been more profitable on a per professional basis than our competitors and dividends on common shares have increased in each of the last ten years. Senior investment banking professionals are directly compensated on a unique performance driven basis, hence the constant focus on generating new business and "getting the deal done." Associates benefit by being involved in all aspects of a transaction and generally work on small teams directly with our most senior professionals. In summary, our system attracts professionals who are highly motivated, extremely talented and fun to work with.

Discuss changes in your firm's revenues (both domestic and international) and professional staff over the past year; over the past five years.

First Marathon's revenues have increased from $85 million in 1992 to $260 million in 1996. Net income increased from $21 million to $58 million over the same period. Investment Banking revenues have increased more than three-fold since 1992 to over $80 million in 1996.

First Marathon has offices across Canada, significant international reach and over 500 employees world-wide. From approximately 12 professionals in 1992 to 34 at the end of 1996, Investment Banking has similarly experienced tremendous growth.

The Finance MBA's Job Description

Describe the career path and corresponding responsibilities for an MBA at your firm.

The company recruits MBAs for career positions in our Investment Banking Division, including Mergers and Acquisitions. Associates are both encouraged and expected to assume as much responsibility in their projects as they can handle. Over time, increased levels of responsibility and decision-making will naturally accrue to the individual.

Associates work with other associates, analysts, vice-presidents, and directors. Associates usually work on small transaction teams of two to three professionals, generally reporting directly to the director overseeing the transaction.

Describe the opportunities for professional mobility between the various departments in your firm.

Each of the departments work closely together and, in particular, the Investment Banking Division interacts on a regular basis with members of equity sales and trading, research and syndication groups.

Discuss the lifestyle aspects of a career with your firm (i.e., average hours per week, amount of travel, flexibility to change offices, corporate culture, etc.).

A career in investment banking can be very demanding albeit both financially and intellectually rewarding. Our commitment to professionalism and client satisfaction creates a dynamic and challenging environment which requires all members of the Investment Banking team to work long hours. Travel is an important part of the job, but it varies from three to four day roadshows or due diligence trips, to day trips for client meetings. Due to the transactional basis of our business, there are natural peaks in the demands placed on one's time.

The Recruiting Process

Describe your recruiting process and the criteria by which you select candidates. Is prior experience necessary?

Recruiting efforts focus on on-campus activities during the fall recruiting season. Finalists are flown to Toronto to tour our head office and meet with other members of the Investment Banking Division.

All candidates should have strong financial, business, communication and interpersonal skills. Prior industry work experience is preferable but viewed in the context of other important criteria. An interest in financial markets is essential as well as the desire and ability to work in a fast paced and challenging environment.

How many permanent associates and analysts do you hire in a typical year? How many summer interns do you expect to hire? If you have a formal summer program, please describe it. Please be sure to indicate whether the summer program is in place for all offices or just some.

Typically First Marathon hires one to three analysts, one to three associates, and one summer intern for our Toronto offices. Our offices in Vancouver, Calgary and Montreal will also hire additional professionals.

What international opportunities does your firm offer for U.S. citizens? For foreign nationals?

All candidates should meet the necessary requirements to work in Canada before applying.

FMC Corporation

200 East Randolph Drive
Chicago, IL 60601
(312) 861-6000
Fax: (312) 861-5913
Web site: www.fmc.com

MBA Recruiting Contact(s):
FMC College Relations

Company Description

Describe your firm's business and the types of clients served by your finance group(s).

FMC is a New York Stock Exchange-listed, $5 billion, Chicago-based multinational corporation producing machinery and chemicals for industry, agriculture, and government. Our worldwide work force of 22,000 staffs 115 manufacturing facilities and mines in 24 countries.

Our competitive edge in manufacturing excellence, technological innovation, cost control, and customer satisfaction has made us a leader in the global markets we serve. Earning a consistently high real return on shareholder equity is a challenge and an imperative. At FMC, the finance function is committed to increasing value today while positioning the company for future profitable growth and strategic development.

FMC is a corporate leader in developing and implementing state-of-the-art analytical techniques for financial planning, performance measurement, and resource allocation. For example, FMC recapitalized in 1986, doubling shareholder value, while enabling FMC to continue its vigorous program of internal development, capital investment, and research and development. We have also adopted an innovative current cost accounting system to assist top management in evaluating performance and strategic investment decision-making. At one of our plants, we are implementing a new activity-based costing, which will give our management a deeper understanding of our product costs.

This philosophy of financial innovation pervades the entire corporation. Financial managers are active leaders of the management team and are required to think and act strategically. They are involved in all facets of managing FMC's complex businesses, from product planning to international investment decisions. Therefore, we seek highly motivated individuals who will become both our future financial leaders and future general managers.

The Finance MBA's Job Description

Describe the career path and corresponding responsibilities for an MBA at your firm.

Financial Business analysts begin their careers in a variety of corporate and site locations, where they are responsible for analyzing, monitoring, and tracking the performance of specific business segments. Analysts also work with line management on a variety of projects that affect management decisions and business performance. After 12–18 months, most analysts assume positions in financial management in one of our line organizations. It is also possible for analysts to pursue other functions at this point. Their choices often depend on their career focus: specializing in a functional discipline or taking advantage of FMC's opportunities for cross-functional career growth. In addition, Financial Business analysts are in demand for a wide variety of offshore opportunities.

The Recruiting Process

How many permanent associates and analysts do you hire in a typical year? How many summer interns do you expect to hire? If you have a formal summer program, please describe it. Please be sure to indicate whether the summer program is in place for all offices or just some.

FMC recruits at eight to ten major business schools. Typically, we hire 15 to 25 full-time MBAs and 12 to 20 interns each year in the Planning, Manufacturing, Human Resources, and Finance functions.

Ford Motor Company

World Headquarters Building
11th Floor—East Wing
The American Road
Dearborn, MI 48121
(313) 323-0850
Web site: www.ford.com

MBA Recruiting Contact(s):
Malcolm Macdonald

Company Description

Describe your firm's business and the types of clients served by your finance group(s).

Ford is the world's fourth-largest industrial corporation and the second-largest producer of cars and trucks. It also ranks among the largest providers of financial services in the United States. Approximately 325,000 employees in our plants, offices, and laboratories serve the automotive and financial services needs of customers in more than 200 countries and territories.

Our two core businesses are the Automotive Group and the Financial Services Group, which consists of Ford Credit, The Associates, and U.S. Leasing. We also are engaged in a number of other businesses, including electronics, glass, electrical and fuel-handling products, plastics, climate control systems, service and replacement parts, vehicle leasing and rental, and land development.

Our Finance Organization serves a broad range of internal and external clients. The primary focus of Finance at Ford is on providing timely and accurate financial analysis to company management in order to support a wide range of business decisions.

Describe your ownership structure.

Ford Motor Company is a widely held, publicly traded corporation. Approximately 40% of the voting shares in the corporation are controlled by the Class B stock—controlled by the Ford family.

How does your approach to finance differ from that of other firms, and what do you consider to be your strengths and distinctive capabilities?

Historically, finance has played a very strong role in the automobile industry, particularly at Ford. In fact, in a recent survey conducted by CFO magazine, over 200 financial executives, executive recruiters, bankers, and consultants identified Ford Motor Company as one of the three companies that best prepares financial managers for the chief financial officer chair.

Finance professionals are involved in every aspect of the company's operations—product development, engineering, sales and marketing, customer service (sale of after-market parts), and financial services—as well as the traditional finance functions, such as treasury, financial planning, and operations analysis. Typically, finance professionals move frequently among the company's different components, developing into well-rounded managers who can fill top-level positions in the Finance Organization or in general management. Examples of the varied experiences of recent Harvard MBAs are Tom Gorman (HBS '87), presently Finance Director of Ford France, whose previous assignments include Dearborn Stamping Plant Controller, Taurus Vehicle Line Controller, and Staff liaison to the Asia-Pacific region. Kathleen Gallagher (HBS '85) is currently Finance Manager at Powertrain Operations, with responsibility for the V Engines and Automatic Transmission businesses. Previous experiences include International Financing Manager in Treasury Operations, Financial Analysis Manager at Ford's Customer Service operations, and numerous assignments in the product development community.

Finance MBAs at Ford can expect a wide variety of challenging assignments that expose them to all the functional areas of the corporation. At Ford, finance is not about abstract theories; it is about real decisions that affect the viability of a multi-billion-dollar new car platform, the investment in hundreds of millions of dollars' worth of plant and equipment, or the pricing strategy of a major product line.

The Finance MBA's Job Description

Describe the career path and corresponding responsibilities for an MBA at your firm.

The Career Foundation Development Program ensures an early diversity of experiences, with the following job rotations (and job responsibilities):

- Year 1: At a vehicle assembly plant or a component manufacturing plant, typically located in the Midwest (manufacturing cost analysis, operations analysis, and special projects)
- Years 2 and 3: At one of the following groups, generally located in Dearborn, MI:

    Product Development (develop proposals for new product programs, analyze product line profitability)

Sales (establish pricing strategies and incentive programs for new and existing products, competitive analysis)
Treasury/Capital Markets (capital structure decisions for acquisitions/joint ventures, dividend policy for parent/foreign affiliates, issuance of debt/equity, foreign exchange)
Manufacturing General Offices (capital project analysis, e.g., review of plant expansion proposals and quality improvement actions)
Parts and Service (financial analysis related to sales of after-market parts)
Ford Motor Credit Company/Financial Services (funding of automotive receivables via asset-backed securities, commercial paper, and/or swaps)

- Year 4: Rotate to a new organization (one of the groups listed above). Future rotations could be expected about every two years.

Long career paths could lead an MBA to become controller of a division, to become treasurer of an affiliate, or to move into general management.

Discuss the lifestyle aspects of a career with your firm (i.e., average hours per week, amount of travel, flexibility to change offices, corporate culture, etc.).

The finance culture at Ford is reflective of the people we hire: highly analytical, aggressive, motivated, and career oriented—with a strong desire to win. Professional development is an integral part of our corporate culture. At Ford, we view our people as an investment, not an expense.

Ford world headquarters is in Dearborn, MI, located about 15 miles from downtown Detroit. Southeastern Michigan offers a wide variety of affordable housing and an easy commute to the office yet has access to all of the cultural amenities one would expect of the nation's sixth largest metropolitan area, including outstanding universities, world-class museums, and four professional sports teams.

The Recruiting Process

Describe your recruiting process and the criteria by which you select candidates. Is prior experience necessary?

Ford is looking for aggressive, intelligent, highly motivated men and women who are looking for a challenge in an exciting, highly competitive industry. As Ford enters the twenty-first century, we face many challenges: globalization, trade barriers, increased regulation, excess capacity, and stiff competition, to name a few. We are looking for people to help us meet these challenges.

Prior technical experience or education is helpful but certainly not essential. A healthy interest in, and a willingness to get close to, our products is more essential to long-term success at Ford.

Our recruiting process includes a recruiting briefing in the fall followed by on-campus interviews in the winter. On-site visits follow a successful on-campus interview. In addition we will arrange a visit for candidates to take a "Ford Finance Test Drive"—an opportunity to spend a day with an MBA who has worked at Ford for two or three years. He or she will show you what a typical day is like. The Ford Finance Test Drive provides an additional opportunity to decide if Ford is the right place to make your career.

How many summer interns do you expect to hire? If you have a formal summer program, please describe it. Please be sure to indicate whether the summer program is in place for all offices or just some.

Ford plans to continue to seek a limited number of talented individuals for a variety of summer positions. Summer positions are designed to provide a challenging short-term assignment that will give an accurate perspective on a full-time career at Ford. The process and qualifications for summer applicants are similar to those for full-time positions.

What international opportunities does your firm offer for U.S. citizens? For foreign nationals?

Ford derives about 40% of its revenues from international operations, offering abundant opportunities for international experience. Overseas assignments, if desired, are possible after completion of the Foundation Development Program. Many Ford executives have had international experience at some point in their careers.

Ford recruits MBAs who are U.S. citizens or are authorized to work full time in the United States.

Furman Selz LLP

230 Park Avenue
New York, New York 10169
(212) 309-8200
Web site: www.secapl.com/FurmanSelz/fs2.html

MBA Recruiting Contact(s):
Diane Kopyscianski, Investment Banking
(212) 309-8653
Fax: (212) 309-8638

Lillian Rinchiuso, Equity Research
(212) 309-8219
Fax: (212) 309-8618

Sarah Hiemen, Private Asset Management
(415) 834-3650
Fax: (415) 834-2410

Company Description

Describe your firm's business and the types of clients served by your finance group(s).

Furman Selz is a full-service investment banking firm, headquartered in New York with offices in Boston, San Francisco, Los Angeles, Chicago, London, and Tokyo. We employ over 700 people in the areas of investment banking, institutional equities and fixed income, institutional services, and investment management.

Describe your ownership structure.

The firm was founded in 1973 as a research boutique. It has grown consistently and today has over $140 million in capital and over $25 billion in assets under management and administration. The firm is privately owned by its employees, and has been profitable in every year since its inception.

How does your approach to finance differ from that of other firms, and what do you consider to be your strengths and distinctive capabilities?

Furman Selz is focused on differentiating itself with regard to providing thoughtful, cutting-edge advice while at the same time delivering personal service. The firm maintains a familial heartbeat as it grows.

We focus on selected industries including: Media & Communications, Healthcare, Shipping, Automotive, Retailing & Consumer Products, Technology, Financial Services & Insurance, and Utilities. Our greatest strengths lie in our knowledge-based approach to our businesses derived from our origins in Research.

The Finance MBA's Job Description

Describe the career path and corresponding responsibilities for an MBA at your firm.

MBA career paths in Investment Banking and Research are open-ended based on the capabilities, diligence, willingness to accept responsibility, and accomplishments of the candidate. Mobility between departments does exist, but usually not until after the first two to three years of employment.

Furman Selz also has an MBA recruiting, hiring, and training program in its Private Asset Management Division. P.A.M. works with wealthy individuals, usually entrepreneurs, to assist them in managing their personal and corporate assets. An interest in investments and the ability to interact successfully with corporate executives are important qualities. The MBA career path in Private Asset Management is highly entrepreneurial and sited to self-starters.

Discuss the lifestyle aspects of a career with your firm (i.e., average hours per week, amount of travel, flexibility to change offices, corporate culture, etc.).

Furman Selz prides itself in terms of employee satisfaction. Average hours per week and amount of travel vary by department. Furman Selz strives to create a positive work environment for all employees.

The Recruiting Process

Describe your recruiting process and the criteria by which you select candidates. Is prior experience necessary?

Candidates are interviewed on campus; some are invited back to be interviewed by business line and senior management. Intellect, academic achievement, work ethic, and the ability to interact with fellow employees are important. Prior experience is an advantage.

How many permanent associates and analysts do you hire in a typical year?

Approximately 10 associates are hired in a typical year.

General Motors Corporation

New York Treasurer's Office

GM Building
767 Fifth Avenue
New York, NY 10153
(212) 418-6193
Web site: www.gmc.com

MBA Recruiting Contact(s):
Niharika Taskar, HBS '96
Dwaine Kimmet, HBS '95

Company Description

Describe your firm's business and the types of clients served by your finance group(s).

General Motors designs, manufactures, and sells automobiles, trucks, vans, locomotives, and other equipment and components related to the worldwide transportation industry. In addition, the corporation is involved in the design and manufacture of satellites, integrated circuits, electronic-optical sensors, guidance systems, and other defense electronics systems, as well as financial services and the application of a wide range of computer systems and software.

The global automobile industry is progressing into an era of unprecedented competition. At General Motors, we are approaching this challenge with a commitment to remaining the premier manufacturer of cars and trucks in North America and the rest of the world. As has been well documented in the press, this commitment has resulted in a period of incredible change, with the entire GM organization being scrutinized and restructured. This process is placing emphasis on the ability of GM's employees to manage its operations and finance effectively.

GM's New York Treasurer's Office plays a vital role in the decisions that affect both the current operations of the corporation and its future direction. The office is extensively responsible for a broad range of financial, strategic planning, and other business matters leading to the execution of transactions, including new business ventures, domestic and international subsidiary financings, investments, divestitures, capital planning, and foreign exchange trading. In addition to developing and executing action plans for top management, the Treasurer's Office is also responsible for presenting such action plans and other information to the Board of Directors and its Finance, Audit, Incentive and Compensation, and Nominating Committees. As such, GM's New York Treasurer's Office distinguishes itself from other corporate treasury staffs by providing individuals with the opportunity to develop and practice corporate finance, consulting, and general management skills.

Furthermore, the appeal of the Treasurer's Office extends beyond that provided by traditional treasury functions. Specifically, GM's Treasurer's Office also functions as GM's in-house consulting firm. As such, the office's responsibilities include developing, assessing, negotiating, and implementing strategic business initiatives of the corporation. Reflecting the Treasurer's Office objectives of developing both the financial and general business acumen of its employees, many alumni have progressed to top financial and general management positions throughout the United States and virtually all of our international locations, including Europe, Asia, and South America.

The Finance MBA's Job Description

Describe the career path and corresponding responsibilities for an MBA at your firm.

A senior financial analyst in the office is exposed to a wide range of strategic and financial assignments that can be matched by very few other companies. For example, a typical business school graduate could immediately be engaged in any of several activities, including structuring an international subsidiary or joint venture, developing an entirely new form of equity or debt offering, managing GM's multibillion-dollar cash portfolio, or trading foreign currency on a global basis. Newly hired MBAs are provided with the opportunity to practice a wide range of corporate finance activities. In this regard, individuals in the Treasurer's Office are rotated from section to section in order to develop their breadth of expertise fully. Senior analysts would typically follow a rotational assignment system through several of nine office sections, which places emphasis on developing general managers proficient in many areas of finance. While the responsibilities of each section and position vary, analysts are expected to develop a broad knowledge of GM's operations, its products, and its markets on a worldwide basis. Key responsibilities within the sections include:

Business Development (Overseas & Domestic)

- Analysis of potential acquisition, mergers & divestitures
- Structuring and negotiating alliances, partnerships & joint ventures

- Devise workout strategies for financially distressed GM suppliers

Capital Planning

- Corporate change initiatives focused on asset management and financial performance accountability
- Forecast & analysis of GM capital structure, cash flows & related strategies
- Structured finance and balance sheet management

Investor Relations

- Communication with Wall Street analysts, rating agencies & global investor community
- Competitive analysis of other major automobile manufacturers

Domestic Finance

- Analysis & implementation of both debt & equity issuances for corporate funding purposes
- Management of interest rate risk via utilizing derivative products
- Investment of corporation's multi-billion dollar cash portfolio
- Foreign exchange/commodities analysis & hedging

Worldwide Pension Funding & Analysis

- Development of funding strategies for worldwide pension & benefit plans
- National negotiations with the United Auto Workers union
- Design & analysis of benefit & compensation plans

Overseas Finance

- Overseas capital planning & liquidity management, including cash repatriation
- Funding for Latin American & Mid-East/African operations
- Export & trade finance
- Global financial policies

Regional Treasury Centers - RTCs (Satellite Offices in Brussels, Singapore & Beijing)

- Foreign exchange & interest rate exposure management of GM's European subsidiaries
- Cash management for European operations
- Risk management advisory work for Asian subsidiaries
- Funding for Asian & European operations
- Corporate finance advisory for Asian & European operations
- Venture development & financing of Chinese projects

Outlined below are the job classifications within the New York Treasurer's Office and the average time at each level:

Job Classification	Average Years in Level
Senior Financial Analyst (entry-level position for MBA)	3 years
Manager (typically supervises 3 or 4 analysts)	2–3 years
Section Director (responsible for 2 to 4 managers and 4–8 analysts)	2 years

Describe the opportunities for professional mobility between the various departments in your firm.

In addition to promotions leading to a successful and rewarding experience at the Treasurer's Office in New York, numerous financial openings occur for Treasurer's Office employees at the regional treasury centers, overseas and domestic subsidiaries and divisions (e.g., GM Hughes Electronics, NUMMI [GM's joint venture with Toyota in Fremont, CA], GMAC, Saturn, GM-Europe, EDS, and GM's North American Operations). Furthermore, many opportunities are available outside the financial side of the business, including general management, personnel, industrial relations, manufacturing, industry-government relations, and our worldwide trading corporation.

The Recruiting Process

Describe your recruiting process and the criteria by which you select candidates. Is prior experience necessary?

GM's Treasurer's Office is staffed with approximately 60 MBAs from the nation's top schools and from around the globe. We seek individuals with initiative and a willingness to assume a demanding workload in a challenging environment, as new analysts are expected to assume a significant amount of responsibility within a very short period of time. A typical senior financial analyst has a strong academic background, with particular emphasis on finance; a background in economics, accounting, engineering, or operations is also valuable. Attractive candidates demonstrate strong analytical and organizational abilities, as well as effective oral and written communication skills. Importantly, they also have a high level of interpersonal skills and an ability to function effectively as part of a team.

If you have a formal summer program, please describe it. Please be sure to indicate whether the summer program is in place for all offices or just some.

GM's Treasurer's Office has an excellent summer program that allows students between years of business school to learn about the New York office and gain valuable knowledge and skills in a particular section. Many of our recent summer analysts have elected to return to the Treasurer's Office upon graduating.

Goldman, Sachs & Co.

85 Broad Street
New York, NY 10004
(212) 902-1000
Web site: www.goldmansachs.com

MBA Recruiting Contact(s):
Goldman, Sachs & Co.
85 Broad Street
New York, NY 10004
(212) 902-1000
Web site: www.goldmansachs.com

Jide J. Zeitlin, Managing Director
Investment Banking Division; for Investment Banking Division and Principal Investment Area

Robert D. Emer, Vice President
J. Aron Currency and Commodities Division; for J. Aron Currency and Commodities Division

Goldman, Sachs & Co.
1 New York Plaza
New York, NY 10004

James Baker, Vice President
Equities Division; for Equities Division and for Global Operations and Technology Division

Goldman, Sachs & Co.
Exchange Place
53 State Street
13th Floor
Boston, Massachusetts 02109

Barry Turkanis, Vice President
Fixed Income Division; for Fixed Income Division

Company Description

Describe your firm's business and the types of clients served by your finance group(s).

Goldman, Sachs & Co. is a full-service international investment banking and securities firm headquartered in New York City. Major offices in London and Tokyo serve as European and Asia/Pacific Basin headquarters, respectively. Other offices are located throughout the United States and in Frankfurt, Hong Kong, Montreal, Paris, Singapore, Sydney, Toronto, and Zurich.

The firm is a leader in virtually every aspect of financing and investing, serving corporations, institutions, governments, and individual clients. A recent survey of U.S. corporate financial officers named Goldman, Sachs the leading investment banking firm for overall service to large public companies. Another survey of U.S. chief financial officers and top institutional money managers names the firm "best broker" for the second consecutive year.

Our leadership derives principally from the dedication, talent, and professionalism of our people. We recruit and train the very best graduates from leading colleges and universities. These individuals become part of our noted team effort, which provides the closely integrated financial skills and services necessary to help our clients meet diverse goals and new challenges in global markets.

The following is a brief overview of the firm's organization and activities.

Investment Banking Division
The Investment Banking Division assists corporations, financial institutions, and governments in planning and executing financial strategies in the global capital markets.

Corporate Finance. Our Corporate Finance Department professionals concentrate the firm's resources on identifying alternative sources of capital and on developing innovative techniques to match the interests of users and providers of capital. Transactions, structured and executed worldwide, include public debt and equity offerings and private placements of debt and equity. The firm is a leading manager of public offerings in the United States and abroad and a major factor in arranging private financings. The firm is also active in corporate workouts and restructurings.

Energy and Telecommunications Group. The Energy and Telecommunications Group provides investment banking services to Goldman, Sachs' clients in four principal industries: Oil and Gas, Pipelines, Utilities, and Telecommunications.

Financial Institutions Group. Professionals in the Financial Institutions Group provide full-service investment banking services to many of the largest banks, insurance companies, money managers, finance companies, and thrift institutions worldwide.

Structured Finance Group. The Structured Finance Group is responsible for the conception, development, promotion, and execution of a variety of types of financing transactions characterized by nonconventional features. These features include noncorporate legal structures, advantageous tax or accounting treatment, nonconventional sources of capital, and contractual mechanics governing business input and output.

Mergers and Acquisitions. The Mergers and Acquisitions Department, consistently a leading advisor in major merger transactions, assists corporations in achieving financial and strategic objectives through sales, acquisition, divestitures, leveraged buyouts, and recapitalizations, and defending against hostile takeovers.

Capital Markets. Professionals in our Capital Markets Groups advise issuing clients on capital-raising strategies and opportunities by communicating current fixed income market and product information generated by our trading, sales, and foreign exchange professionals worldwide.

Real Estate. The Real Estate Department serves the world's leading corporations, real estate developers, and institutions. The firm is dominant in arranging sales and financings of investment-grade office, retail, hotel, industrial, and multifamily properties. These transactions frequently involve foreign investors and lenders and include capital markets instruments such as securitized offerings, interest rate swaps, and credit enhancements.

Investment Banking Services. The Investment Banking Services Department is the marketing arm of the Investment Banking Division. Professionals are responsible for maintaining and strengthening client relationships and developing new relationships and business. In cooperation with each execution department, professionals create and implement marketing plans for specific products as well as strategies to enhance the firm's overall presence and reputation worldwide.

Principal Investment Area

Principal Investment professionals are responsible for the principal investing activities of the firm, including the firm-sponsored investment funds. All principal investments are made so as not to conflict with client objectives.

Fixed-Income Division

The Fixed-Income Division serves investing and issuing clients as a leader in marketing and trading fixed income securities and derivative products in all major financial markets. A majority of the division's professionals are involved in sales, trading, and research. The division also includes Municipal Finance and Asset-Backed Finance professionals.

Sales and Trading. Sales and Trading professionals work within groups that concentrate on such specific fixed-income products as government and agency securities, corporate securities, mortgage-backed securities, high-yield securities, municipal securities, futures and options, and preferred stock.

Sales professionals play a key role in the firm's capital markets transactions. They assist institutional investors in planning and implementing portfolio strategies. As a critical link between the firm's issuing and investing clients, they ensure the successful distribution of new issues and the firm's ability to underwrite the debt of corporations, governments, and other major borrowers.

Trading professionals make markets in major debt securities as well as in derivatives of those securities. They commit the firm's capital to ensure liquidity for investing clients. Traders are continually in touch with sales professionals, soliciting investor opinions and suggesting investment strategies. Traders also advise capital markets, investment banking, and syndicate professionals on the pricing, structuring, and timing of new issues, as well as on debt repurchase, synthetic securities, and asset swaps.

Fixed Income Research. The Fixed Income Research Department uses sophisticated analytical, mathematical, and computer capabilities to develop new ideas, products, and approaches for trading, hedging, and investment strategies as well as for asset-liability management. Professionals work in specialized sections covering debt options, trading systems, asset-liability management, risk management, sales support, financial modeling, hedging, portfolio optimization, new product development, and research.

Municipal Finance. Professionals in our Municipal Finance Department are responsible for developing new business opportunities, structuring and executing transactions, and providing ongoing financial advisory services for issuers of municipal bonds. Clients include states, state agencies, local governments, hospitals, health care systems, airports, public power authorities, colleges and universities, housing finance agencies, mass transit systems, and cultural institutions. The department originates and underwrites the full spectrum of tax-exempt and taxable municipal debt, ranging from tax-exempt commercial paper, variable-rate demand notes, and put bonds, to long-term, fixed-rate bonds.

Asset-Backed Finance. Our Asset-Backed Finance professionals—who are part of the Mortgage Securities Department—provide a full range of investment banking services to clients, including thrift institutions, mortgage bankers, federal agencies, home builders, commercial banks, and insurance, finance, and industrial companies.

Equities Division

Through its Equities Division, Goldman, Sachs underwrites, distributes, and trades equity securities and derivative products on a worldwide basis. Goldman, Sachs' position in the global equities marketplace results from its product innovation, distribution capability, and willingness to commit capital in response to clients' needs. The division has long-standing relationships with a wide range of institutional investors and wealthy family groups.

As a member of the New York, London, Frankfurt, and Tokyo stock exchanges, Goldman, Sachs is a trader and market maker in U.S., European, U.K., Japanese, and other global equities. Trading and execution activities are conducted as both agent and principal.

Institutional Investor Services. The Institutional Investor Services Department provides trading and research coverage, through product-focused specialists, to institutional clients, including public and private pension funds, insurance companies, mutual funds, hedge funds, banks, investment advisors, endowments, and foundations in the United States, Europe, and Asia.

Global Convertible Securities. The Global Convertible Securities Department distributes, makes markets, and conducts arbitrage in U.S., yen-denominated, and Euroconvertible bonds and in a substantial portion of U.S.-convertible preferred stocks. Equity warrants specialists in New York, London, and Tokyo make markets and conduct arbitrage in U.S., Japanese, and European warrant issues.

Equity Derivatives. The Equity Derivatives Department distributes and trades listed and unlisted options and futures on market indexes, industry groups, and individual companies. The department develops quantitative strategies to effect portfolio hedging and restructuring, asset allocation, equity index swaps, and the construction of synthetic instruments. These instruments enable sophisticated investors to undertake desired hedging strategies and establish or liquidate investment positions not otherwise available in the financial markets.

Equity Capital Markets. The Equity Capital Markets Department advises corporate and governmental clients worldwide with regard to equity financing opportunities, privatization strategies, capital structure, and equity product design. Through the Equity Capital Markets Department, Goldman, Sachs manages international equity offerings, U.S. common stock offerings, and issues of ADRs by international companies.

Private Client Services. The Private Client Services Department provides comprehensive equity, fixed income, and cash management services, as well as securities safekeeping, margin lending, portfolio reporting, and principal investment opportunities to wealthy family groups, medium-size institutions, corporations, and professional investors worldwide.

Investment Research. The Investment Research Department consists of more than 80 analysts, located in New York, London, Frankfurt, and Tokyo, who provide quantitative and qualitative analyses of global economic, currency, and financial market trends; portfolio strategy; asset allocation recommendations; industry weighting; and investment options on 1300 companies in over 80 different industries in the United States, Japan, Europe, and elsewhere.

J. Aron Currency and Commodity Division

The J. Aron Currency and Commodity Division, with offices in New York, London, Tokyo, and Singapore, is a leading market maker in foreign exchange and commodities worldwide, providing complete trading, hedging, and advisory services to corporations, institutions, and governments. The division's activities include:

Foreign Exchange Trading Department
Foreign Exchange Sales Department
Oil and Natural Gas Trading Department
Coffee Trading Department
Grain Trading Department
Metals Trading Department
Currency and Commodity Investment Products Department

Global Operations and Technology Division

Integral roles in firmwide activities are played by our information technologies, securities operations, controllers, credit, treasury, and personnel professionals.

Information Technologies. Information Technologies serves the business, operations, and administrative areas of the firm by managing the delivery of high-quality computer systems.

Controllers. The Controllers Department designs and monitors all internal financial functions. The department is responsible for internal financial analysis and consulting, external financial reporting, monitoring internal trading positions and regulatory compliance, and general accounting for the firm.

Credit. The Credit Department approves and monitors the credit/exposure limits of many companies with which Goldman, Sachs does business. The department participates in the solicitation, structuring, and selling of commercial paper and conducts due diligence investigations.

Treasury. Worldwide funding of the firm's operations is the responsibility of the Treasury Department. The firm is rated A1+, the highest ranking for commercial paper issuers assigned by Standard & Poor's.

Personnel. Our Personnel professionals ensure that Goldman, Sachs maintains the highest standards in all human resources activities. Functional areas include benefits and compensation, employment and employee relations, training and professional development, personnel systems and administration, and international personnel operations.

Describe your ownership structure.

Founded in 1869, Goldman, Sachs is the only remaining private partnership among the major Wall Street organizations. Our partnership structure fosters a culture that is characterized by teamwork, aggressive pursuit of business opportunities, compensation that is commensurate with responsibility and performance, and sound financial management. We have historically been among the most profitable investment banking firms.

How does your approach to finance differ from that of other firms, and what do you consider to be your strengths and distinctive capabilities?

Commitment to client interests and teamwork are the most distinctive characteristics of our approach to investment banking. We emphasize relationships rather than the completion of individual transactions. Our success is directly related to our ability to provide our clients with exceptional service. Among our key strengths are the following:

The skill, experience, and dedication of our people
Leadership in financial markets worldwide
Strong capital position
Technological resources
Reputation for excellence

Most important, we believe our ability to integrate all facets of the firm's areas of excellence through teamwork is unique in the industry.

The Finance MBA's Job Description

Describe the career path and corresponding responsibilities for an MBA at your firm.

The firm recruits MBAs for career positions in all divisions and operating entities. Initial training will depend on the new associate's background and functional area. Training emphasizes on-the-job learning, which is complemented by formal instruction. Professionals throughout the firm serve as instructors and mentors. During training, associates prepare for any registration exams that may be required for their specialization. They begin training in their functional areas after they complete those exams. Associates are encouraged to assume as much responsibility in their assignments as they can handle.

Associates play an integral role in planning, structuring, and executing transactions that range from a single private placement of equity or debt to a major portfolio restructuring or corporate reorganization. They work with partners, vice presidents, other associates, and analysts in an open atmosphere in which ideas are shared and creative thinking is encouraged. Because the firm has only three levels of professionals, new associates have significant contact with its senior members.

Describe the opportunities for professional mobility between the various departments in your firm.

As part of career development, we foster a working environment in which professionals are encouraged to explore their interests and develop their skills continuously. Believing that diversity of experience is beneficial not only to our professionals but also to the firm and its clients, we provide opportunities to work in other areas of the firm and to transfer to other departments, divisions, or offices.

We are diligent in evaluating professionals for career advancement and financial reward. Yearly reviews are made by teams of superiors and peers to ensure thoroughness and objectivity.

Discuss the lifestyle aspects of a career with your firm (i.e., average hours per week, amount of travel, flexibility to change offices, corporate culture, etc.).

A career at Goldman, Sachs is a challenging one that places significant demands on time and energy. Professionals are encouraged to make their lifestyle decisions within the context of doing the best job possible. The amount of travel varies greatly. In areas requiring the most travel, our professionals can average two or three days on the road each week.

As a result of our care in hiring, developing, challenging, and rewarding our people, the turnover rate for our professionals has consistently been one of the lowest in the industry.

The Recruiting Process

Describe your recruiting process and the criteria by which you select candidates. Is prior experience necessary?

In recruiting, we look for professionals who will flourish in a team-oriented environment. There is no single type of individual who fits in at Goldman, Sachs. We are an amalgam of people from around the world with different cultural and educational backgrounds and professional orientations. What we have in common are creativity, the confidence and willingness to take initiative and responsibility, an interest in being a part of a highly motivated group, and a desire to achieve beyond the norm.

Although each area of specialization requires certain qualities, most of our professionals demonstrate a keen interest in the financial markets; strong interpersonal, analytic, and communication skills; and an ability to respond creatively and quickly in a fast-paced, changing environment.

We believe that academic achievement is a good indication of potential, but it is not the most important criterion. Prior experience is usually not a major consideration for MBAs.

How many permanent associates and analysts do you hire in a typical year? How many summer interns do you expect to hire? If you have a formal summer program, please describe it. Please be sure to indicate whether the summer program is in place for all offices or just some.

We offer a two-year financial analyst program for college graduates. Each year, we hire a significant number of college graduates in the Investment Banking Division worldwide. In addition, there are select analyst positions elsewhere in the firm. As with MBAs, most of the training of college graduates is on the job. Many of our analysts earn an MBA and return to the firm as associates. The contact for the program is Andrea Baum, Investment Banking Division (212) 902-0003.

The firm actively recruits for its summer associate program. Our summer associates gain broad exposure to many areas of our business, and many return as full-time employees.

What international opportunities does your firm offer for U.S. citizens? For foreign nationals?

Investment banking has become an international business, and Goldman, Sachs is fully committed to the business on a worldwide basis. In addition to our headquarters in New York City, we have major offices in London and Tokyo, which serve as our European and Asian/Pacific Basin headquarters, respectively. We have other offices located throughout the United States, as well as in Frankfurt, Hong Kong, Montreal, Paris, Singapore, Sydney, Toronto, and Zurich. Consequently, we offer many international opportunities for both U.S. citizens and foreign nationals.

HBK Investments L.P.

777 Main Street, Suite 2750
Fort Worth, TX 76102
(817) 870-6100

MBA Recruiting Contact:
Laurence H. Lebowitz, Principal
Fax: (817) 870-6190
E-mail: llebowitz@hbk.com

Company Description

Describe your firm's business and the types of clients served by your finance group(s).

HBK Investments L.P. is a private investment management firm that is responsible for a portfolio of securities with a market value in excess of $3 billion. We manage two investment funds: HBK Fund L.P., an investment partnership organized in 1991; and HBK Offshore Fund Ltd., an investment fund organized in March 1996.

How does your approach to finance differ from that of other firms, and what do you consider to be your strengths and distinctive capabilities?

Our investment program emphasizes arbitrage and relative value opportunities throughout the world. The portfolio is managed 24 hours per day to cover all major securities markets, including the United States, Europe, and Asia. Our investment expertise includes convertible securities, fixed income securities, emerging market debt instruments, risk arbitrage and other special situation investments, bankrupt and distressed securities, and equity securities.

Discuss changes in your firm's revenues (both domestic and international) and professional staff over the past year; over the past five years.

We commenced operations in 1991 with $30 million of equity capital and four employees. As of April 1996, the firm managed $425 million of equity capital and had 36 employees.

HBK Investments is controlled by the principals of the firm.

The Finance MBA's Job Description

Describe the career path and corresponding responsibilities for an MBA at your firm.

Investment Analyst
HBK Investments is seeking investment analysts in its securities investment and trading operation. We use fundamental analysis to evaluate companies involved in mergers, acquisitions, and bankruptcies; the creditworthiness of issuers of fixed income and convertible securities; and the relative merits of competing investment opportunities. The successful applicant will work with principals of the firm who are responsible for all different areas of the investment program.

Firm Management Position
HBK Investments is also considering qualified MBA candidates for a managerial position in its back office operations, which are responsible for trade accounting, financial accounting and reporting, regulatory reporting and compliance, and investor relations. The position involves development and implementation of efficient operating procedures relating to all aspects of the firm's activities other than securities investment and trading.

The Recruiting Process

Describe your recruiting process and the criteria by which you select candidates. Is prior experience necessary?

HBK Investments seeks highly motivated individuals who have a demonstrated record of achievement and the ability to work effectively with others. Relevant work experience is beneficial, but not a prerequisite. We offer a Summer Associate Program for students who are completing their first year of business school. Summer internships are flexible and designed to permit us to evaluate your skills while giving you an opportunity to demonstrate the ability to add value. The firm also will consider permanent offers for graduating MBA candidates.

Hewlett-Packard Company

Employment Response Center
3000 Hanover Street/ms: 20APP
Palo Alto, CA 94304-1181
Web site: www.hp.com or www.jobs.hp.com
(415) 852-8473

MBA Recruiting Contact(s):
Employment Response Center

Company Description

Describe your firm's business and the types of clients served by your finance group(s).

Hewlett-Packard (HP) is a leading international manufacturer of computing and electronic measuring equipment for people in business, industry, science, engineering, health care, and education. The company's more than 12,000 products include computers and peripheral products, test and measuring instruments and computerized test systems, networking products, electronic components, handheld calculators, medical electronic equipment, and instruments and systems for chemical analysis.

HP's basic business purpose is to help accelerate the advancement of knowledge and fundamentally improve the effectiveness of people and organizations worldwide.

Describe your ownership structure.

HP is a publicly owned company and is one of the 20 largest industrial corporations in America. HP stock is traded on the New York Stock Exchange.

How does your approach to finance differ from that of other firms, and what do you consider to be your strengths and distinctive capabilities?

HP's combination of strength and structure enables us to offer a broad spectrum of financial career opportunities and early responsibility.

HP's unique corporate culture, often referred to as the "HP Way," is a combination of organizational values, corporate objectives, and company practices. The company is built upon values such as honesty, teamwork, and respect that are reflected in everything we do.

One of our guiding objectives as a company is profit. The profit we generate from our operations is the ultimate source of the funds we need to prosper and grow. It is the one absolutely essential measure of our corporate performance over the long term. Without profit, the company is unable to grow or fulfill the rest of its objectives.

Our long-standing policy has been to reinvest most of our profits and to depend on this reinvestment, plus funds from employee stock purchases and other cash flow items, to finance our growth.

The day-to-day performance of each individual adds to—or subtracts from—our profit. Profit is seen as the responsibility of all HP employees.

Discuss changes in your firm's revenues (both domestic and international) and professional staff over the past year; over the past five years.

In fiscal year 1996, ending October 31, 1996, net revenues rose 25% to $38.5 billion, following a 23% increase in fiscal year 1993.

HP employs approximately 112,000 people.

The Finance MBA's Job Description

Describe the career path and corresponding responsibilities for an MBA at your firm.

Financial analyst positions are typically in HP product divisions, field sales organizations, or corporate functions. These initial experiences lead to careers in financial management or in other functional areas such as marketing and manufacturing.

In the divisions, financial analysts work closely with other functional areas. Tasks may include product/process cost analysis, financial planning and reporting, product pricing and profitability analysis, asset evaluation, and the design and implementation of financial models that will simulate division operations.

Financial analysts in the sales regions are responsible for financial planning and reporting, customer leasing arrangements, credit analysis and accounts receivable management, inventory analysis and control, and contracts and order administration.

In our corporate headquarters, responsibilities may include many of the activities described above plus cash, debt, and foreign exchange management; pensions and investment analysis; coordination of long-range plans; the development of corporate financial policy; external shareholder and Securities and Exchange Commission reporting; and internal audit tasks.

Describe the opportunities for professional mobility between the various departments in your firm.

The company is committed to giving people the flexibility to reach well-defined goals. HP believes that freedom encourages the creativity and initiative of every employee. Career paths are not defined formally at HP; rather, they are flexible by design. We strive to help our people succeed and move on to greater challenges and responsibilities. An extensive internal job posting system allows employees to change jobs within their site (both within their function and across functions) and to move to other sites.

Discuss the lifestyle aspects of a career with your firm (i.e., average hours per week, amount of travel, flexibility to change offices, corporate culture, etc.).

HP trusts individuals and believes that people are committed to doing a good job given the right environment. To create this environment, HP offers pay based on performance, pleasant and open work environments, flexible work hours, cash profit sharing, and recognition for achievement.

The Recruiting Process

Describe your recruiting process and the criteria by which you select candidates. Is prior experience necessary?

HP recruits highly motivated, successful MBAs with initiative and a strong desire to make a significant impact on our business. Prior experience is preferred although not mandatory. Candidates must have a thorough knowledge of financial and accounting principles and proficiency in PC-based analytical tools. We look for outstanding analytical and problem-solving ability, as well as flexibility and excellent communication skills.

How many permanent associates and analysts do you hire in a typical year? How many summer interns do you expect to hire? If you have a formal summer program, please describe it. Please be sure to indicate whether the summer program is in place for all offices or just some.

The number of openings varies from year to year, but we typically have several finance openings distributed among many of our operations.

HP's Student Employment and Educational Development (SEED) Program enables students who have completed their first year in business school to gain hands-on experience as contributing members of our Finance team.

What international opportunities does your firm offer for U.S. citizens? For foreign nationals?

Overseas employment opportunities are limited to foreign nationals.

IBM Corporation

IBM Staffing Services
3808 Six Forks Road
Raleigh, NC 27609
(800) 964-4473
Web site: www.ibm.com

Company Description

Describe your firm's business and the types of clients served by your finance group(s).

IBM is a unique organization—a major multinational corporation that takes pride in its small-team atmosphere.

Consider that the company stands at the leading edge of one of the world's most dynamic industries: information processing. Consider that it does business in over 130 countries.

Consider, also, that IBM is an organization known worldwide for its respect for the individual and its environment for personal and professional growth. Consider that it is a market-driven company dedicated to providing the best possible customer service and that it is committed to excellence in all activities. Consider that it is a dynamic organization constantly striving to be competitive, to be responsive, to push decision making down to manageable levels.

In fact, IBM is a number of things. It is products and services designed to help customers solve problems through the application of information solutions. It is mainframe, mid-range, and personal computer systems; software for systems, applications, communications, and application development; telecommunications products; office systems; and related supplies and services. All are products and services designed to help record, process, store, retrieve, and communicate information.

In addition, IBM is a technological leader—an innovator with over 32,000 patents worldwide and major contributions at all levels of information processing. The company invented FORTRAN, RAMAC, the floppy disk, the relational database concept, systems network architecture, RISC technology, and much more. It has continually increased the density of circuit packaging, recently producing the first 4-million-bit chip. IBM scientists have earned Nobel Prizes for advances in superconductivity and scanning tunneling microscopy. The company is exploring sub-half-micron lithography, optical storage, speech recognition, artificial intelligence—and a host of other technologies.

But IBM is also open communications channels and respect for privacy, career flexibility and promotion on merit, personal growth and recognition, shared employee/company responsibility, a balance of work and personal life, corporate citizenship, and a benefits program considered one of the finest in industry. In other words, IBM is a special place to work.

Within IBM, Finance is its own team, a function that cuts across organizational lines. A cadre of over 5,000 professionals in the United States, IBM Finance offers opportunities at U.S. plant, laboratory, marketing, and subsidiary locations, as well as at headquarters facilities. Joint ventures and business alliances are also mutually staffed with an IBM and partner financial team.

Working in IBM Finance, you will gain exposure to all aspects of the business. Financial decisions affect research, engineering, manufacturing, programming, marketing, administration, personnel, communications—all the basic functions of the company. As a member of an IBM financial team, you will be in frequent contact with senior management early in your career. From the start, you will also interact with your counterparts at other locations.

In the process, you will gain an understanding of the business and what makes it work. To build a career in IBM Finance, you need a perspective that cuts across functional lines. A pricing decision in Raleigh, NC, can affect accounting controls in Boca Raton, FL. Financial planning for the IBM Credit Corporation can affect the treasury function at corporate headquarters in Armonk, NY. Equity investments can have worldwide implications.

The Finance MBA's Job Description

Describe the career path and corresponding responsibilities for an MBA at your firm.

Career paths in IBM Finance are characterized by a variety of experience and responsibilities, with advancement on merit. The path you follow depends on your objectives and how well you do in the variety of job responsibilities you will be given. You can move ahead as fast as your capabilities permit.

You will most likely start in financial planning or accounting—with later assignments in these areas plus pricing, treasury, and controllership—and rotate assignments for balanced experience. You could start as a cost accounting analyst, become a planning manager, move on to be a product pricer in an international headquarters in Paris—all while moving up in your career. An assignment in the IBM Credit Corporation might be in the picture. Ideally, your performance will lead you to first-line management in an operation unit, then on toward executive positions in financial or general management or increased professional staff responsibility.

Throughout your career, training will be largely on the job, enriched by formal classroom work within and outside the company. In fact, your training and education will never stop.

Looking Ahead with Financial Planning

A major entry-level area is financial planning—the development of basic financial strategies by which IBM runs its business. Financial planning is to IBM management what flowcharting is to the programmer. It establishes short-range projections of income and expense—the operating plan—and long-range strategic planning for the business environment.

IBM financial planning starts with determination of the goals and objectives of the business deliberately set at challenging but realistically attainable levels. Basic inputs are the following: customer requirements, competitive analysis, industry opportunity, technology trends, and available resources (both dollars and people). From goals and objectives, financial planners develop strategies for the business. This demands analysis of the company's current position and the availability of alternate strategies for the future.

In this area, you will work hand-in-hand with the IBM engineering, manufacturing, marketing, and general management communities to understand requirements, analyze IBM's and competitors' strengths and weaknesses, and realistically assess opportunities. You will interact closely with product planners; forecasters; and development, marketing, and service organizations. You may develop business models with desired returns, do portfolio analysis, or make investment decisions.

Aside from overall short- and long-term evaluations, your work can extend to specific IBM lines of business. Here the focus is on discrete markets and products, including the impact of competition. Developing, implementing, and controlling IBM financial plans calls for rigorous objectivity. Every recommendation must be judged by one basic criterion: Is this a sound business decision for IBM?

Financial planning at IBM helps convert goals to reality. Your experience in this area can make a real difference. You will develop creative ability, business judgment, and strong communications skills.

Accounting: The Language of the Business

A function of the office of the controller, accounting also offers a range of opportunities. State-of-the-art tools and technologies are used to collect, record, and report the company's economic transactions; the accountant's skills are used to interpret past business performance and to present recommendations for management decisions. The function is highly communications-oriented, with data consolidated from many sources for analysis and reporting in commonly understood terms.

Accounting fills many roles at IBM, from measurements and planning to government reporting and preparation of financial statements. Schedules are sensitive and demanding, logistics complex. The work demands teamwork and communication. You must accurately record financial results, comply with government regulations, and report earnings in a variety of ways. You must also ensure consistent presentation of accounting data and compliance with generally accepted accounting principles.

Accounting plays a vital, creative role in the management decision-making process at IBM. In an accounting position, you not only affect all basic operational areas—engineering, programming, marketing, administration—but also play a key role with IBM Treasury, international operations, and internal business partnership arrangements.

IBM also offers internal education to help you prepare for and take the Certified Management Accountant (CMA) exams. IBM is a corporate leader in the number of CMA certificates in its financial ranks.

IBM Pricing: Much More Than Finance

The pricing of IBM products and services is one of the most important responsibilities of the business. It is much more than finance—it is business itself. To ensure an adequate profit and return on investment, the pricing function must manage a product or service throughout its life, from conception to withdrawal from the market.

In simple terms, the role of pricing is to select IBM offerings and their prices to maximize the corporation's profitability. The major challenge is to ensure recovery of all costs and expenses, direct or indirect, associated with the development, manufacture, marketing, and maintenance of IBM products and services. In addition, IBM hardware, software, and service offerings must be understood within the context of a global marketplace where product strategies vary from country to country.

In fact, the pricing area is instrumental in initial selection of IBM products to be developed. Pricing analysts work side by side with the product management and marketing teams to ensure that new product offerings will meet the needs of IBM customers. The pricing function takes a financial and general management role in the decision about a program's financial viability and match to IBM's strategic objectives.

Pricing has an impact on all stages of a product's life. In the introduction stage, price selection, and terms and conditions involve detailed analysis of several areas: business area opportunity, product function, strategy, positioning, price elasticity, supply constraints, cost trends in technologies, manufacturing process, research and development strengths, marketing support plans, and selection of cost-effective distribution channels. The product must be positioned with respect to competition, with respect to the needs of the customer, and within IBM's product line.

Once introduced, a product is open to competitive moves: new products, price cuts, discounting, creative marketing, and promotional tactics. Pricing's responsibility is to anticipate these actions and prepare appropriate responses. During the growth stage of the product life cycle, the generation of sales is paramount. This often means that competitive bid situations, existing prices, terms, conditions, and methodologies are constantly subject to review and fine tuning.

If you work in this area, you will draw on the full repertoire of financial skills acquired in business school. You will coordinate the efforts of many groups, including product managers, market requirements specialists, business planning managers, and product forecasters. It is a unique opportunity for cross-disciplinary exposure within IBM and excellent experience in the IBM Finance career.

Treasury: Providing Capital for the Business

The IBM Treasury function is responsible for managing the company's capital structure and securing funds needed to operate the business. This demands reliable forecasting of cash receipts and disbursements, up-to-the-minute knowledge of international money markets, selection of funding vehicles, and maintenance of relationships with investment banking and commercial banking institutions.

In effect, Treasury is a focal point for the evaluation of a broad range of complex financial alternatives. IBM is concerned with worldwide liquidity, asset safety, currency management, tax optimization and compliance, risk/insurance management, optimal capital structure, investor perceptions, portfolio returns, and cost of capital.

The worldwide nature of IBM's business also requires techniques to protect the company from fluctuation in the value of foreign currencies. The ultimate objective is to optimize the use of cash, to keep any excess funds appropriately invested until needed, and to ensure access to funds when needed at the most favorable terms possible.

Other activities within the Treasury organization include internal audit, retirement fund management, short-term investment supervision, intercompany relations, and IBM's corporate citizenship programs.

Opportunities in the IBM Credit Corporation

Opportunities are also available for recent graduates in the IBM Credit Corporation, a wholly owned corporate subsidiary. By helping customers acquire IBM products and services through competitive financing offerings, IBM Credit plays a pivotal role in providing complete customer solutions.

IBM Credit provides leases and other financing products, remarketing services, end-of-lease options, and—for IBM Business Partners—inventory financing programs. It also provides IBM employees with financial services such as a money market account and mutual funds.

IBM Credit contributes significantly to the corporation's competitiveness and to the growth and stability of IBM earnings.

Since IBM Credit's products are financing offerings, financial professionals are involved in every stage of product development and delivery. These stages include the following:

- Development of new financial offerings that respond to customer requirements and competitive opportunities
- Assessments of credit risk and recovery of investment in high-risk situations
- Pricing of specific customer proposals for financing, including unique terms and conditions and competitive tactics
- Borrowing of debt funds via commercial paper, medium-term notes, and bond issues; relationships with investment-banking advisors
- Managing capital structure, including asset and liability matching and relations with the principal rating agencies
- Planning, accounting, and modeling financial performance, including publication of annual reports and supporting external financial communications

The Recruiting Process

Describe your recruiting process and the criteria by which you select candidates. Is prior experience necessary?

Within this environment, IBM Finance needs talented people with MBA degrees. The qualities sought are leadership, intelligence and awareness, interpersonal skills, creativity and ingenuity, energy, business maturity and judgment, integrity, personal enthusiasm, a goal-setting outlook, a desire to compete among the best—and the ability to be yourself.

The International Finance Corporation

2121 Pennsylvania Avenue, NW
Room 11K-290
Washington, DC 20433
(202) 473-7972
Web site: www.ifc.org

MBA Recruiting Contact(s):
Cornelis de Kievit, Manager
Recruitment

Total Number of Professionals (U.S. and worldwide):
1,200

Company Description

Describe your firm's business and the types of clients served by your finance group(s).

The International Finance Corporation (IFC) seeks to carry out its mandate—helping developing nations achieve sustained economic growth—by supporting private sector development. It proves this support through three types of operations.

Project Financing

The most traditional of IFC's operations, project financing, is also the largest. IFC commits over $1 billion in new project financing yearly. IFC finances the creation of new companies, as well as the expansion or modernization of established companies in virtually all sectors, from agribusiness to manufacturing to energy and mining. A significant number of projects backed by IFC, intended to help developing countries build up their financial sectors, involve the creation of institutions such as investment banks and venture capital, insurance, and leasing companies, as well as other specialized enterprises. IFC also provides lines of credit to financial intermediary institutions for onlending to enterprises too small to be the object of a direct investment by IFC. The Africa Enterprise Fund (AEF) directly finances small and midsize projects in sub-Saharan Africa.

The type of financial package provided by IFC is tailored to project requirements—IFC can provide loans, equity and quasi-equity, and guarantees, or a combination of these. Loans are offered at commercial rates with maturities and terms that vary with the needs of client companies. IFC finances only projects unable to obtain adequate funding from other sources and typically limits its loan or investment to 25% of total project costs, as it seeks not to replace private investment but to catalyze it. IFC does not accept government guarantees; it shares project risks with its investment partners. Before going ahead with a project, IFC undertakes a thorough technical, financial, and economic appraisal to verify that the project is viable and likely to benefit the economy of the host country.

Mobilization of Finance

IFC mobilizes funds from other investors and lenders in a variety of ways. It actively seeks partners for joint ventures and raises additional finance for the projects in which it has invested, either by encouraging other institutions to make loans or equity investments in parallel to its own or by arranging syndicated loans for groups of commercial banks.

IFC also raises capital for companies in developing countries in the international financial markets by underwriting security offerings and by promoting vehicles for foreign portfolio investment such as country funds. IFC's in-house financial engineering expertise is applied to designing innovative financial products such as swaps, options, and convertible instruments to mobilize needed risk capital.

Advisory Services and Technical Assistance

Advisory services and technical assistance are frequently provided in the context of IFC's project-related activities. In the course of conducting project appraisals, for instance, IFC may provide technical assistance to project sponsors. IFC may also help in finding foreign partners, structuring transactions, and facilitating negotiations between foreign and domestic financiers and governments.

IFC provides advisory services to both government and corporate clients independently of project finance. IFC's Capital Markets Department advises member governments on the establishment of fiscal, legal, and regulatory frameworks that support the development of a market-oriented financial sector. IFC's Corporate Finance Services Department provides advice, often on a fee-earning basis, to private companies with heavy debt-servicing burdens on balance sheet restructuring, as well as to state-owned companies undergoing privatization. The Foreign Investment Advisory Service, operated jointly by IFC and the Multilateral Investment Guarantee Agency (MIGA), another member of the World Bank Group, advises member governments on policies, regulations, and institutions that can help them attract more foreign direct investment to priority sectors.

The Africa and Caribbean Project Development Facilities (APDF and CPDF), established in collaboration with the United Nations Development Programme (UNDP) and other donor organizations, provide technical assistance to entrepreneurs in regions seeking to develop bankable projects and obtain financing. IFC has also established a similar facility for the South Pacific (SPPF). Most recently, the Mekong Project Development Facility (MPDF) was established.

The Finance MBA's Job Description

Describe the career path and corresponding responsibilities for an MBA at your firm.

As an IFC staff member, you will be part of a team of highly qualified and motivated professionals from around the world seeking creative—and profitable—solutions to complex business problems. You will face the challenges and earn the satisfactions of helping to further economic progress in the developing world through private sector development. And you will be working for a unique institution: IFC has a businesslike approach to development and believes that development and profitability go hand in hand.

Each staff member's performance is reviewed annually. Opportunities to maintain and expand individual skills are provided through an in-house training program particularly in technical subjects, finance, communications, and office technology.

IFC's more than 1200 staff members come from about 70 different countries, including over 50 developing countries.

Discuss the lifestyle aspects of a career with your firm (i.e., average hours per week, amount of travel, flexibility to change offices, corporate culture, etc.).

Staff normally join IFC on fixed term appointments, although appointments for a regular position can also be arranged on an exceptional basis. The majority of staff are based in Washington, DC. Operational staff are likely to spend about one-fourth of their time on overseas travel.

The Recruiting Process

Describe your recruiting process and the criteria by which you select candidates. Is prior experience necessary?

In addition to outstanding academic and professional qualifications, IFC's work requires creativity, flexibility, and imagination. Staff members are expected to take initiative and make sound independent judgments. Tact and sensitivity are critical, as staff will be working with private and public sector officials from many countries, often in very different cultural settings. Fluency and the ability to write cogently in English are required, and working knowledge of another language, particularly French, Spanish, Portuguese, Arabic, or Chinese, is an added advantage. Computer literacy is highly desirable.

IFC recruits professional staff on an international basis. The selection process is very competitive. Many of the professionals recruited by IFC are already in mid-career. However, IFC also recruits directly from leading business schools around the world to fill the growing number of openings for investment and financial officers. Recruitment teams visit a number of schools each year to conduct on-campus interviews. IFC is interested in interviewing MBA candidates in their last year of school who have at least a few years of experience relevant to IFC's needs and requirements.

J.P. Morgan & Co. Incorporated

60 Wall Street
New York, NY 10260
(212) 483-2323
Web site: www.jpmorgan.com

MBA Recruiting Contact(s):
Andrea Beldecos, Vice President
Investment Banking Recruiting

Hiromi Kishi, Vice President
Markets Recruiting

Susan J. Baisley, Vice President
Private Client Services Recruiting

Company Description

Describe your firm's business and the types of clients served by your finance group(s).

J.P. Morgan provides sophisticated financial services to corporations, governments, financial institutions, private firms, not-for-profit institutions, and wealthy individuals throughout the world. Our activities include advising on corporate financial structure; arranging financing in capital and credit markets; underwriting, trading, and investing in an array of currencies and the full range of securities and derivative instruments; serving as investment advisor; and providing select trust, agency, and operational services.

J.P. Morgan advises its clients on the financial implications of corporate strategy and executes transactions when appropriate. These transactions include mergers, acquisitions, divestitures, other forms of corporate restructurings, and privatizations. The firm's global presence and experience are increasingly important to our advisory business as the focus shifts to cross-border transactions.

The firm is an expert on raising money for clients through the full range of instruments—equity and debt underwriting, loan syndications, private placements, and others—in all world markets. We advise clients on their optimal capital structure and implement that advice through transactions in local capital markets or through global offerings.

Morgan is active in the highly liquid debt and equity markets of the established markets, as well as in the markets of the emerging economies. We are a leader and innovator in the derivative business.

All of Morgan's business activities are supported by a strong research capability. In some cases, dedicated research units support specific business areas, such as Taxable Credit Research, Markets Research, and Equity Research, which provides sell-side research as part of our U.S. equity sales and distribution function.

Morgan works within the context of a few long-standing and fundamental strategic strengths. We always put our clients' interests first. We take advantage of our deeply rooted and long-standing global network in approaching the needs of our clients. A team approach gives our clients the benefit of the breadth of our capabilities. We operate always with the belief that our reputation for fair dealing is our greatest asset, and we are committed to maintaining the highest standard of conduct.

Investment Banking
A matrix of client and product specialists forms the core of J.P. Morgan's investment banking business. Client specialists are responsible for understanding a client's overall business and financial strategy, as well as for developing an understanding of Morgan's full range of products and services. Product specialists develop expertise in a specific financial area. Investment banking professionals counsel clients on and execute the full range of restructuring transactions, including mergers, acquisitions, divestitures, recapitalizations, and privatizations. As the leading international firm doing business in Latin America, Morgan provides advisory services to local governments and businesses. Morgan is extending its expertise to emerging markets elsewhere in the world, including Eastern Europe and the Asia Pacific region. J.P. Morgan offers a full range of financing options to its clients, including public and privately placed debt and equity securities, syndicated loans, and other credit products in all major world financial markets.

Markets
J.P. Morgan's markets businesses engage in sales and distribution, market making, proprietary risk taking, and investment on a global basis. Morgan has built a well-managed global network of trading locations, supported by decentralized research and a solid infrastructure of communications. The firm makes markets in 21 locations worldwide and takes positions in debt and equity securities, foreign currencies, derivative instruments, government bonds, and developing-country debt. Morgan traders manage risk, liquidity, and interest rate exposure. Morgan has become a strong market leader in the global derivatives business, including swaps, forwards, options and their derivatives, and equity and commodity derivatives, which we use to help clients manage risk as well as for

our own account. The firm has focused on building a global sales capability. Sales professionals cover a portfolio of clients based on product/instrument or geography. Research plays a critical role in our markets-related activities, and our research professionals work closely with our traders, sales force, and clients.

Private Client Services

In our private client division, J.P. Morgan assists wealthy individuals make investment selections from among the increasingly complicated and often conflicting choices available in the market. Client managers work with clients to help them optimize their wealth by working through three closely related sets of issues. One is investment strategy: mapping out an overall allocation of assets and recommending specific investment vehicles geared to a client's appetite for risk and desire for involvement in day-to-day portfolio management decisions. Client managers also help clients unlock the full value of their assets by exchanging them for more liquid alternatives or by placing them in tax-advantaged structures that facilitate the transfer of wealth to philanthropic organizations and heirs. With wealth invested and structured, we provide vehicles that give clients control over the management of liquid assets to meet current needs. Morgan is a leader in this business, offering a full range of investment-related services, including portfolio management, securities brokerage, mutual funds, direct investments, fiduciary services, and liquidity management.

The Finance MBA's Job Description

Describe the career path and corresponding responsibilities for an MBA at your firm.

Business units within Investment Banking, Markets, and Private Client Services employ MBAs. Morgan professionals usually have the opportunity to work in various areas of the firm during the course of their career. This helps them better understand the needs of Morgan's clients and enables them to maximize the firm's abilities to meet these needs.

The first assignment for MBAs hired for Investment Banking is in Investment Banking Services (IBS), a group of professionals who work with client and product teams in the marketing, structuring, and execution of financing and advisory assignments. New associates will be assigned on a rotation to a specific business area. The IBS assignment is followed by an assignment to one of a number of areas such as clients, mergers and acquisitions, and debt or equity capital markets. An MBA associate's career will continue to evolve as the individual develops a broad and solid base of knowledge and experience. The direction of the evolution will be the result of several factors, including an individual's skills and interests as well as the needs of the firm. Some individuals may have the opportunity to experience an assignment in one of our international offices.

MBAs hired for Markets will begin their careers in the positions for which they were hired in one of our Markets areas. Careers in Markets are flexible, and, after gaining some hands-on experience, an individual may have the opportunity to transfer his or her skills to a new market or product.

Private Client Services hires MBAs for positions in domestic and international client management and in security sales. Client managers are the primary business developers and are responsible for the overall client investment relationship with the firm. Security sales people work with clients to provide markets research and advice and to execute their brokerage needs. Individuals hired by our Private Client Services group attend our six-month training program and, upon completion, begin working with clients immediately.

The Recruiting Process

Describe your recruiting process and the criteria by which you select candidates. Is prior experience necessary?

Morgan seeks outstanding, creative, analytical, and committed individuals who work well with others and who are willing to assume responsibility. The firm offers hardworking individuals the opportunity to make a significant contribution quickly. Morgan operates with a team approach, which promotes an open discussion of ideas and enables its professionals to learn about parts of Morgan's business outside their own. Members of the firm stress dealing honorably and responsibly with others to maintain the firm's high-quality work environment and high standard of integrity.

J.P. Morgan's Investment Banking, Markets, and Private Client Services groups conduct on-campus interviews for full-time and summer positions. Prior experience in the financial services industry is not required or expected for employment. Foreign language skills are considered an asset but are not a requirement.

How many permanent associates and analysts do you hire in a typical year? How many summer interns do you expect to hire? If you have a formal summer program, please describe it. Please be sure to indicate whether the summer program is in place for all offices or just some.

Summer Intern Program

J.P. Morgan's extensive program for MBA students during the summer between their first and second years of business school provides a broad exposure to the firm and its businesses. Summer associates are hired for a general area, based on interests, skills, and past experience, as well as the needs of the firm. Summer associates have the opportunity to learn about other areas through presentations by Morgan managers and are briefed by senior managers on the firm's business strategy and management philosophy. We also encourage summer associates to take the time to meet with officers throughout the firm to identify areas for further exploration. Candidates for the summer associate program should have a serious interest in finance and the financial markets. Most positions are in New York, though opportunities to work abroad may exist for students with the right to work in other jurisdictions. Positions last 10 to 12 weeks and are scheduled between mid-May and mid-September.

What international opportunities does your firm offer for U.S. citizens? For foreign nationals?

J.P. Morgan recruits MBAs primarily for positions in New York. The firm also hires MBA students with the right to work overseas for positions in Morgan's offices in Asia, Europe, and Latin America.

Lehman Brothers

Three World Financial Center
New York, NY 10285
(212) 526-2000

MBA Recruiting Contact(s):
Rita Haring
Investment Banking
(212) 526-4162

Sarah Seaman
Sales, Trading & Research
(212) 526-4895

Company Description

Describe your firm's business and the types of clients served by your finance group(s).

Lehman Brothers is one of Wall Street's premier investment banks, serving the needs of corporations, institutions, governments, and high-net-worth individuals in the United States and throughout the rest of the world. Lehman Brothers' business lines include investment, fixed income, equities, commodities and foreign exchange (as well as derivatives of these products), and private client services.

Lehman Brothers has major operating centers in New York, London, and Tokyo, and over 35 additional offices worldwide.

Describe your ownership structure.

Lehman Brothers has been a publicly traded company since May 31, 1994, when it was spun off from American Express. As of the end of 1994, 10% of Lehman Brothers' common stock was employee owned.

How does your approach to finance differ from that of other firms, and what do you consider to be your strengths and distinctive capabilities?

Lehman Brothers' goal is to build upon the firm's 145-year history of success and to be a leader in all the markets and businesses in which it participates. We will achieve this goal by having the right people in our organization and by adhering to clearly defined objectives and our stated values.

These values are grouped around four major themes:

1. acting as one firm,
2. characterized by teamwork,
3. with effective and flexible leadership and management,
4. making the firm a world class organization known for its global presence, profitability, client service, integrity, and superior people.

Lehman Brothers' approach is to work in concert with clients, integrating our efforts with theirs to provide superior service across the investment banking and capital markets businesses. The firm has a long, well-earned reputation for serving its clients and for the professionalism and creativity of its employees. We are continually striving to improve our ability to work as a team, to heighten awareness of client needs, and to deliver still higher levels of service excellence.

Building relationships with clients is the foundation of Lehman Brothers' business philosophy. Toward this end, the firm organizes investment bankers by industry group to enable them to develop expertise in a specific industry, and thus understand and anticipate client's needs.

The contributions of our people are critical. We maintain a professional atmosphere that fosters cooperation rather than competition without stifling individuality. We place a strong emphasis on teamwork and on leveraging one another's skills, while encouraging each individual's unique creativity and entrepreneurial spirit.

Discuss changes in your firm's revenues (both domestic and international) and professional staff over the past year; over the past five years.

Lehman Brothers' net revenues for the eleven month reporting period ended November 30, 1994, totaled $2.7 billion. Net operating income, excluding special charges related to severance, expenses for the spin-off from American Express, and a change in accounting principle, was $156 million. Net income after these charges totaled $113 million.

Despite the challenging market environment in 1994, Lehman Brothers strengthened its franchise and market position. This is evident in the various industry rankings achieved during the year:

- Lehman Brothers was the number two ranked underwriter for lead-managed debt and equity offerings in the United States and the number three ranked lead manager for offerings worldwide.*

* Source: Securities Data Company.

- Lehman Brothers lead managed $84.1 billion of fixed income securities globally in 1994, ranking third among underwriters.*
- Lehman Brothers lead managed $5.8 billion of common stock and convertible securities worldwide in 1994, ranking fifth among underwriters.*
- In 1994, Lehman Brothers acted as advisor on 115 completed mergers and acquisition transactions, ranking fourth by number of transactions and sixth by dollar volume among investment banks. Thirty-five of these transactions were cross-border.
- Lehman Brothers is a leader in origination, distribution, and trading of municipal securities. In 1994, the firm lead-managed $17.8 billion in long- and short-term municipal securities, ranking third among competitors with an 8.8% market share.
- Lehman Brothers continued to grow some of its high margin businesses such as derivatives, assisting approximately 1,300 clients and customers worldwide in over 7,500 fixed income derivatives transactions in 1994.
- Lehman Brothers was awarded 21 positions on *Institutional Investor*'s 1994 All-America Research Team, ranking first for the third year in a row.

Over the past years Lehman Brothers has pursued a strategy of growing revenues and profitability outside the United States. Under this strategy, net revenues derived from international sources increased in 1994 to more than $1.1 billion, accounting for 42% of total net revenues. During 1994, the firm significantly strengthened its position in its targeted European and Asian markets. Lehman Brothers became a reporting dealer, or CVT, in France and a primary dealer in Italy. The firm opened new offices in Beijing and Tel Aviv, expanded the scope of its operations in Singapore, and received regulatory approvals or banking licenses to expand its operations in various international locations.

The Finance MBA's Job Description

Describe the career path and corresponding responsibilities for an MBA at your firm.

Lehman Brothers prides itself on the variety of backgrounds and range of achievements represented by its professionals. Before joining the firm, many Lehman Brothers' professionals had careers in areas such as law, medicine, public service, and private industry, as well as in finance. This diversity instills creativity in and provides depth to the firm.

Lehman Brothers is committed to developing well-rounded professionals and encourages associates to take on as much responsibility as they can handle. Each associate is given the opportunity to build a broad base of skills, and the firm constantly monitors each associate's development, working with him or her to help achieve specific career goals.

All Investment Banking, and Sales, Trading & Research associates begin their career at Lehman Brothers participating in a "One Firm" training program that introduces them to Lehman Brothers, its clients, products and services. Classroom training during the first two months enables associates to hone their skills in finance and accounting and to develop the analytical tools they will use throughout their careers. Specific training is also provided in fixed income, equity, foreign exchange, commodities and derivative products. In addition, associates share in team-building activities and social events. This strategy helps build internal networks and working relationships among professionals throughout the organization.

Following the training program, Investment Banking associates rotate through various industry coverage and product specialty groups. During the rotation, they will gain exposure to several groups within Investment Banking and are able to apply the analytical tools developed during the training program. The rotation is followed by a six-month assignment in a specific group. The associates may then choose to continue with the same group or move into another area. International associates benefit from the same training and rotation as U.S. associates. At the end of this 18-month period in Lehman Brothers' New York headquarters, the international associates begin their permanent assignments in Lehman Brothers' international offices.

Associates for Sales, Trading & Research move from the training program into a two-month generalist rotation. There they will be exposed to a variety of product areas before joining a specific business. High Net Worth Sales associates also benefit from the generalist rotation, prior to joining Private Client Services. International Sales, Trading & Research associates also begin their careers in Lehman Brothers' New York headquarters. Following classroom training, associates complete a rotation through various product areas. This rotation may take place in New York, the international offices, or both, and provides associates with an overview of the product areas.

After completing the training program, Public Finance associates serve as generalists during their entire first year, working with a variety of municipal clients. Associates then join either a specialty group, such as Housing,

---

* Source: Securities Data Company.

Education, or Health Care, or a regional group covering a geographically defined area of the United States.

The Recruiting Process

Describe your recruiting process and the criteria by which you select candidates. Is prior experience necessary?

In our recruiting efforts we look for individuals who possess a keen intellect, a powerful desire to succeed, and the resourcefulness to produce results. Because of the emphasis on teamwork, we also want people who can cooperate and leverage one another's skills while encouraging each individual's unique creativity and entrepreneurial spirit.

How many summer interns do you expect to hire? If you have a formal summer program, please describe it. Please be sure to indicate whether the summer program is in place for all offices or just some.

Lehman Brothers' Summer Associate Program provides students at the midpoint of their graduate school education an opportunity to evaluate the working environment and career opportunities at the firm.

Investment Banking and Public Finance summer associates work as full members of client teams on a variety of transactions. They also enjoy extensive contact with Lehman Brothers' professionals at all levels through discussion groups, seminars, and informal social functions.

Sales and Trading summer associates are assigned to a 10-week placement in an individual business unit, although they spend one day of each week in different product areas, covering a variety of businesses over the course of the summer. In addition, they attend lectures by senior professionals and participate in weekly market update sessions.

Merrill Lynch & Co., Inc.

World Financial Center
250 Vesey Street
New York, NY 10281-1331
(212) 449-8790
Web site: www.ml.com

MBA Recruiting Contact:
Roslyn N. Dickerson
Vice President & Manager
Corporate & Institutional Client Group Recruiting

Company Description

Describe your firm's business and the types of clients served by your finance group(s).

Merrill Lynch is a global investment banking firm, headquartered in New York with a presence in 35 countries worldwide. It is the leading underwriting and brokerage firm in the United States.

Merrill Lynch acts as principal, agent, underwriter, market maker, broker, and financial advisor to its clients. The firm is fundamentally client driven, bringing together issuers and investors.

Our institutional businesses—Investment Banking, Institutional Investment Management Services, Institutional Client, Debt Markets, Capital Markets, Municipal Markets, and Equity Markets—offer an expansive range of services to 6,000 corporate, institutional, and governmental clients worldwide. These groups are based in New York with major offices in London, Tokyo, and Hong Kong and representation in other major financial centers. Our individual investor business—Private Client—provides investment, banking, credit, money management, and insurance products and services to 7 million individuals and small businesses worldwide. These groups are headquartered in Princeton, NJ.

In a little over a decade, the firm has built a premier institutional franchise with clients on a worldwide basis. Since 1988, Merrill Lynch has been the leading global underwriter of debt and equity securities. Two major trends are creating new opportunities for the firm globally: the spread of capitalism and an increasing variety of financing alternatives. In Latin America, Eastern Europe, and Asia-Pacific, we expect growth to outpace that of more developed regions.

Describe your ownership structure.

Merrill Lynch & Co. is a publicly owned corporation, trading on the principal stock exchanges in New York, London, Toronto, Paris, and Tokyo. Stockholders' equity at December 27, 1996, totaled $6.9 billion, with 164 million shares outstanding.

Merrill Lynch was the first member firm of the New York Stock Exchange to go public in June 1971, and a month later it became the first member firm whose own stock was traded on the Big Board. Previously it had been a partnership.

How does your approach to finance differ from that of other firms, and what do you consider to be your strengths and distinctive capabilities?

The strength of our organization is based on leadership in both the institutional and retail sectors. Merrill Lynch's ability to capitalize on the synergies that exist between these sectors—specifically, a strong distribution function complementing an origination and trading capability—distinguishes its strategy from that of its competitors. With the largest distribution capabilities on Wall Street and an integrated global network, the firm has the unique ability to place deals and facilitate transactions worldwide.

Discuss changes in your firm's revenues (both domestic and international) and professional staff over the past five years.

1996 was a profitable year in Merrill Lynch history. Net earnings to common shareholders were $1.61 billion, our third consecutive year of billion-dollar profits. Shareholders' equity rose to $6.9 billion. The firm's return on average common equity was 26.8%. The firm employs 49,800 people worldwide.

The Finance MBA's Job Description

Describe the career path and corresponding responsibilities for an MBA at your firm.

Merrill Lynch invests substantial resources in identifying and recruiting superior candidates. In the graduating class of 1997, the firm hired 160 Associates: 91 in Investment Banking, 18 in Debt Markets, 18 in Institutional Client, 9 in Equity Markets, 6 in Municipal Markets, 9 in Asset Management, and 9 in Capital Markets.

The following businesses recruit the most MBAs:

- Investment Banking is responsible for corporate and institutional client relationships worldwide. Through the delivery of advisory services and financial products, the division focuses on the needs of issuer clients. Included in this division are mergers and acquisitions, leveraged buyout fund management, real estate, project financing, relationship management, and several specialty functions.

- Debt Markets offers issuing and investing clients a complete array of debt financing alternatives in short-, medium-, and long-term debt products. The division is integrated vertically to include origination, trading, fixed income, marketing, research, and new product development. Major product areas are money markets, global debt financing, mortgage capital, financial futures and options, U.S. governments and agencies, foreign exchange, and municipal markets.
- Equity Markets is structured to provide institutional investor clients with origination, trading, syndication, and wholesale services worldwide. The division also works with investment banking in serving corporate and government issuers.
- Municipal Markets encompasses all activities related to the origination, pricing, sales, and trading of tax-exempt debt instruments. These include fixed rate bonds and notes, commercial paper and other variable rate products, interest rate swaps, hedges, and embedded derivative products.
- Capital Markets has primary responsibilities in product origination in coordination with Investment Banking; and product innovation and marketing in coordination with Debt and Equity Markets as well as Institutional Client.
- Institutional Client includes a network of teams specializing in selling or trading a specific fixed-income or equity product. This business unit serves institutional accounts worldwide.

Career paths and corresponding responsibilities vary depending on the business division. An MBA joining Investment Banking, for example, typically enters as an associate, responsible for the details of executing transactions and preparing proposals. After approximately four years, associates are eligible for promotion to vice president. Vice presidents manage the execution of transactions and identify new opportunities with clients. About three years later, vice presidents become eligible for promotion to director, or the more senior title of managing director. Directors and managing directors are responsible for maintenance of client relationships and identification of new business opportunities.

New associates generally join the firm in early August and complete a five-week firmwide development program; besides serving as an orientation to Merrill Lynch, the program builds strong ties among the participants. The academic component includes team assignments, case studies, simulations, and hands-on interaction with trading games.

Describe the opportunities for professional mobility between the various departments in your firm.

New associates work in a specific department, though they have much contact throughout the firm. As their interests change and as our businesses evolve, new opportunities are often available firmwide.

Discuss the lifestyle aspects of a career with your firm (e.g., average hours per week, amount of travel, flexibility to change offices, corporate culture, etc.).

Lifestyles vary depending on which business unit an MBA joins. Requirements for each division are typical for the financial services industry.

The Recruiting Process

Describe your recruiting process and the criteria by which you select candidates. Is prior experience necessary?

Merrill Lynch participates in on-campus presentations and events, and on-campus interviews. Successful candidates are called back for final interviews in New York.

We seek individuals with a record of achievement and excellence. Successful candidates have strong analytical skills and an understanding of strategic issues. They communicate effectively, think creatively, work well with others, and act decisively. Academic performance and prior work experience are also important criteria, though prior work in the industry is not necessary.

In a typical year, how many permanent associates and analysts do you hire? If you have a formal summer program, please describe it.

Hiring is based on the needs of each business division, and recruiting goals are set early in the fall for the coming recruiting season. In 1997, we hired 160 full-time Associates.

Most business divisions of the firm participate in the summer associate program. Summer associates have significant responsibilities and are involved with a variety of transactions. Scheduled activities and seminars with senior management offer summer associates frequent exposure and the opportunity to expand their knowledge of the firm. In 1997, 140 summer associates were hired across the firm.

Montgomery Securities

600 Montgomery Street
San Francisco, CA 94111
(415) 627-2000
Web site: www.montgomery.com

MBA Recruiting Contact(s):
Maggie Woodward, Vice President
(415) 627-2314

Company Description

Describe your firm's business and the types of clients served by your finance group(s).

Montgomery Securities is a San Francisco-based investment banking, institutional brokerage, and asset management firm. Privately held, Montgomery Securities is the nation's premier equity-focused broker/dealer specializing in growth companies. In .996, the firm managed over $44 billion in public and private offerings and merger and acquisition transactions and traded over 6.1 billion shares in the listed and over-the-counter markets, ranking tenth. Montgomery's activities are conducted through four departments: Investment Banking, which includes underwritings, mergers and acquisitions, private placements and high yield; Research; Sales; and Trading. In addition, Montgomery's Private Client Department, with assets of over $11 billion, handles the money management needs of corporations and high-net-worth individuals.

The activities of each of the firm's departments are closely coordinated and are focused on five industries: technology, media and communications, consumer, health care, and financial services. Montgomery's investment banking clients consist of emerging and established growth companies located throughout the United States. The firm's institutional brokerage clients include over 1,700 institutions worldwide, including the top 200 in the U.S. which control more than 80% of all institutional assets.

Investment Banking

The Investment Banking Department initiates, develops and maintains relationships with the premier growth companies in each of the industry groups Montgomery focuses on. Investment Banking professionals have extensive experience in analyzing and identifying a company's financing requirements and executing transactions including public and private equity offerings, mergers and acquisitions, and public and private debt. The department is staffed with over 198 professionals whose skills combine specific industry experience and investment banking expertise. The department is organized along industry lines to take advantage of the firm's research and trading strengths in technology, media and communications, consumer, health care, and financial services.

Research Department

The foundation for Montgomery's success in serving both its investment banking clients and its institutional brokerage customers is its strong Research Department. The department is staffed with forty-nine senior analysts and sixty-one analyst associates whose skills combine industry-specific focus and expertise covering large and small capitalization companies. Montgomery covers 629 companies, with a total market cap of more than $2.4 million. The department is organized along five industry groups: technology, media and communications, consumer, health care, and financial services and its primary goal is superior performance for Montgomery clients.

Sales Department

Montgomery Securities' effectiveness as an underwriter owes much to the strength and reputation of its Institutional Sales Department. This reputation has been built over two decades through relationships with clients that are based on trust, knowledge of the markets, past money-making performance, and superior service. Montgomery's institutional sales force covers more than 1,700 domestic and international institutions.

The Private Client Department of Montgomery Securities was founded to service the investment needs of wealthy individuals, families, and corporations. The Private Client Department has approximately $11.0 billion of corporate and private assets in custody.

Montgomery Prime Brokerage Services (MPBS)

Montgomery created its Prime Brokerage Services Department in 1995 to provide investment partnerships with a wide range of services. MPBS clients, who include hedge funds, family offices, large individual investors and various other partnerships, are offered clearing, custody, accounting and administrative services and also have access to Montgomery's research, execution and cash management capabilities. MPBS has more than 150 clients, with total custodial assets of over $3.2 billion.

Montgomery Clearing Services (MCS)

Established in 1996, Montgomery Clearing Services provides high-quality, fully integrated clearing services to a select group of brokerage firms in a "strategic clearing" approach that extends well beyond the processing of trades. In addition to the clearing of brokerage transactions, MCS offers its clients access to the firm's research, collaboration on investment banking opportunities, use of Montgomery's advanced technology platform, and a range of advisory services.

Trading Department

The Trading Department, one of the largest outside New York, complements and enhances the Corporate Finance, Research and Sales Departments. Montgomery is a major market maker in common stocks traded in the over-the-counter market. In addition, Montgomery is very active in the block trading of common stock for companies listed on the New York Stock Exchange and other national securities exchanges. The trading focus is on the stocks of companies that are actively covered by the Research Department. These activities provide the after-market trading support that is essential in ensuring a successful public offering and maintaining an efficient market for a company's stock.

Fixed Income

As the firm's client base continued to expand and its clients continued to grow, Montgomery made a strategic decision to enter the fixed income market in 1993. Since the inception of this group, Montgomery has completed 31 straight debt offerings, totaling over $4.4 billion in proceeds. In early 1997, Montgomery greatly expanded its high yield capabilities. The firm hired several of Wall Street's senior high yield professionals to head up high yield sales, trading, research and bridge lending departments. Montgomery intends to expand each of these divisions to create a high yield operation that meets the same standards of excellence as it currently provides in the equity area.

Describe your ownership structure.

Montgomery Securities is a privately-held general partnership.

How does your approach to finance differ from that of other firms, and what do you consider to be your strengths and distinctive capabilities?

Montgomery Securities differentiates itself by combining focus and specialization in research and investment banking with bulge bracket capabilities in global distribution and large-block trading. The firm's industry-focused orientation allows Montgomery professionals to become experts in specific sectors, enhancing the investment banking relationships and providing quality research. The close communication among the firm's investment banking personnel, research analysts, and sales force gives Montgomery a unique ability to communicate a client's story to institutional investors effectively and to distribute that company's securities efficiently. Montgomery's after-market support for its investment banking clients, including ongoing research coverage, institutional road shows, investment conferences, investment banking advice, and trading of the clients' stock, is superior and again reflects the combination of a focused approach and bulge-bracket execution capabilities. This combination differentiates Montgomery from the larger New York-based investment banks and the smaller boutique firms and is the primary reason for Montgomery's tremendous growth and profitability in its twenty-seven year history.

The Finance MBA's Job Description

Describe the career path and corresponding responsibilities for an MBA at your firm.

In the Investment Banking Department, an MBA begins her or his career as a generalist associate before specializing in one of Montgomery's five business sectors. Montgomery's client teams are traditionally lean, so an associate is ensured significant client contact and responsibility from the start. An associate's responsibilities focus primarily on analyzing, structuring, and executing transactions, as well as assisting in new business development. Advancement and success are contingent on personal performance. As an individual advances, that individual's responsibilities for clients and new business development increases.

Upon the completion of a comprehensive training program in the Private Client Department, associates help facilitate long-term investment relationships with wealthy individuals and family groups. Interacting closely with the research and trading departments, associates will provide a portfolio approach for private clients' investment needs. Associates will be trained as product generalists, knowledgeable in all markets and supported by a network of specialists in each. The Associate Program offers individuals a unique entrepreneurial experience with compensation tied directly to one's efforts.

In the Research Department, entry-level associates are assigned to work directly with research analysts and may come in on many different levels, depending on prior knowledge and experience. Working with the analyst, the associate develops her or his expertise researching industries and analyzing companies, with the goal of being promoted to an analyst with a specific industry and company focus.

Entry level MBAs joining the Sales and Trading Departments begin their career at Montgomery as junior traders with the goal of being promoted to a senior trader with their own group of stocks.

Discuss the lifestyle aspects of a career with your firm (i.e., average hours per week, amount of travel, flexibility to change offices, corporate culture, etc.).

A career in investment banking at Montgomery is exciting and rewarding and requires a significant commitment of time and energy. The hours can be long and the travel extensive. Montgomery is, however, located in San Francisco and this location reflects a commitment to a lifestyle outside the office. The hours worked and the extent of travel vary depending on an individual's workload.

The Recruiting Process

Describe your recruiting process and the criteria by which you select candidates. Is prior experience necessary?

Because of its size and corporate philosophy, Montgomery offers an unstructured investment banking environment. Montgomery is seeking bright, hard-working, personable candidates who are self-motivated. Strong analytical and communication skills, as well as creativity and initiative, are important. Prior investment banking experience is not necessary. Advancement and success are contingent upon personal performance.

How many permanent associates and analysts do you hire in a typical year? How many summer interns do you expect to hire? If you have a formal summer program, please describe it. Please be sure to indicate whether the summer program is in place for all offices or just some.

The firm expects to hire a significant number of undergraduates and MBAs to work in the San Francisco, Boston and New York offices. The Investment Banking Department will be hosting a summer program in the San Francisco office providing a hands-on summer experience working in 1–2 industry groups during the 10–14 week program.

Morgan Stanley & Co. Incorporated

1585 Broadway
New York, NY 10036
(212) 761-4000
Web site: www.ms.com

MBA Recruiting Contact(s):
Bruce Cohen, Principal
Firmwide Recruiting

Suzanne Gallagher, Recruiting Manager
Equity Research

Jane Jacobi, Recruiting Manager
Equity Sales & Trading

Patricia Dever, Recruiting Manager
Fixed Income Sales, Trading and Research
Foreign Exchange

Katherine Hill, Recruiting Manager
Private Client Services

Locations of Offices:
28 principal offices in 23 countries

Total Number of Professionals:
over 11,000 worldwide

Company Description:

Describe your firm's business and the types of clients served by your finance group(s).

Morgan Stanley & Co. Incorporated is a global firm providing a wide range of financial services to corporations, governments, financial institutions, and individual investors. Our businesses include securities underwriting, distributions, and trading; merger, acquisition, restructuring, real estate, and other corporate finance advisory activities; merchant banking and other principal investment activities; brokerage and research services; asset management; trading foreign exchange, commodities, and structured financial products on a broad range of asset categories; and global custody, securities clearance services, and securities lending.

Morgan Stanley's finance groups provide the following services to our clients:

Equity Research
Equity Research provides timely, high-quality, in-depth analysis to enhance the performance of Morgan Stanley's clients' global portfolios. Using economic market, industry and company studies, Equity Research Analysts, Economists, and Strategists strive to anticipate developments that will affect security values worldwide. New Research Analysts are assigned to a specific industry at the very outset. Our program is designed to develop proficiency in one to two years, with the ultimate goal of our Analysts becoming recognized experts in their respective industries. Equity Research Professionals analyze company financial data, industry trends, and macroeconomics factors; forecast earnings and stock prices; write research reports and updates on companies and industries; and make independent buy and sell recommendations. Research Analysts work closely with Equity Salespeople and Traders, Investment Banking Professionals, Clients, and Institutional Investors.

Equity Sales and Trading
The Equity Division provides Morgan Stanley clients with global distribution capabilities, liquidity, and a high level of trading expertise in all major world markets. It also offers sophisticated analysis and ready access to a broad range of equity products and issues. Associates in Equity Sales and Trading are involved in the worldwide selling and trading of equity and equity derivative securities. After a two month training program conducted in New York, associates immediately go to work on their assigned desk covering either the traditional stock business, equity derivatives, or convertible securities. New Associates are assigned their own accounts and act as backup to some of our major accounts; they also have the opportunity to work with many different investors, products, and areas of the firm.

The Equity Division consists of three major areas:

Core Equity. Core Equity consists of the traditional stock business and encompasses the sales and trading of equity securities around the world. Customers include banks, insurance companies, private pension funds, mutual funds, investment advisors, endowments, foundations, and hedge funds. There are two main sources of revenue: sales and primary and secondary offerings, and trading commissions (which customers pay in return for liquidity, the firm's trading expertise, and access to equity research).

Convertible Securities. Convertible Securities plays a leading role in both the primary and secondary markets in global convertible securities, one of the earliest forms of equity derivative instruments. Through its operations in New York, London, Tokyo, and Hong Kong, Morgan Stanley is able to exercise its expertise in domestic and global markets.

Equity Derivatives. Equity Derivatives executes stick index futures and options on global basis. In addition, it executes customer trading programs for institutions wishing to liquidate, invest, or restructure large equity portfolios. The group offers a range of services in synthetic equity products, including executions of long-dated options, index-linked bonds, and equity swaps. The global equity derivatives sales force advises institutional clients on the use of listed equity derivatives portfolio trading strategies and synthetic equity products to meet their unique risk profiles. Our equity derivative sales and trading activities have increased substantially in recent years and will continue to expand to meet the changing needs of our client base. The group now reaches all major international listed markets, while also supporting the latest techniques in structured financial engineering.

Fixed Income Sales, Trading, Research and Foreign Exchange

Morgan Stanley's Fixed Income Division offers clients a wide range of products and services, including government securities, capital markets, products (corporate debt, preferred stock, and money markets), high-yield securities, mortgage- and asset-backed securities, derivative products, tax-exempt securities, and fixed income research. The division's sales and distribution teams are organized geographically and supported by product specialists. Using a broad and growing range of financial products, Fixed Income Associates working in sales assist Institutional Investors plan and implement portfolio strategies. Associates working as Traders commit the firm's capital to ensure liquidity for our clients. Research Associates provide fixed income strategy and corporate credit research and develop quantitative models for analytical support.

The Fixed Income Division consists of seven principal global product areas:

Government Bonds. Trades, makes markets, and has specialists in many of the world's government securities. Morgan Stanley is one of a select group of primary dealers in the U.S. and French government debt and participates in underwriting syndicates for domestic bond issues in Germany, Italy, and Japan. The financing desk finances the firm's inventory of government securities and money market and mortgage- and asset-backed securities through repurchase and reverse repurchase agreements.

Capital Markets Products. Products include intermediate- and long-term corporate debt, medium-term notes, commercial paper, floating-rate notes, certificates of deposit, and preferred stock for industrial corporations, utilities, banks, thrifts, and finance companies. Makes markets in securities to provide liquidity for institutional investors; provides investment strategies for institutional investors; advises Morgan Stanley's capital markets services group on pricing and timing of new issues; develops portfolio swapping strategies for customers; and assists corporations in repurchasing debt.

Global High Yield/Emerging Markets Securities. Focuses on noninvestment grade debt and LDC debt securities; objective similar to the capital markets product group. Distributes, trades, and has specialists in straight and zero-coupon high-yield bonds. Expert in placing and making markets in complex high-yield securities issued for start-up ventures in emerging markets.

Tax Exempt Securities. Sells and trades new and secondary issues of tax-exempt securities issued by U.S. cities, states and other public authorities. Tax exempt area also includes public finance, which originates and structures negotiated new issues, and syndicate, which is responsible for setting the prices and yields on competitive and negotiated new issues and research.

Mortgage- and Asset-Backed Securities. Originates, structures, and trades mortgage- and asset-backed securities, which are collateralized by residential first mortgages, commercial mortgages, aircraft leases, and such consumer receivables as auto loans, credit card balances, and home equity loans.

Derivative Products. Integrates the origination and trading of structured products, currency and interest rate swaps, and synthetic securities. In January 1994, the group launched Morgan Stanley Derivative Products Inc. (MSDP), which is triple-A rated by Moody's Investors Service and Standard & Poor's Corporation. MSDP gives the firm access to the credit-sensitive sector of the derivatives market at a time when the credit ratings of derivatives providers are coming under increasingly close scrutiny.

Fixed Income Research. Provides global research and analytical support for traders, salespeople and customers. There are four major areas: Credit Research (industry and company credit prospects), Modeling (quantitative models such as optimization and trading strategies), Mortgage-Backed (analytical support for the mortgage-backed securities salespeople and traders), and Portfolio Strategy (fundamental trends).

Foreign Exchange

Foreign Exchange is a market maker in a number of foreign currencies including deutsche marks, yen, pound sterling, French francs, Swiss francs, lire, and Canadian sterling. We actively trade currencies in the spot, forward, and options markets. We are also involved in arbitrage where we seek to profit from inefficiencies between the future and spot markets. Foreign Exchange is a client-driven business in which associates work with senior producers on existing Morgan Stanley accounts and are also given the opportunity to prospect for new client business.

INVESTMENT BANKING

Morgan Stanley's Investment Banking Division utilizes both traditional and innovative financing techniques to help corporations and governments around the world make and execute decisions regarding their capital. New Associates begin in Investment Banking as generalists, gaining broad exposure to a variety of the division's products, services and clients. Associates work on a mix of assignments ranging from transaction execution to business development initiatives. Associates have the opportunity to work directly with the senior-level financial and strategic decision-makers of some of the world's largest corporations, as well as with smaller, emerging growth clients. After a one-year generalist experience, Associates begin to specialize in either an industry, product area or geographic region.

The Investment Banking Division consists of five closely related business units: Corporate Finance; Mergers, Acquisitions and Restructuring; Morgan Stanley Realty; Debt Capital Market Services; and Equity Capital Markets Services.

Corporate Finance. Corporate Finance is responsible for initiating, developing and maintaining the firm's investment banking relationships with clients worldwide; for providing financial advice; and, in partnership with other specialized areas of the firm, for executing specific client transactions. The Corporate Finance Department is organized into teams of regional and industry specialists. The regional coverage groups provide a strong Morgan Stanley presence in the United States, Canada, Western and Eastern Europe, Latin America, the Middle East, the Far East and Australia. The industry groups provide special expertise in the following sectors: commercial banking, financial entrepreneurs, food and consumer products, health care, insurance, media, natural resources, public utilities, retail, technology, telecommunications and transportation. Within Corporate Finance, there is the Client Services Group (CSG) which is responsible for the execution of all equity offerings, complex debt issuances, and other capital markets-related business. We also advise government and private sector clients on the privatization of state-owned enterprises.

Mergers, Acquisitions and Restructuring (MARD). MARD provides corporate and financial clients with financial advisory services in situations involving mergers, acquisitions, defenses, proxy contests, divestitures, spin-offs, joint ventures and restructuring. Many of our MARD assignments involve complex, competitive situations that require a high degree of creativity, analytical skills and judgment. M&A professionals must be proficient in a wide range of technical skills (e.g., legal, tax and accounting) and understand an extensive number of strategic alternatives in the context of any particular transaction. Within MARD is the Private Investment Group which manages an investment partnership, Princes Gates Investors, L.P. This partnership invests globally in special situations that help to facilitate the strategic or financial objectives of companies.

Morgan Stanley Realty (MSR). MSR is a full service real estate investment banking group which provides a broad range of financial services to public and private clients. With offices in New York, San Francisco, London, Tokyo and Hong Kong, MSR's real estate activities are focused in three primary areas: Advisory Services; Principal Investing; and Real Estate Debt Capital Markets (REDCM). MSR's Advisory Services include: commercial property portfolio and asset sales; mergers, acquisitions and restructurings; and debt and equity underwritings. Principal Investing is done through the Morgan Stanley Real Estate Funds which have raised over $2.0 billion of discretionary capital and invest in real estate operating companies, property and mortgage portfolios, discrete assets, new developments and international opportunities. REDCM is an MSR/Fixed Income Division joint venture which focuses exclusively on the origination, distribution and trading of whole loans and commercial mortgage backed securities.

Debit Capital Markets Services (DCMS). DCMS is responsible for the solicitation and execution of Morgan Stanley's primary debt and related products business. The group consists of Syndicate, Continuously Offered Products, Market Coverage, High Yield, Private Placements, Asset and Equipment Finance, Tax Products, Liability Management and Preferred Stock. Together these groups provide a sophisticated global capital markets service, including product development, marketing and execution from Morgan Stanley offices in New York, London, Hong Kong, Tokyo, Frankfurt and Paris.

Equity Capital Markets Services (ECMS). ECMS has global product responsibility for corporate equity-related transactions, including common stock, initial public offerings, subsidiary initial public offerings, convertibles, warrants and share repurchases in the domestic and global markets. The specific functions of the group include product development, syndicate (execution of transactions), business development, and strategic advice from Morgan Stanley offices in London, Tokyo, Hong Kong and New York.

PRIVATE CLIENT SERVICES

Private Client Services (PCS) provides world-class brokerage and investment advisory services to high-net-worth individuals and smaller institutional investors. PCS offers its clients the same services the firm provides to large banks, pension funds, governments and multinational corporations. After a six-month training program, new investment representatives begin to develop their own brokerage and asset management businesses with the support of the firm's sales, trading, research and advisory resources. Investment representatives develop and manage relationships with clients, review their portfolios, identify opportunities and evaluate and execute investment strategies. Investment representatives sell and manage products in every asset class including global equities, fixed income securities, currencies and commodities.

Describe your ownership structure.

The common stock of Morgan Stanley Group Inc. is listed on the New York Stock Exchange and several other U.S. stock exchanges. Employees and directors of the company own approximately 39% of the common stock.

The Finance MBA's Job Description

Describe the career path and corresponding responsibilities for an MBA at your firm.

Regardless of the business area in which one works, most Morgan Stanley careers share similar characteristics. New hires spend their initial years learning about our technology, products, services and clients. Thereafter, they take on more operational responsibility and coach the junior people who are entering the business. We encourage professionals to start developing new business opportunities and client relationships, whether those clients are external or internal, as soon as their abilities permit.

The firm is committed to the recruitment of MBAs and to creating an environment for individuals to achieve professional and personal growth in the context of diverse career challenges and opportunities. When it makes sense, we encourage specialization—but we do not mandate it. We have a tradition of developing our people and matching our best people with our best opportunities, relying on the transferability of skills among businesses.

The Recruiting Process

Describe your recruiting process and the criteria by which you select candidates. Is prior experience necessary?

Each year the firm seeks to recruit and hire a diverse group of highly motivated, intelligent MBAs to join us in a number of business areas. Prior experience in the investment banking industry is not a prerequisite. We typically conduct a traditional recruiting process including campus presentations and interviews followed by final round in-office interviews for selected students.

How many permanent associates and analysts do you hire in a typical year? How many summer interns do you expect to hire? If you have a formal summer program, please describe it. Please be sure to indicate whether the summer program is in place for all offices or just some.

In addition to full-time hires, many areas of the firm seek to hire summer interns. Full-time position initial placement and summer internships are generally available in New York, London, Tokyo and Hong Kong, although availability varies by business area. International opportunities exist both initially and later in one's career based on the firm's needs and individual qualifications.

The firm works through the school's placement office and interested students should look for our advertisements and announcements both there and in the campus newspaper.

Morgan Stanley is an Equal Opportunity Employer.

NationsBank

100 N. Tryon Street
NC1007-21-10
Charlotte, NC 28255
Web site: www.nationsbank.com

MBA Recruiting Contact(s):
Ms. Stanley Merriwether
Assistant Vice President
(704) 386-4258

Ms. Angela Hubbard
Assistant Vice President
(704) 388-7237

Locations of Offices:
Offices are throughout the United States as well as in Frankfurt, London, Tokyo, Taipei, Seoul, Jakarta, Hong Kong, Singapore, and Mexico City.

Total Number of Professionals (U.S. and worldwide):
Approximately 60,000

Company Description

Describe your firm's business and the types of clients served by your finance group(s).

NationsBank Corporation is one of the largest financial services companies in the United States, well-known for its capital strength, market position, and bias for doing business in all sectors of the communities and markets it serves.

The company is organized by three major business groups:

- **Global Finance Businesses**—A diverse organization that provides a broad range of financial services to large domestic and international corporations and institutions.
- **General Bank**—The NationsBank retail banking network that spans the Southeast, Southwest, and Mid-Atlantic states.
- **Financial Services**—A growing unit, with specialized services in corporate finance, commercial real estate, project finance, and capital assets, as well as business inventory financing and consumer credit for customers who traditionally do not use banks.

From its historical roots as a Southern bank dating back to the early 1800s, the company has grown into what has been called an emerging model for financial services in the twenty-first century. Today, NationsBank serves clients throughout the United States and international markets with a broad spectrum of financial products.

Such an evolution would not have been possible without an executive commitment to grow NationsBank Global Finance into a leading provider of credit, investment banking, capital markets, and specialized financial services to corporate clients in America and around the world.

Having brought the capabilities of Wall Street to its investment, international, and corporate banking businesses—as well as in global trading and distribution—NationsBank remains committed to the culture and heritage that is uniquely its own.

NationsBank Global Finance Businesses
NationsBank meets the needs of the domestic and international corporate marketplace through its Global Finance Businesses. The company has a long and distinguished track record in corporate banking, built on one of the largest client bases of any American financial institution.

Recent years have been pivotal at NationsBank. Investment banking, capital raising, and risk management capabilities have been dramatically expanded and strengthened. In short, NationsBank set a goal to move beyond its traditional, regional focus and into direct competition with Wall Street firms. That goal has now been achieved.

Global Finance Businesses are comprised of two groups:

Corporate Finance Group

- Corporate Finance (including specialty industry groups)
- International Banking
- Leveraged Capital
- Mergers and Acquisitions
- Loan Syndications
- Depository Services
- Real Estate Finance
- Private Placements
- High Yield

Capital Markets

- Corporate Securities
- Risk Management
- Structured Transactions

- Primary Dealer
- Research
- Real Estate/Mortgage Finance
- Capital Markets Advisory Services

The Client Management Process
At the core of the NationsBank approach is the Client Management Process. Teams from Corporate Finance, Capital Markets, and other areas join together and focus on clients' 3–5 year strategic objectives. These teams bring the best ideas to clients to meet their strategic and tactical financial needs. These ideas create opportunities to deliver creative, value-added solutions to clients' needs.

The Finance MBA's Job Description

Describe the career path and corresponding responsibilities for an MBA at your firm.

Global Finance Associate
Global Finance professionals at NationsBank provide a full array of sophisticated products and services to the largest American and international corporations and institutions. Success depends on their ability to proactively identify current and future client needs—and then make sure those needs are met.

Global Finance Associates work closely with Client Managers and Product Specialists to analyze client needs and develop and execute solutions—the backbone of the Client Management Process.

The Recruiting Process

Describe your recruiting process and the criteria by which you select candidates. Is prior experience necessary?

These positions are for the MBA interested in corporate finance, specialized financing, advisory services, and capital markets. At least two years of related work experience and an MBA qualifies applicants for these programs. Strong analytical, communications, and teamwork skills are necessary along with a willingness to relocate.

How many permanent associates and analysts do you hire in a typical year? How many summer interns do you expect to hire? If you have a formal summer program, please describe it. Please be sure to indicate whether the summer program is in place for all offices or just some.

Historically, 25–50 graduating MBAs are hired into the Global Finance Associate Program each year.

Our Summer Associate Program enables candidates to spend 10–12 weeks under the leadership and guidance of senior staff. Our goal is to create a mutually beneficial partnership that will result in permanent hire after graduation.

Candidates must be legally able to work in the United States. NationsBank does not sponsor people for work authorization visas (H-1).

NationsBank is an Equal Opportunity Employer.

Nesbitt Burns Inc.

1 First Canadian Place
4th Floor
P.O. Box 150
Toronto, Ontario
M5X 1H3 Canada
(416) 359-4000

MBA Recruiting Contact(s):
Jeff Watchorn
Yahphen Yvonne Chang

Company Description

Describe your firm's business and the types of clients served by your finance group(s).

On September 1, 1994, Nesbitt Thomson Inc. and Burns Fry Limited, merged to become one of Canada's largest full-service investment firms—Nesbitt Burns. Each of Nesbitt Burns' predecessor companies had developed a strong reputational franchise as a leader in serving the needs of individual, corporation, government and institutional clients. As Nesbitt Burns, the firm is positioned to become a premier Canadian investment bank in North America with a significant presence in Europe and Asia.

Nesbitt Burns is committed to excellence in each and every area of its businesses. We are determined to build, in partnership with the Bank of Montreal, a prominent North American investment bank with strong global capabilities.

Nesbitt Burns aspires to be recognized for the highest standards of excellence, integrity, and professionalism. As an organization committed to learning, we will continue to foster a culture that is challenging, rewarding and entrepreneurial.

With the power of knowledge, teamwork, creativity and innovation, we create value and wealth for our clients. We contribute meaningfully to the economy and the well-being of the communities in which we work.

- Nesbitt Burns employs over 3,700 individuals who are located in over 100 offices across Canada and in 12 international locations. The firm is one of the largest Canadian investment firms in terms of capital employed.
- Close to 1,300 Investment Advisors serve the needs of individual investors by providing them with top-ranked research information, timely advice, the highest quality service and the broadest selection of products. The firm is recognized for having the most comprehensive Investment Advisor training program in the industry.
- In 1996, Nesbitt Burns managed or co-managed over $25 billion of financings or 71% of all offerings in Canada and was the leading underwriter in 1996 of all Canadian corporate new issues of all types (common equity, preferred equity and debt) based on a full credit to lead basis.
- Nesbitt Burns' Institutional Equity Sales and Trading is the top trader and distributor of Canadian equity securities throughout the world.
- Nesbitt Burns' Fixed Income team is one of Canada's largest and offers the greatest depth of any Canadian firm. The group provides bond sales and trading, money market, fixed income research, derivative products, and securitization services to its domestic and international clients.
- Nesbitt Burns is Canada's leader in advisory services including: mergers, acquisitions and divestitures, valuations and fairness opinions, and restructuring and recapitalization.
- Nesbitt Burns is a manager for nine out of the ten provinces which represents nearly all of provincial borrowing and is a leading advisor to governments, government agencies and Crown Corporations in Canada.
- Jones Heward, the firm's wholly owned investment management company, founded in 1925, provides investment counselling services to individuals, estates, foundations, and corporations resident in Canada and abroad. Jones Heward has displayed strong asset growth and performance in each of its three distinct businesses: private wealth management, mutual funds and pension fund management.

Describe your ownership structure.

Nesbitt Burns is part of the Bank of Montreal financial group and operates autonomously to offer securities-related services on its behalf. Our partnership with the Bank reinforces our capital base, increases our distribution capabilities, and greatly enhances our ability to compete effectively in the global capital markets.

How does your approach to finance differ from that of other firms, and what do you consider to be your strengths and distinctive capabilities?

Our focus on uncompromising quality and integrity is incorporated in all aspects of the way we do business. It underpins the success we have had in identifying financing opportunities and designing new products, the preeminence we have achieved as a major market maker in Canadian corporate and government securities, and the stature we have attained as a world-ranked mergers and acquisitions financial advisor. Our work throughout has been supported by our top-ranked economics and investment research team.

Nesbitt Burns' Investment Banking group consists of over 161 professionals in Canada based in Toronto, Montreal, Calgary, and Vancouver and more than 50 professionals located in offices in New York, Chicago, and London. Nesbitt Burns has also recently opened offices in Houston and San Francisco. The Investment Banking department provides a broad range of services, including corporate finance, mergers, acquisitions and divestitures, restructuring, and consulting and advisory services to corporations, governments, and other organizations. We achieve success for our clients by having a thorough understanding of client needs combined with a sensitivity and swift response to market opportunities. For Nesbitt Burns, a corporate client relationship is a long-term partnership. Conscious of our continuing obligation to provide financial services, a team of highly skilled individuals is assembled to ensure full client coverage. Our team approach to assignments serves as a catalyst to combine experience and knowledge with innovation and creativity.

Investment Banking includes industry specialists who focus on the real estate, mining, financial services, forest products, communications, utilities, oil and gas, and consumer products industries. Industry specialists work closely with product specialists. The approach of our Investment Banking group is to combine an in-depth knowledge of our clients' needs and goals with creative thought, a thorough understanding of the capital markets, and integrity.

The Finance MBA's Job Description

Describe the career path and corresponding responsibilities for an MBA at your firm.

Career opportunities are available in all areas of the firm, including Investment Banking and Fixed Income and Equity Sales and Trading.

Nesbitt Burns encourages Investment Banking Associates to generalize during their first two years in order to develop a broad range of investment banking skills. Associates work with senior members of the department on a variety of corporate financing and M&A-related projects, including drafting prospectuses or offering memorandums, analyzing a corporation's financing needs, creating corporate presentations, assisting on valuations and fairness opinions, managing solicitations, and assisting in the marketing of new issues, both public and private. As an Associate gains more experience and product knowledge, he or she may decide to specialize in a particular industry or product group.

A career in Fixed Income or Institutional Equity begins directly on the sales and trading floor. Working alongside an experienced professional, the trainee will master an understanding of market behaviour and will develop marketing skills and strategies for arbitrage, market making, and taking positions as both principal and agent.

Nesbitt Burns offers a dynamic, challenging work environment with tremendous career opportunities. Nesbitt Burns stresses a team-oriented approach to assignments and encourages an environment open to providing innovative solutions for clients.

Discuss the lifestyle aspects of a career with your firm (i.e., average hours per week, amount of travel, flexibility to change offices, corporate culture, etc.).

The time commitment required to provide the quality of work required in the competitive investment banking environment is considerable, particularly of new recruits.

The Recruiting Process

Describe your recruiting process and the criteria by which you select candidates. Is prior experience necessary?

We look for highly motivated individuals with strong analytical skills, sound judgment, and a high level of integrity. Academic achievement is important. Prior related work experience is an asset.

In a typical year, Nesbitt Burns hires three or four Associates, four or five Analysts, and others as required. In the past, we have also hired Summer Associates and Summer Analysts.

For MBA candidates from U.S. schools, eligibility to work in Canada is a prerequisite.

Nomura Securities International, Inc.

2 World Financial Center
Building B
New York, NY 10281
Web site: www.nomurany.com

MBA Recruiting Contact(s):
Human Resources Department

Company Description

Describe your firm's business and the types of clients served by your finance group(s).

Nomura Securities International, Inc. (NSI) is a wholly owned subsidiary of the Nomura Securities Co., Ltd. (Nomura), the world's largest securities firm. With shareholder equity exceeding $14 billion and total assets of more than $23.2 billion, Nomura is the most profitable financial institution in the world.

A medium-size investment banking company, NSI employs more than 800 people in the United States. NSI has evolved from a company handling primarily Japanese-related securities into a full-fledged member of the American financial community and also is a member of the major securities and commodities exchanges, as well as a primary dealer in U.S. Treasury securities. U.S. operations, which began in 1927, have expanded to include two branch offices in Chicago and one in Los Angeles. Today, NSI offers a wide range of products and services: sales, trading, investment banking, mutual funds, and portfolio and asset management.

NSI is continually in a state of evolution as the firm works to develop new businesses, such as the high-yield and Latin American departments. Two years ago, 80% of NSI's investment banking revenues were due to Japanese-related business (country funds distributed in Japan, Tokyo Stock Exchange listing fees, etc.). This past year over 40% of revenues were from non-Japan-related business (Compania Cervecerias Unidas S.A., Chic by H.I.S., and JAFCO II). Our investment banking group was active with numerous initial public offerings and private placements and created innovative financing structures such as ROSA II and Ivory.

In addition to its financial strength and the breadth of its capabilities, Nomura is internationally renowned for its innovation in finance:

- Nomura introduced and popularized the Gensaki, a Japanese bond sale and repurchase agreement that has developed into an important short-term investment instrument.
- Nomura pioneered the expansion of the Japanese financial community by introducing foreign companies to the country's rapidly growing capital markets. The firm designs and implements investor relations programs for client companies and arranges the listing of their shares on the Tokyo Stock Exchange. In the past, Nomura has listed Anheuser-Busch, AT&T, General Electric, Kraft, and J.P. Morgan, among others.
- With the increase in global investing, more and more institutional and individual investors rely on Nomura's international research, sales, and trading capabilities. Nomura's leadership position in the Japanese market as a broker/dealer and market maker provides an unparalleled resource for investors.
- Working to meet clients' needs, Nomura has established relationships with financial institutions to help ensure the development of innovative products in the areas of leveraged leasing, project financing, real estate investing within the United States, and mergers and acquisitions.
- NSI's Equity Derivatives group is constantly at the top of the New York Stock Exchange chart of 15 most active firms in program trading volume.

The growing importance of investment management has led NSI to form additional companies to provide service to clients. Nomura Corporate Research and Asset Management (NCRAM) is a money management firm with a worldwide client base specializing in high-yield bond investments. Combining the credit expertise of NCRAM with Nomura's tremendous capital base and global distribution capability has helped the firm to achieve a preeminent position in asset management. Expertise in corporate credit also provides the foundation for our aggressive worldwide expansion into proprietary trading, structured finance, and other related merchant and investment banking activities.

With our mortgage-backed securities business continuing to grow, Nomura created a subsidiary, Nomura Asset Capital Corporation (NACC), to conduct our real estate and nonagency trading and financing. NACC, though initially focusing on commercial mortgages, will transact in the commercial and residential loan markets, as well as the asset-backed securities market.

Emphasizing an empirical, problem-solving approach to its studies, Nomura Research Institutes conducts fundamental research on a wide range of socioeconomic and socioscientific issues, as well as on matters of long-term relevance to the securities industry.

The Finance MBA's Job Description

Describe the career path and corresponding responsibilities for an MBA at your firm.

Full-time associates receive global finance training in such areas as investment banking and sales and trading through our associates program. As a sales and trading associate, individuals undergo a six-month training program during which they rotate through various sales and trading areas and participate in intensive product training seminars. In investment banking, associates are expected to become a contributing member of the department immediately. Most of the training is conducted on the job by teaming senior executives in the department with the associates. Since the firm encourages initiative, the degree of responsibility of an associate's assignment is determined to a large extent by an individual's desire and ability to learn and contribute.

The Recruiting Process

Describe your recruiting process and the criteria by which you select candidates. Is prior experience necessary?

NSI seeks people with strong academic records and excellent analytical and communication skills. Demonstration of leadership, high levels of self-motivation, initiative, and commitment, and the ability to work effectively with others in an intense and demanding environment are crucial.

How many permanent associates and analysts do you hire in a typical year? How many summer interns do you expect to hire? If you have a formal summer program, please describe it. Please be sure to indicate whether the summer program is in place for all offices or just some.

NSI's summer associate program provides a select group of students with an intense, hands-on view of the securities industry, as well as the extensive global operations at Nomura. After choosing to work in one of the following areas—investment banking, derivative products or fixed income, or equity sales and trading—the summer associate is quickly integrated into the department's daily operations. In sales and trading, there is a rotation through the different sales and trading areas. Investment banking and derivative products tend to be more project oriented. Additionally, through a series of weekly seminars with senior managers, the MBAs have the opportunity to be exposed to the many facets of our business.

What international opportunities does your firm offer for U.S. citizens? For foreign nationals?

NSI does not recruit for the other overseas offices. Individuals interested in working internationally should contact NSI for additional information.

PaineWebber Incorporated

1285 Avenue of the Americas
New York, NY 10019
(212) 713-2000
Web site: www.painewebber.com

MBA Recruiting Contact(s):
Kelly A. Decker, Investment Banking Recruiter
(212) 713-3406
Fax: (212) 713-1054
email: Kelly_decker@painewebber.com

Company Description

Describe your firm's business and the types of clients served by your finance group(s).

PaineWebber is an independent, full-service securities firm with a leadership position in individual and institutional businesses and a reputation for outstanding research and quality client service. With assets of over $45 billion, total capitalization in excess of $4 billion, and more than 15,900 employees in this country and in eight offices overseas, PaineWebber services the investment and capital needs of over two million clients, including individuals, institutions, corporations, state and local governments, and public agencies in the United States and abroad. Among the firm's key businesses are private client brokerage, investment banking, public finance, real estate, institutional equity and fixed income sales and trading, research, international, asset management, and transaction services.

PaineWebber's core strengths set it apart from the competition. With a distribution capability that is one of the strongest in the industry, PaineWebber is uniquely positioned to quickly and fully meet the needs of both its institutional and retail clients. Our renowned Research Group keeps a close watch on nearly 900 companies in 62 industries, and serves as a vital resource for Investment Banking, the Private Client Group, and Capital Markets.

The Finance MBA's Job Description

Describe the career path and corresponding responsibilities for an MBA at your firm.

Investment Banking
PaineWebber's Investment Banking Division is built on a strong client-oriented philosophy. We keep apprised of the fast-moving financial markets, enabling us to serve our clients' increasingly diverse and complex needs. We concentrate our resources in specifically targeted industries—notably consumer products, energy and natural resources, utilities, technology, telecommunications, and healthcare—in order to leverage our full range of financing products, as well as our capabilities such as mergers and acquisitions advice.

Our strategy for the future is to continue to focus on those selected areas where we have achieved a competitive edge, bringing together for our corporate clients the resources we have developed in areas such as research, trading, and distribution, in addition to our investment banking expertise in these targeted industries.

Associates are exposed to a broad range of industries and transactions through a six to nine month rotational program. During this time, they work with several of the Division's industry and product groups. This environment provides a strong foundation on which to hone financial skills, choose an area of specialization, and evolve into a senior investment banker.

Associates participate in all aspects of a transaction and have the potential opportunity to play a key role in maintaining client relationships. In addition to research and financial analysis, Associates help to develop new business proposals, work on structuring and documenting a deal, and learn to negotiate as well as close a transaction.

Public Finance
The role of an Associate involves extensive client interaction. The Associate advises clients on the most efficient way to access capital, assists in the creation and presentation of new ideas on innovative financing techniques for municipal issuers, and communicates with syndicate members, underwriting professionals, attorneys, and financial advisors. The Associate's quantitative expertise will extend to cash flow, arbitrage, derivative product, and yield analysis. Each Associate is assigned to a specific project team that best matches his or her own career interest.

Real Estate
Associates are expected to apply what they have learned in business school and through prior work experience to become productive and contributing members of a deal team. Associates play an integral role in creating new business presentations and directly contribute to the structuring, documentation, marketing, and closing of transactions. Associates have the responsibility of meeting the day-to-day requirements of transactions and, through direct client contact, gain important client-relationship skills.

The Recruiting Process

Describe your recruiting process and the criteria by which you select candidates. Is prior experience necessary?

Investment Banking
PaineWebber looks for approximately 12–15 individuals who demonstrate a high level of motivation, outstanding scholastic, extracurricular, and professional achievement, excellent communication and interpersonal skills, good judgment, and the ability to take initiative. A background in finance or investment banking is helpful. Advancement is determined by individual performance.

Public Finance
The Municipal Securities Group hires about 3–4 Associates out of business school who go through an intensive 10-week Municipal training program. The training program is taught by PaineWebber employees and well-respected industry experts, and is one of the most renowned on Wall Street. Quantitative experience along with prior public finance or finance experience is requested.

Real Estate
The Real Estate Group hires 2–4, self-motivated individuals who are able to accept a great deal of responsibility and complete tasks in an accurate and efficient manner. Individuals need both strong qualitative and quantitative skills. Candidates should have prior work experience, a background in finance or real estate, and an advanced academic degree.

If you have a formal summer program, please describe it.

The Investment Banking Summer Associate Program serves as an introduction to the Associate position. Summer Associates act as generalists and are given similar responsibilities to those of a full-time Associate during their 11 weeks. Each Summer Associate is staffed on several transactions in a broad range of industries and product areas. In a typical year, PaineWebber hires 10 to 15 Summer Associates for the New York office.

Peter J. Solomon Company

767 Fifth Avenue, 26th Floor
New York, New York 10153
(212) 508-1600
Web site: www.pjsolomon.com

MBA Recruiting Contact(s):
Diane M. Coffey, Chief Administrative Officer

Company Description

Describe your firm's business and the types of clients served by your finance group.

Peter J. Solomon Company (PJSC) is among the leading independent investment banking firms. Headquartered in New York City, the firm of thirty-five professionals including twenty-two bankers provides investment banking and senior advisory services to owners, chief executives, and senior management of public and private companies. PJSC initiates and completes merger and acquisition transactions, advises clients on raising public and private debt and equity capital, and assists creditors and owners of financially distressed companies with bankruptcy and restructuring advice.

A Singular Focus

Every investment banking firm has its own unique culture that embodies its values and the way it approaches transactions. The characteristic that differentiates PJSC is a single-minded focus on our clients' strategic needs. Since we do not underwrite or trade securities or provide investment research, we are free to explore every conceivable way for our clients to accomplish their strategic goals. Our specialty is sound, unbiased advice. Our firm thrives on complexity and is recognized by our clients for original, creative thinking and an ability to deal with the most difficult, multi-faceted transactions. We approach every assignment with a fresh outlook. We seek innovative solutions. Finally, our degree of persistence is exceptional. PJSC bankers will stick with a difficult transaction for as long as it takes to get it done.

The Clients of Peter J. Solomon Company

Since its establishment in 1989, Peter J. Solomon Company has performed more than 100 advisory assignments for leading United States and foreign corporations in a wide range of industries. As such we have applied our strategic merger and acquisition, restructuring and corporate finance skills to transactions in the retail and consumer product industries, in media and communications, in health care, as well as real estate, paper, forest products, and diversified manufacturing industries. Indeed, our firm's keen understanding of influential individual and institutional shareholder concerns which affect corporate decisions is equally acute in shaping strategies for young entrepreneurial concerns and family-owned or controlled businesses where special sensitivity to intergenerational and intra-family issues is both welcome and needed.

Describe your ownership structure.

Founded in 1989 by Peter J. Solomon whose distinguished career spans more than thirty-five years in investment banking, PJSC's senior investment bankers include Kenneth T. Berliner, Henry D. Jackson, and Jeffrey H. Kuhr, Managing Directors; David L. Resnick, Principal; and Jeffrey A. Hornstein, Darryl E. Wash, and Mitchell G. Hara, Vice Presidents. Mssrs. Solomon, Berliner, Hornstein, and Hara are graduates of Harvard Business School.

With PJSC's extensive experience in mergers, acquisitions, recapitalizations, restructurings, accounting, and strategic analysis, each of our bankers provides a different and valuable perspective gained through their work at major investment banks and financial institutions including Goldman, Sachs & Co., Salomon Brothers, Credit Suisse/First Boston, Lazard Freres, and GE Capital Corporation. In addition, PJSC's bankers bring established credentials from big six accounting firms, law firms, and corporations.

Peter Solomon's illustrious career which includes two periods of government service—to the City of New York as Deputy Mayor for Economic Policy and Development under Mayor Edward I. Koch and to the federal government as Counselor to the United States Treasury under President Jimmy Carter—began at Lehman Brothers where he served in various capacities including Chairman of the Mergers and Acquisitions Department, Co-Chairman of the Investment Banking Group, Chairman of the Merchant Banking Group, and Vice Chairman of the firm. Mr. Solomon is also a frequent guest on CNN's *Before Hours,* where he provides regular commentary on merger activities.

How does your approach to finance differ from that of other firms, and what do you consider to be your strengths and distinctive capabilities?

From the beginning of an engagement a select team of our senior bankers focuses on meeting each client's special needs. That same team remains with that client throughout the relationship and is always available. As senior advisors, our bankers apply their expertise to understanding our clients' businesses and industries, long-term strategic and financial objectives, marketing and competitive environments and to assessing the cost and feasibility of alternatives and opportunities. Often we function as unofficial members of our clients' management teams and in some instances we serve on their boards. Because of PJSC's size and the fact that we accept a limited number of assignments, senior bankers are not distracted by administrative concerns, allowing them to devote their undivided attention to client matters. This personal, highly responsive approach emphasizes *relationships,* not transactions, and is at the heart of our concept of investment banking.

Our strengths are many. Let's begin with our *independence:* since we are free from the potential conflicts of underwriting, research and trading, our advice is candid and unbiased. Our *size* is optimal: large enough to field teams of experienced, senior-level people to work on major transactions, yet small enough to preserve our intense involvement with our clients. Unlike the integrated investment banking firms where separate groups focus on particular industry sectors, or transactions, our bankers interact easily, constantly sharing their ideas, judgments and collective knowledge with one another. PJSC's size also permits a more rapid response to client needs, greater flexibility when market conditions require a change in strategy and, of course, confidentiality. With fewer people aware of a deal, clients can be sure their discussions will remain confidential. Our *experience* in mergers, acquisitions, recapitalizations, restructurings, accounting, and strategic analysis is extensive and the quality of PJSC's bankers is exceptionally high.

The Finance MBA's Job Description

Describe the career path and corresponding responsibilities for an MBA at your firm.

The firm recruits associates from the nation's leading business schools and although career training is essentially on-the-job, it is coupled with formal instruction from professionals within and outside the firm. Associates also are provided ample time and opportunity to prepare for any required registration examinations. The size of our firm is particularly advantageous for associates as it offers a rapid and diverse learning experience. Associates work in small client project teams, generally with a managing director or principal of the firm and an analyst to plan, analyze, and execute a wide variety of investment banking and principal investment transactions. Because of the entrepreneurial nature of the firm, we encourage associates to assume increasing levels of responsibility commensurate with their abilities. As a result, we believe our associates develop significant client and deal experience earlier than at larger, more structured investment banking firms.

Our firm is assiduous in evaluating associates as well as senior bankers. Notwithstanding the excellence of our professionals, we are vigilant in seeking ways to improve ourselves and the quality of our work. Associates receive annual reviews by senior and junior members of the firm for objectivity as well as guidance. Advancement and financial reward are dependent on one's initiative, performance and contribution to the firm. Again, the size of our firm permits considerable latitude for diversity in assignments as well as the opportunity to assume substantial responsibility.

Such responsibility is naturally accompanied by solid commitments of time and energy. An investment banking career at PSJC is intellectually and physically demanding yet exciting, stimulating and financially rewarding.

The Recruiting Process

Describe your recruiting process and the criteria by which you select candidates.

PJSC's philosophy is to pursue individuals with diverse backgrounds who are highly motivated and possess exceptional interpersonal and analytical skills. People who have demonstrated leadership skills; who can flourish in a team environment; who are flexible by nature and creative in their thinking, will thrive at our firm. As our firm continues to expand these are the types of individuals who will be welcome.

Piper Jaffray Inc.

222 South Ninth Street
Minneapolis, MN 55402
(612) 342-6000
Web site: www.piperjaffray.com
Email: applicant@piperjaffray.com

MBA Recruiting Contact(s):
Jennifer Piehl

Company Description

Describe your firm's business and the types of clients served by your finance group(s).

Piper Jaffray Inc., a full-service investment banking firm headquartered in Minneapolis, MN, is one of the leading investment banks based outside New York City. Established in 1895, it has over 3,200 employees. Piper Jaffray services consist of Equity and Fixed Income Capital Markets and Retail Distribution, with 1,140 brokers located in 80 offices across the western and southern United States.

Piper Jaffray's capital markets activities encompass corporate finance, equity research, public finance, debt and equity trading, and equity and fixed income sales. The Corporate Finance Department consists of 44 professionals who are divided along industry or functional specialties. The Research Department has 25 professionals who, with their Corporate Finance peers, lead industry teams. Piper Jaffray has five industry teams—HealthCare, Financial Institutions, Technology, Consumer, and Industrial Select—as well as functional specialists performing private placements, mergers and acquisitions, venture capital, and valuations. The majority of these services originate from the company's Minneapolis headquarters.

Describe your ownership structure.

Piper Jaffray's stock is listed on the New York Stock Exchange. Approximately 41% of the company's common shares are owned by its employee stock ownership trust. Another 15% is held by employees directly.

How does your approach to finance differ from that of other firms, and what do you consider to be your strengths and distinctive capabilities?

The ownership structure of Piper Jaffray is a distinctive strength. Because much of Piper Jaffray's equity is broadly owned by its employees, there is a strong sense of loyalty to the company and commitment to its professionalism and profitability. Consistent with its focus on servicing the financial needs of emerging-growth companies, Piper Jaffray is also able to commit its own capital to new ventures. It has made a number of venture capital investments in recent years and intends to increase investment in this area in the future.

Piper Jaffray places strong emphasis on the importance of long-term investment banking relationships. The company devotes substantial resources to trading, research coverage, and corporate finance expertise to provide its investment banking clients with the highest levels of service. Piper Jaffray also has one of the industry's lowest turnover rates, which is important to maintaining long-term banking commitments.

The Finance MBA's Job Description

Describe the career path and corresponding responsibilities for an MBA at your firm.

Piper Jaffray emphasizes hiring good people and giving them as much freedom and responsibility as is possible, consistent with general corporate objectives, to determine their own focus and goals. The good people rise to the top on their own initiative, and they remain with Piper Jaffray, in many instances because no other organization can offer them as much latitude to exercise their initiative. This unstructured atmosphere and emphasis on the individual, coupled with our employee ownership structure, have made it possible for entrepreneurial people to satisfy many of their goals within the corporate structure. For example, the Corporate Finance Department has built a partnership mechanism whereby its people, along with other members of management, can build capital by participating in some of the investment opportunities developed in the department.

New associates are hired as generalists and given substantial latitude to develop industry expertise and functional specialties that are compatible with their particular interests and capabilities. Associates are immediately assigned to a wide variety of projects and given as much responsibility as their experience and capabilities permit. A senior officer in the department supervises all client relationships and engagements. Associates generally choose a particular industry or functional specialty area after a couple of years at Piper Jaffray.

The Recruiting Process

Describe your recruiting process and the criteria by which you select candidates. Is prior experience necessary?

The most successful people in Corporate Finance have come to Piper Jaffray with some significant financially related working experience. This experience has enabled them to contribute effectively to the department at an early stage in their development. Members of the group also must have the confidence, maturity, and personal attributes necessary to develop successful client relationships. In most instances, the current professionals in the department are people who have spent time in financial centers such as New York, or would have done so, but preferred the working environment and growth opportunities that a smaller organization can offer and the lifestyle available in the Twin Cities or Seattle area.

How many permanent associates and analysts do you hire in a typical year? How many summer interns do you expect to hire? If you have a formal summer program, please describe it. Please be sure to indicate whether the summer program is in place for all offices or just some.

New associates are hired primarily into the Corporate Finance Department. Because of the department's size, it is not possible to offer a formal training program. Piper Jaffray typically hires two to five MBA graduates each year.

For information on the summer intern program, call (612) 342-1099 or visit our web site.

Raymond James & Associates, Inc.

880 Carillon Parkway
St. Petersburg, FL 33716
Web site: www.rjf.com

MBA Recruiting Contact(s):
Gerald K. Hwasta, Assistant to the Chairman
Raymond James Financial, Inc.
ghwasta@mba1996.hbs.edu

Company Description

Describe your firm's business and the types of clients served by your finance groups(s).

Raymond James Financial is a diversified financial services holding company whose subsidiaries engage in investment banking services. Since its founding in 1962, Raymond James has grown dramatically by providing these services to our clients and customers with a superior level of execution and integrity. Today, Raymond James is one of the preeminent investment banking and brokerage firms in regard to quality of service and reputation. The firm maintains the eighth largest retail brokerage network in the United States.

Raymond James & Associates, a subsidiary of Raymond James Financial, provides investment banking services to emerging-growth companies throughout the United States. The primary emphasis is on companies within targeted industries such as information technology, healthcare/biotechnology, consumer, energy, among others, where sufficient industry knowledge has been developed to deliver an extremely high level of value-added service. Investment banking services include: public underwritings; private placements; merger, acquisition, and divestiture representation; and various advisory services.

Describe your ownership structure.

Raymond James Financial, the parent company of Raymond James & Associates, is a publicly-traded corporation whose shares are traded on the New York Stock Exchange (NYSE: RJF).

How does your approach to finance differ from that of other firms, and what do you consider to be your strengths and distinctive capabilities?

Raymond James has developed a reputation for providing capital and advice to emerging-growth and medium-sized companies in targeted industries. Members of the Investment Banking Department work closely with our highly-acclaimed Research Department to develop an in-depth understanding of our clients and their businesses in order to provide the highest level of value-added services.

Discuss changes in your firm's revenues (both domestic and international) and professional staff over the past year; over the past five years.

Raymond James is one of the leading growth companies in the country with a compound growth rate in revenues and earnings in excess of 20% per year during most of the firm's history. In our most recently completed fiscal year, revenues exceeded $721 million and profits totaled $66 million. All major areas of the firms have grown dramatically in the past five years, including expansion of our institutional sales effort to seven offices in Europe, publishing research from our South African joint venture and managing assets through our joint venture in India. Today, there are 31 Investment Banking professionals, 31 Equity Research analysts, 70 Domestic and International Equity Salesmen, 24 Equity Traders, 20 Public Finance professionals, 75 Fixed Income Salesmen and 30 Fixed Income Traders.

The Finance MBA's Job Description

Describe the career path and corresponding responsibilities for an MBA at your firm.

Raymond James hires MBAs for a variety of positions within the firm, including Investment Banking, Equity Research, Sales and Trading, Asset Management, and Corporate Staff positions. By virtue of its growth and entrepreneurial environment, Raymond James provides a recently hired MBA more rapid exposure to transactions and client contact than other firms.

Describe the opportunities for professional mobility between the various departments in your firm.

There are numerous examples of MBAs moving from one department to another within the firm as their interests change. Our philosophy is to hire people who are highly qualified and choose to live in Florida for the lifestyle alternative. Thus, we are flexible in meeting their needs over time in recognition of their contributions to the success of the firm.

Discuss the lifestyle aspects of a career with your firm (i.e., average hours per week, amount of travel, flexibility to change offices, corporate culture, etc.).

Raymond James offers an attractive alternative to the

lifestyles offered by other firms. All MBA positions are located at the firm's spacious headquarters in St. Petersburg. A typical workweek is 60–70 hours, and travel ranges from 30% to 50% of the MBA's time. The real benefit is the warm climate of Florida, where many leisure activities can be pursued year-round. The corporate culture at Raymond James can best be described as "work, work, play."

The Recruiting Process

Describe your recruiting process and the criteria by which you select candidates. Is prior experience necessary?

Raymond James conducts on-campus recruiting at several of the country's finest business schools for full-time positions in Investment Banking, Equity Research, Sales and Trading, Asset Management, and Corporate Staff. In each of these departments, the firm seeks individuals with a track record of superior achievement who wish to work in an entrepreneurial environment. All aspects of a candidate's background are considered and measured against a high set of standards. Personality fit is also an important factor. Prior experience in financial services is not required.

How many summer interns do you expect to hire? If you have a formal summer program, please describe it. Please be sure to indicate whether the summer program is in place for all offices or just some.

Each summer, Raymond James also offers a number of summer internships in positions throughout the firm. These internships provide students with an opportunity to work alongside senior management on special projects that will impact the ongoing success of the company.

RBC Dominion Securities Inc.

P.O. Box 50
Royal Bank Plaza, South Tower
Toronto, Ontario
M5J 2W7
Canada
(416) 842-7588
Fax: (416) 842-7555
Web site: www.rbcds.com

MBA Recruiting Contact(s):
H. Martin Kent, Vice President and Director
Nitin Babbar, Associate

Company Description

Describe your firm's business and the types of clients served by your finance group(s).

RBC Dominion Securities is a fully integrated Canadian investment bank that enjoys a leading position in all segments of the securities business in Canada. Its principal investment banking activities are general corporate and government finance, mergers and acquisitions, corporate restructuring, real estate, fixed income and equity sales and trading, international financing, commercial paper, and foreign exchange. The firm has an extensive retail sales network of approximately 1,600 registered representatives located in over 70 cities across Canada. RBC Dominion Securities also has a strong international presence, with offices in New York, Boston, London, Paris, Lausanne, Hong Kong, and Tokyo.

RBC Dominion Securities has grown through a series of mergers over the past two decades to become one of the largest, most profitable investment banks in Canada. The firm's investment banking clients include most of Canada's largest and fastest-growing companies, as well as the 10 Canadian provinces, the federal government, and numerous government agencies. Over the past several years, RBC Dominion Securities has lead-managed over 25% of all public Canadian corporate debt and equity offerings in Canada. The firm has demonstrated a consistent ability to meet the changing needs of its many clients while maintaining a superior rate of return on its own capital, a performance that is of interest to potential employees, as 20% of the firm is owned by professional-level employees. RBC Dominion Securities has been able to take advantage of its strong capital base and exceptional distribution capability to compete effectively and profitably.

The firm's corporate strategy is to be the leading investment bank to Canadian clients in both domestic and international markets and to be the leading investment bank to foreign clients in the Canadian market. The firm achieves this goal through its ability to view client interests as paramount and to deliver superior services that integrate the various areas of strength throughout the firm. This integrated, client-oriented approach has distinguished RBC Dominion Securities in terms of both its reputation and its performance over the past several years.

Describe your ownership structure.

As a consequence of financial services deregulation in Canada and certain acquisitions, the firm has sold an 80% equity interest to the Royal Bank of Canada, Canada's largest commercial bank. The transaction provided the firm with access to the Royal's international network, as well as the financial backing of a major financial institution. The remaining 20% of RBC Dominion Securities' shares are owned by employees and traded at book value. Professionals in investment banking are typically first offered an opportunity to purchase shares in the firm within the first several years of their careers.

Unlike some other commercial bank-investment bank relationships in Canada, RBC Dominion Securities has maintained a high level of independence of operations. Career opportunities and compensation structures for professional staff have and will remain unchanged.

The Finance MBA's Job Description

Describe the career path and corresponding responsibilities for an MBA at your firm.

The firm employs approximately 120 investment banking professionals located in Toronto, Montreal, Calgary, Vancouver, Regina, and New York, as well as in London and other overseas offices. RBC Dominion Securities devotes a great deal of time and consideration to its search for associates. The firm's intention is to hire outstanding graduates who will continue with the firm throughout their careers. It has among the lowest turnover rates in the industry.

Associates who join the investment banking group at RBC Dominion Securities generally do not specialize in any one particular industry or product group. The firm prefers to develop well-rounded professionals who have participated in a wide variety of transactions, whether debt or equity, domestic or international, private or public.

Associates are nevertheless encouraged to develop expertise in areas that interest them, and the firm makes every effort to satisfy a professional's ambitions in a particular specialty area. The firm is large enough to be able to offer both a generalist approach to the business and the opportunity to specialize in specific areas of interest but small enough to take a flexible approach in the career development of high-performing employees.

Other aspects of RBC Dominion Securities would be of interest to potential associates, including the firm's reputation for excellence, innovation, and high ethical standards. Moreover, there are comparatively few associates, which results in new professionals being given substantial responsibilities early in their careers. RBC Dominion Securities' position in the domestic underwriting league table affords new associates the deal flow necessary to develop well-rounded professional skills.

Discuss the lifestyle aspects of a career with your firm (i.e., average hours per week, amount of travel, flexibility to change offices, corporate culture, etc.).

An open and collegial atmosphere prevails throughout the firm. There is a genuine concern on the part of senior management that young professionals develop a number of outside interests and have the ability to devote a significant portion of time to their families. While the highest value is placed on productive output by professionals, the firm does not encourage long hours when they are unnecessary.

The Recruiting Process

Describe your recruiting process and the criteria by which you select candidates. Is prior experience necessary?

RBC Dominion Securities is highly selective in its hiring program. The firm has made a consistent commitment over the years to hire from the top business schools in both North America and Europe. A number of criteria are applied, including academic excellence, energetic presentation, evidence of strong outside interests, and overall fit with the firm. Grades by themselves are not given undue consideration. No prior investment banking experience is necessary, and the firm encourages applicants from a wide variety of academic disciplines and work experience. Successful candidates are typically persistent self-starters with a keen interest in financial markets and a good sense of humor.

How many permanent associates and analysts do you hire in a typical year? How many summer interns do you expect to hire? If you have a formal summer program, please describe it. Please be sure to indicate whether the summer program is in place for all offices or just some.

Each year three to five full-time associates and a smaller number of summer associates are hired into investment banking. There is no formal training program. Associates are immediately assigned to client transaction teams to learn on the job.

The Robinson-Humphrey Company, Inc.

Atlanta Financial Center
3333 Peachtree Road, NE
Atlanta, GA 30326
(404) 266-6000

MBA Recruiting Contact(s):
Pam Smith, Assistant
(404) 266-6919
Jim Birkholz, Associate
(404) 266-6759

Company Description

Describe your firm's business and the types of clients served by your finance group(s).

The Corporate Finance Department at Robinson-Humphrey consists of 50 professionals. The entire department is located at Robinson-Humphrey's headquarters in Atlanta. Essentially, everyone in the Corporate Finance Department is regarded as a generalist in terms of product. Teams of professionals focus on certain industries (e.g., technology, health care, retailing, financial institutions), but a flexible approach to industry coverage is maintained at the junior level. Robinson-Humphrey attempts to position itself as a full-service investment banker to its clients. Robinson-Humphrey's primary corporate finance clientele are middle-market, emerging-growth companies.

Describe your ownership structure.

The Robinson-Humphrey Company, Inc. was purchased by American Express in 1982 and operated as a wholly owned subsidiary of Shearson Lehman Brothers, Inc. As part of Primerica's acquisition of Shearson in 1993, Robinson-Humphrey operates today as an essentially autonomous subsidiary of Smith Barney Inc.

How does your approach to finance differ from that of other firms, and what do you consider to be your strengths and distinctive capabilities?

Robinson-Humphrey positions itself as a full-service investment bank to emerging-growth and middle-market companies. Because of its outstanding retail distribution system (55 branches across 10 states), as well as its ability to tap the worldwide resources of Smith Barney, Robinson-Humphrey has capabilities unique among regional investment banking firms. The Corporate Finance Department has grown from approximately 20 people to 50 people over the past six years. Robinson-Humphrey is the largest corporate finance and investment banking operation in the Southeast, an area realizing tremendous gains in economic growth and in the origination of capital.

Discuss changes in your firm's revenues (both domestic and international) and professional staff over the past year; over the past five years.

Robinson-Humphrey, like most other investment banking firms, has benefited over the past year from the surge in public underwriting and merger and acquisition activity. Robinson-Humphrey has been a particularly active underwriter of new equity issues, both initial public offerings and issues for companies whose stocks are already publicly traded. The Corporate Finance Department, however, still maintains a balance between public underwriting and other activities, such as mergers and acquisitions and private capital raising. Over the past five years, merger and acquisition work has comprised from 20% to 80% of the department's business.

By the summer of 1997, our department will have over 50 professionals, including three new MBA associates. Of our three new MBA associates, one is from the Harvard Business School. These additions continue the growth that the department has experienced during the past six years.

The Finance MBA's Job Description

Describe the career path and corresponding responsibilities for an MBA at your firm.

An associate works as a key member of transaction teams typically comprising two to three professionals. The associate's primary responsibilities consist of transaction execution duties, including financial analysis and project management. The associate also works with senior professionals to develop new business by meeting with and making presentations to prospective clients. An associate's degree of responsibility depends on the type and scope of a project and on his or her particular capabilities.

Describe the opportunities for professional mobility between the various departments in your firm.

There is very little mobility between the various departments within Robinson-Humphrey, although corporate finance associates are exposed to other areas of the firm on a regular basis.

Discuss the lifestyle aspects of a career with your firm (i.e., average hours per week, amount of travel, flexibility to change offices, corporate culture, etc.).

People who work at Robinson-Humphrey generally seem to enjoy the lifestyle offered by a career with the firm and fostered by its location in the Southeast. In addition, the relatively small size of the department and of the firm by Wall Street standards tends to encourage close relationships among co-workers. While investment banking inevitably demands a significant time commitment, one's average hours worked and travel schedule will vary depending on market conditions and the number and types of projects on which one is working.

The Recruiting Process

Describe your recruiting process and the criteria by which you select candidates. Is prior experience necessary?

The company hires graduating MBAs to entry-level positions every year, depending on market conditions. Our annual recruiting effort usually begins in the fall, when we solicit cover letters and résumés from interested, qualified candidates. We are scheduled to conduct off-campus interviews in early November with another round at our headquarters in Atlanta to follow. Typically, an entering MBA will have some experience in investment banking or a closely related financial services business. All factors such as grades, prior experience, and personal attributes are taken into consideration in the decision process. However, final recruiting decisions are based on interviews with several people in the department who make judgments concerning a candidate's ability to make a meaningful contribution to the department.

How many permanent associates and analysts do you hire in a typical year? How many summer interns do you expect to hire? If you have a formal summer program, please describe it. Please be sure to indicate whether the summer program is in place for all offices or just some.

Hiring decisions are based solely on current and perceived market conditions and an assessment of the department's overall needs. The department has hired from two to five associates each of the past four years. Most likely, we will hire two to four entry-level MBAs in the upcoming year.

The firm does not have a summer program and does not interview for summer associates or analysts.

Rothschild Canada Limited

1 First Canadian Place
Suite 3800
P.O. Box 77
Toronto, Ontario
M5X 1B1
Canada
(416) 369-9600
Fax: (416) 864-1261

MBA Recruiting Contact(s):
Stephen L. Shapiro, Vice President

Company Description

Describe your firm's business and the types of clients served by your finance group(s).

Rothschild Canada provides independent investment banking, corporate finance, and financial advisory services to selected Canadian and international clients in Canada and offers the global capability and expertise of the Rothschild Group around the world. Our range of experiences to date includes advising on acquisitions, mergers, divestitures, reorganizations, financings, spin-offs, privatizations, and restructurings. In addition, Rothschild Canada is involved in valuing and selling, both nationally and globally, private and public companies as a whole, operating units of large companies, and, in some cases, specific assets.

Rothschild Canada works with the other offices in the Rothschild Group to identify target companies for acquisition or investment purposes for current and prospective clients. There is a steady flow of ideas between Rothschild's offices with respect to opportunities in the mergers and acquisitions market in Canada and internationally.

As part of our long-term relationships with our clients, we advise them on their ongoing corporate and financial strategies and corporate finance activities and on the implementation of their strategic plans.

Rothschild Canada is not associated with commercial banks, financial institutions, or industrial groups in Canada, nor does it engage in public underwriting, market trading, arbitrage, or principal investing. Rothschild Canada is able to provide unbiased judgments free from potential conflicts of interest.

Describe your ownership structure.

Rothschild Canada Limited is the Canadian member of one of the world's leading independent merchant banking organizations, the Rothschild Group. The main operating company of the Rothschild Group in the United Kingdom is N M Rothschild & Sons Limited, the merchant bank that has been based at New Court in the City of London for nearly 200 years. The Rothschild Group has expanded globally to meet the increasingly diverse needs of its clients and now has offices in over thirty countries worldwide. The Canadian office was opened in 1990 and has grown each year.

How does your approach to finance differ from that of other firms, and what do you consider to be your strengths and distinctive capabilities?

Rothschild Canada's independence and professional client-related approach to its focused business of providing advisory services differentiates it from its competitors in Canada. In addition, the international reach of the Rothschild Group allows it to offer truly global investment banking services.

The Finance MBA's Job Description

Describe the career path and corresponding responsibilities for an MBA at your firm.

A new member of the investment banking team has the opportunity to gain experience quickly in a vast number of transactions. Our experience to date has covered all major industries in Canada and a wide range of various types of transactions. Our professionals do not specialize in industrial sectors or products, although the majority of our professionals have brought years of experience to Rothschild Canada in all aspects of industry. All professionals begin as generalists, gathering as wide a portfolio of experiences as possible. As the firm grows, professionals naturally develop areas of particular expertise upon which the Canadian office, as well as our international group, will draw in dealing with various clients' needs.

Describe the opportunities for professional mobility between the various departments in your firm.

There are opportunities to meet and work with professionals from Rothschild's other offices, or the Rothschild Group, as well as opportunities to consider extended assignments in other offices.

Discuss the lifestyle aspects of a career with your firm (i.e., average hours per week, amount of travel, flexibility to change offices, corporate culture, etc.).

While the lifestyle of an investment banker is renowned for its hard work and long hours, Rothschild Canada maintains a friendly and cooperative atmosphere. Within a very short period, every new associate will have worked with all members of the office. The professionals are relatively young, and this allows for common interests and non-work-related activities.

The Recruiting Process

Describe your recruiting process and the criteria by which you select candidates. Is prior experience necessary?

The recruiting process at Rothschild Canada has identified certain characteristics that we feel are crucial to having a successful and long-term career in investment banking. While strong academic performance is not in itself a requirement, it does tend to indicate the dedication and commitment that recruits have made in their past endeavors. Experience in the industry or in related fields will also act as guidance in identifying those recruits who have decided to make investment banking their career choice. A third requirement, of course, is that recruits be familiar and knowledgeable of the Canadian business environment and be able to work in Canada.

Salomon Brothers Inc.

Seven World Trade Center
New York, NY 10048
(212) 783-7000
Web site: www.salomon.com

MBA Recruiting Contact(s):
Maureen Horan, Recruiting Manager
Investment Banking Recruiting
(212) 783-5924

Susan H. Glendon, Vice President
Sales and Trading Recruiting
(212) 783-6197

Company Description

Describe your firm's business and the types of clients served by your finance group(s).

Salomon Brothers is a full-service financial institution engaged in investment banking, market making and trading of financial instruments, fixed income and equity market research, and institutional money management. Salomon's services and activities include advisory services provided for mergers and acquisitions and financial restructurings; capital-raising activities, including the underwriting and distribution of debt, equity, and derivative securities; trading and arbitrage strategies using debt, equity, and derivative instruments; entering into contractual commitments, such as forward securities and currency agreements, interest rate swap cap, and floor agreements; options, warrants, and derivative products; fixed income and equity market research; institutional money management services; precious metals trading; and mortgage banking. Salomon Brothers conducts its business globally, with offices in Australia, Canada, France, Germany, Hong Kong, Japan, South Korea, Spain, Switzerland, Taiwan, Thailand, the United Kingdom, and the United States. Its customer base consists primarily of large- and medium-size corporations, governments, and financial institutions. Financial services are also provided to individuals on a limited basis.

Investment Banking
Salomon Brothers' investment banking activities consist principally of raising capital and providing strategic advisory services. Capital-raising activities include underwriting and distributing debt and equity securities and involve the development, underwriting, and distribution of derivative products. These products include warrants linked to a variety of instruments, such as debt securities, equity securities, baskets of equity securities, indexes based upon stock markets throughout the world, and commodities such as gold and oil. Strategic advisory services are provided in connection with mergers and acquisitions, leveraged buy-outs, financial restructurings, and privatizations.

Sales and Trading
Salomon Brothers is a major dealer in government securities in New York, Tokyo, London, and Frankfurt and is a member of major international securities, financial futures, and options exchanges. It has extensive distribution capabilities and one of the largest capital bases in the U.S. securities industry. Salomon Brothers is a major underwriter of securities for governments and high-grade primary issuers and is capable of executing trading strategies on behalf of its customers and for its own account requiring significant commitments of capital.

Salomon's trading expertise, which dates back more than 80 years, together with the ability to execute a high volume of transactions with counterparties, enables it to provide liquidity to investors across a broad range of markets and financial instruments. Salomon Brothers' ability to execute arbitrage strategies is enhanced not only by its established presence in international capital markets but also by its utilization of information technology, quantitative methods, and risk management tools; its research capabilities; and its leadership position in the development and use of financial derivative products.

Describe your ownership structure.

Salomon Brothers Inc. is the investment banking/brokerage subsidiary of Salomon Inc., a New York Stock Exchange-listed firm. A substantial portion of Salomon Inc.'s equity is owned by its employees and Berkshire Hathaway, Inc. In 1990, Salomon Inc. implemented the Equity Partnership Plan for Key Employees (EPP), designed to provide participants, including newly hired MBAs, with a continuing long-term investment in common stock of Salomon Inc. Through the EPP and other programs designed to increase employee ownership, Salomon Inc. expects that within the next few years, its employees will own 30% of the firm's common stock.

How does your approach to finance differ from that of other firms, and what do you consider to be your strengths and distinctive capabilities?

Several areas of competence distinguish the businesses of Salomon Inc.: our ability and willingness to commit capital for our clients and for ourselves; our superior risk management and financial engineering capabilities; our geographic breadth, with strong customer and proprietary businesses on four continents; our first-class financial advisory and analytical skills and databases; and the character of our professionals.

Discuss changes in your firm's revenues (both domestic and international) and professional staff over the past year; over the past five years.

The financial services industry is characterized by change. Increasingly, the businesses of Salomon Brothers are becoming global. A number of products, markets, and clients that contribute significantly to the revenue and profitability of Salomon Brothers today were nonexistent five years ago. The establishment of a Tokyo office, where Salomon Brothers has become the leading non-Japanese competitor in terms of both revenue and profitability, and the development of its derivative product businesses are illustrative of such markets and products. A hallmark of Salomon Brothers has been its willingness to commit capital, both financial and human, to the development of promising emerging businesses such as these.

As of April 1, 1997, Salomon Brothers employed approximately 6,400 employees worldwide, approximately the same number employed as of December 31, 1986.

The Finance MBA's Job Description

Describe the career path and corresponding responsibilities for an MBA at your firm. Describe the opportunities for professional mobility between the various departments in your firm.

New associates, as well as senior investment bankers, have identified career mobility, cohesiveness, early professional responsibility, and comprehensive training as salient considerations in their decision to join Salomon Brothers.

Flexibility and Options

Flexibility is the hallmark of a professional career at Salomon Brothers. In Investment Banking, several options are available. In contrast with a number of other major investment banks, Salomon does not compel a candidate to choose a specific functional specialty in order to get an offer.

Associates who join Investment Banking enter the generalist associate program, where they have the opportunity to work with many product and coverage areas to develop a broad banking competence. During their first year at the firm, generalists typically spend approximately 25% of their time on financings, 30% on mergers and acquisitions assignments, 25% on financial advisory and restructuring work, and 20% on business development.

After their first one to two years in Investment Banking, associates usually select an initial specialization that best fits their interest and background. Areas of specialization include the following:

- Capital Market Services (synthesizes the efforts of Corporate Finance, Sales, and Trading in new product development and public debt offerings)
- Mergers and Acquisitions
- Leveraged Finance
- Specialty Industries (i.e., media, telecommunications and technology, forest products/paper, retailing, transportation, utilities, and regional industrial and high-yield coverage in the eastern United States)
- Specialty Finance Products (high yield, private placements, project finance, and leasing)
- International (coverage of foreign and international corporations and governments: London, Tokyo, Frankfurt, Sydney, New York)
- Financial Institutions (insurance coverage, depository institutions, diversified financials, government finance, insurance, and real estate)

Similarly, Salomon takes the generalist approach in hiring for sales and trading. All interns are recruited for the training program and then choose their areas of specialty after exposure to all facets of sales and trading through our intensive training and rotation process. These areas of specialization include:

- Corporate Bonds
- Derivative Securities
- Emerging Markets
- Finance
- Foreign Exchange
- Government Bonds
- High Yield
- Mortgage Bonds
- Syndicate
- Equity Derivatives
- Equity Convertibles
- Equity Sales Trading
- Equity Syndicates
- Equity Block Trading
- Equity Over the Counter

A career at Salomon Brothers is dynamic. Many of today's most important product lines and services either did not exist or were relatively small portions of our business a few years ago. Many of our people are now working in product areas that did not exist at the time they joined the firm. We are confident that Salomon's flexibility will enable the organization to continue to capitalize on emerging market opportunities and challenges.

Integration and Teamwork

The integration of the firm's investment banking, research, sales, and trading capabilities is responsible for Salomon's performance. Our achievements reflect the combined expertise of many areas within Finance, as well as contributions from other departments and our international network.

Teamwork is ingrained in Salomon Brothers' professionals. Investment Banking professionals work closely with members of the Sales, Trading, and Syndicate Departments on the trading floor, as well as with Research. For example, while working on an initial public offering, an associate will interact extensively with Syndicate, Equity Sales, and Stock Research.

Salomon's performance-based compensation policy underscores the fact that teamwork and cooperation are the basis of our business success. Unlike many of its competitors, Salomon Brothers does not pay commissions to sales and trading professionals. Instead, a broad group of senior managers carefully assesses each person's contributions to the firm's overall performance.

Responsibility and Participation

Although the number of professionals has grown to meet new market opportunities, Salomon remains committed to a leanly staffed organization. The firm emphasizes small working groups that give new associates room in which to operate and develop.

A first-year Finance associate works closely with a managing director and a vice president on each of his or her important assignments. Rapid client responsibility is encouraged. We are anxious to bring new associates into client contact at the earliest possible stage so that they will cultivate the relationships that are critical to the firm's long-term success.

In Sales and Trading, a first-year associate's exposure to managing directors and vice presidents is also immediate. Sales units and trading desks are run by managing directors who spend most of their time on the sales or trading desk. Furthermore, sales units and trading desks are broken down into small subunits run by experienced vice presidents who act as mentors to train the young associates. Salespeople are given account assignments soon after their placement on a desk, and traders receive risk-taking responsibilities at a very rapid pace. Hands-on training and significant early responsibility are hallmarks of the Salomon sales and trading program.

The Recruiting Process

Describe your recruiting process and the criteria by which you select candidates. Is prior experience necessary?

Salomon's character is reflected in the diversity, talents, and various backgrounds of its new associates. Salomon recruits associates who have displayed exceptional talent at whatever they have set their minds to. Rather than seeking a particular résumé, experience, or personality, we look for individuals with a proven record of achievement, entrepreneurial initiative, outstanding integrity, and continuing desire to work hard and excel. Salomon's 1996 class includes representatives from a large number of business, law, and other graduate schools, of which a significant proportion were international.

Professional development has always been a top priority of the firm. New members of all departments—from Investment Banking and Research to Sales and Trading—complete the firm's training program, widely considered the broadest in scope and most challenging of its kind on Wall Street. The program has three basic components:

1. Two months of classroom training, which is conducted at the firm's New York headquarters for all new associates in Investment Banking and Sales and Trading worldwide. Senior managers provide instruction on all firm capabilities and organizations. Trainees are expected to complete assignments and rotate responsibilities for monitoring and summarizing market activities to the class each morning.
2. Rotation among sales and trading desks in key product areas to work alongside senior managers.
3. Preparation for the Registered Representative examination given by the National Association of Securities Dealers and the New York Stock Exchange.

Training modules continue for three weeks in Investment Banking and eight weeks in Sales and Trading.

Salomon Brothers' compensation policy reflects the firm's belief in a team approach to business. Bonuses and salaries are based on each professional's overall contribution to the firm's performance, which includes such factors as creativity and imagination, management potential, and the ability to train others within the firm.

How many permanent associates and analysts do you hire in a typical year? How many summer interns do you expect to hire? If you have a formal summer program, please describe it. Please be sure to indicate whether the summer program is in place for all offices or just some.

In 1996 our Investment Banking Department plans to hire approximately 30–35 summer and 35–40 full-time associates. In addition, our Sales and Trading Department estimates that it will hire 15 summer and 20–25 full-time MBA candidates.

The Salomon summer program is designed to identify candidates for full-time positions. More than 75% of

Salomon summer associates have received offers, filling approximately half of our full-time hiring needs.

The Investment Banking summer program provides a realistic introduction to the firm and work experience comparable to that of a full-time associate. Summer professionals function as full-time associates and become integral team members working on financings, mergers and acquisitions, and new business presentations.

The Sales and Trading summer program is a flexible, unstructured program that allows associates to rotate to different areas of the firm in both equities and fixed income. Presentations and product-specific classes are an integral part of the program, giving the associate an introduction to a full range of security products, as well as a realistic experience in Sales and Trading.

What international opportunities does your firm offer for U.S. citizens? For foreign nationals?

Salomon Brothers' Investment Banking operations in Asia include offices in Bangkok, Beijing, Hong Kong, Jakarta, Melbourne, New Delhi, Osaka, Seoul, Singapore, Sydney, Taipei, and Tokyo. In addition, there are professionals based in our New York office who are dedicated to servicing the requirements of our Asian clients in the United States. This network enables Salomon to maintain regular contact with governments and major industrial and financial institutions throughout the region. These offices are staffed with Investment Banking professionals with both regional and product expertise, including capital markets, mergers and acquisitions, project and lease finance, and real estate.

Europe is a key component of Salomon Brothers' global investment banking network. Salomon Brothers' activities in Europe are headquartered in London, and Salomon Brothers is also supported by offices in Berlin, Frankfurt, Madrid, Milan, Moscow, Paris, and Zurich. In Europe, Salomon Brothers provides a full range of investment banking services to corporations and to sovereign and supranational organizations. The Investment Banking group in London is staffed primarily by European nationals and includes individuals from over a dozen countries. Salomon Brothers' continuing commitment to Europe reflects the importance of the European economies on the world stage and the vital role Europe plays in the international financial markets.

For further information, contact Joanne Hogan, Salomon Brothers International Limited, Victoria Plaza, 111 Buckingham Palace Road, London SW1W0SB England.

Schroder Wertheim & Co. Incorporated

787 Seventh Avenue
New York, NY 10019
(212) 492-6000

MBA Recruiting Contact(s):
Basil Bliss
Senior Vice President
Human Resources
(212) 492-6290
Fax: (212) 492-7188

Location of Offices:
Schroders worldwide: offices in 46 cities in 33 countries, headquartered in London. Schroder Wertheim headquartered in New York, with other offices in Los Angeles, Chicago, Boston and Philadelphia, London, Paris, Geneva, and Amsterdam.

Total Number of Professionals (U.S. and worldwide):
4,700 worldwide, 1,100 in the United States

Company Description

Describe your firm's business and the types of clients served by your finance group(s).

Schroder Wertheim & Co. Incorporated is part of Schroders, an international investment banking group with extensive operations in the three major financial centers of the world: North America, Europe, and the Asia Pacific region. Schroder Wertheim, founded as Wertheim & Co. in 1927, is a full-service major bracket investment banking firm, based in New York. The firm is actively involved in all aspects of investment banking, including corporate finance, mergers and acquisitions advisory, sales and trading, and securities research.

The group employs approximately 300 investment banking professionals worldwide, with approximately 90 bankers based in North America. The Schroder Wertheim Corporate Finance Department is actively involved in all major areas of investment banking. Specific areas of expertise include mergers and acquisitions, both domestic and cross-border, public offerings of debt and equity securities, private placements of debt and equity securities, financial restructurings, and general financial advisory services. The firm is active in the public and private capital markets and Schroders has consistently ranked in the top 10 M&A advisors worldwide. Schroders provides investment banking services to companies in all industries. Schroder Wertheim has teams of corporate finance and research professionals with particular expertise in the chemical, energy, healthcare, industrial manufacturing, lodging and gaming, media, restaurant, and transportation industries.

The partnership with Schroders has served as the foundation for Schroder Wertheim to participate in the growing international financing and mergers and acquisitions markets. Schroders is and historically has been one of the preeminent merchant banks in Europe and the Far East, with 4,700 employees in offices in 46 cities in 33 countries worldwide, including London, Paris, Milan, Amsterdam, Frankfurt, Warsaw, Tokyo, Singapore, Hong Kong, Shanghai, and Sydney.

Describe your ownership structure.

Schroder Wertheim & Co. Incorporated is a wholly owned subsidiary of Schroders plc, the leading global investment bank based in London. Schroders is publicly traded on the London Stock Exchange and has an equity market capitalization of approximately $4 billion.

How does your approach to finance differ from that of other firms, and what do you consider to be your distinctive strengths and capabilities?

The business of Schroder Wertheim is creating value for clients. The firm conducts its business in a personalized manner, building long term client relationships founded on value creation over time. The Corporate Finance Department focuses its efforts on its particular areas of expertise, which are institutionalized in a number of industry groups. Senior professionals are very actively involved in serving clients, ensuring the highest level of client service. The firm has a strong research tradition and is often among the top rated research organizations relative to its size. The industry group organization promotes strong cooperation and coordination between research and corporate finance.

Mergers and acquisitions has traditionally been a strength of the firm and Schroders traditionally ranks among the most prominent firms in transactions worldwide. With respect to capital raising, the firm is a major bracket underwriter of public equity and debt, with particular strength in institutional sales and trading. The firm brings this same level of expertise to the private financing markets.

Discuss changes in your firm's revenues and professional staff.

The firm has grown steadily over the past ten years and has not been subject to the volatility and erratic expansion and contraction that have typified many other investment banks. Because of Schroder Wertheim's orientation to long-term relationships and a relatively lower level of proprietary trading (and therefore lower level of exposure to the volatility of the financial markets), revenues and profitability have tended to be relatively stable compared to many of our competitors.

The Finance MBA's Job Description

Describe the career path and corresponding responsibilities for an MBA at your firm.

Schroder Wertheim offers its associates the opportunities inherent in a growing international investment banking firm with the atmosphere of a traditional Wall Street partnership.

Though the career path is similar to that of most investment banks, the role of an associate in Schroder Wertheim's Corporate Finance Department differs significantly from the role of an associate in a bulge bracket investment bank. Though there are opportunities for early industry specialization, the firm encourages associates in their early years to obtain as broad an experience as possible, before developing a specific industry or product specialization. Schroder Wertheim endeavors to ensure that all incoming associates obtain experience in all major areas of investment banking: general financial advisory, mergers and acquisitions, public and private placements of securities and financial restructurings. Most associates become involved with clients in a diverse group of industries.

Because of the size and open structure of our department, associates are encouraged to learn as much as possible and develop responsibility early. Rarely is a transaction or client serviced by more than three professionals or more than one associate. Associates in Research work closely with senior analysts.

Describe the opportunities for professional mobility with the various departments in your firm.

The best opportunities for mobility are among the numerous Schroders corporate finance offices around the world. Within the limits of the requirements of the business and availability of positions, international movement is encouraged as a way of enhancing an individual's career development.

Discuss the lifestyle aspects of a career with your firm.

The firm supports a collegial, supportive culture in a professional environment. Professionals work as part of relationship or transaction teams (which may vary project to project) and successful investment bankers should have both strong individual and team skills. Hours and travel are typical for an investment bank and vary according to the demands of particular clients and projects. Travel tends to be one or two days at a time, as opposed to extended stays away from home.

The Recruiting Process

Describe your recruiting process and the criterion by which you select candidates. Is prior experience necessary?

Schroder Wertheim interviews at the top MBA programs to find the select group of associates it hires each year. Schroder Wertheim seeks highly motivated individuals with a record of business and academic achievement. Schroder Wertheim maintains a collegial atmosphere which supports initiative at all levels and Schroder Wertheim seeks individuals who will succeed in this environment. Prior experience in finance or financial analysis is considered helpful, but not required. Interested candidates should send their resumes and cover letters to our recruiting contact.

How many permanent associates and analysts do you hire in a typical year?

Schroder Wertheim's Corporate Finance Department expects to hire approximately ten associates and fifteen analysts this year, primarily for the New York office, with the possibility of additional hiring for the Los Angeles office. These levels are equal to 1996 hiring. Schroders does additional hiring for its other offices around the world. Interested persons should send their resumes to the recruiting contact in New York. Research is expected to hire six associates in New York; Sales and Trading should hire five.

If you have a formal summer program, please describe it.

Schroder Wertheim has a ten-week Summer Associate Program within the Corporate Finance, Research, Sales and Trading Departments in New York. Summer associates function as full members of the department and contribute to several transaction teams as part of a program designed to introduce the summer associate to as broad a client and transaction base as possible. The program gives students an opportunity to learn or expand their experience in the various areas of investment banking.

We expect to hire at least ten summer associates for the New York office for the summer of 1998.

What international opportunities does the firm offer U.S. citizens? For foreign nationals?

Our employees have the opportunity to seek positions in Schroder offices around the world. Within the limits of the requirements of the business and availability of positions, international movement is encouraged as a way of enhancing an individual's career development. Foreign nationals are encouraged to apply for opportunities in our foreign offices.

Simmons & Company International

700 Louisiana, Suite 5000
Houston, TX 77002
(713) 236-9999
Fax: (713) 223-7800

MBA Recruiting Contact(s):
Matthew R. Simmons, President
Charles S. Bratka, Vice President

Company Description

Describe your firm's business and the types of clients served by your finance group(s). Describe your ownership structure.

Simmons & Company International is a privately owned full-service investment banking firm based in Houston. The firm was founded in 1974 by Matt Simmons, an HBS graduate from the Class of 1967, to serve the financial needs of the worldwide oil and gas service and equipment industry ("oil service industry"). Twenty-three years later, Simmons & Company remains focused on providing investment banking services to the oil service industry and its investment community.

Simmons & Company's corporate finance activities include merger and acquisition advisory services, private placements of equity and debt, financial restructuring advisory work, and a variety of strategic consulting assignments. The firm has worked with public and private participants in every industry sector, from pre-exploration to downstream transportation and processing. The firm extended its practice in the downstream oil industry during 1996 through the addition of senior personnel with extensive sector experience. Simmons & Company has implemented approximately 300 transactions with an aggregate value of over $20 billion.

The firm established its Capital Markets division in 1992. Simmons & Company underwrites and co-manages public equity and debt offerings, provides equity research and institutional sales support, trades listed securities, and makes markets in selected over-the-counter stocks. Since mid-1993, Simmons & Company has co-managed over $3.2 billion of public securities offerings.

Simmons & Company conducts its business worldwide. Approximately one third of the firm's clients are internationally headquartered.

How does your approach to finance differ from that of other firms, and what do you consider to be your strengths and distinctive capabilities?

Simmons & Company's success is enhanced by its exclusive focus on the worldwide oil service industry. Through industry specialization, the firm has a unique knowledge base of developments and trends in an historically volatile industry.

The oil service industry is large and diverse. It includes companies supplying products and services for the exploration, production, transportation, and processing of hydrocarbons. The industry is comprised of thousands of participants, including onshore and offshore manufacturing and service companies serving a range of geographical markets.

Simmons & Company is considered the preeminent financial advisor to the oil service industry with its specialization serving as a distinctive competitive advantage over its competition, the large Wall Street investment banking firms. Simmons & Company's market share for transactions in the oil service industry is more than five times any other investment bank.

Several other aspects of the firm's business are different from the majority of its competitors. First, Simmons & Company has a team approach to its business, and in any given year, each Associate has the opportunity to participate as a team member with virtually all other professionals in the firm. Second, the firm maintains strict control over the number and types of projects it undertakes, and has a close rate on committed projects which is as high as any other firm in its business.

Discuss changes in your firm's revenues and professional staff over the past year; over the past five years.

The oil service industry has proved to be one of the more volatile segments of the world economy. Since 1980, the industry has experienced a boom and then a depression of a magnitude unprecedented in any other industry in any historical period. Recently, the operating environment for the industry has improved significantly, particularly in certain offshore and international sectors. This unparalleled volatility has created tremendous opportunities for Simmons & Company. Over the past five years, the firm has doubled its professional staff and revenue base, and increased the international component of its activities.

While growth is expected to continue, the firm intends to remain relatively small and specialized. Simmons & Company's staff now includes eight managing directors, 25 other executives, and a support staff of approximately 20 people. Among our executive group are five HBS graduates.

The Finance MBA's Job Description

Describe the career path and corresponding responsibilities for an MBA at your firm.

The primary objective for an incoming Associate is to gain the experience, judgment, and maturity necessary to assume a leadership role in managing the firm's projects and marketing the firm's services effectively. As an Associate, an MBA can expect to progress through assignments of increasing responsibility toward partnership and ultimate ownership in the firm.

An MBA can expect to have immediate and substantial client contact, including written and oral presentations. Simmons & Company emphasizes analysis, so an Associate should anticipate considerable quantitative work. All projects are organized on a team basis, with one or more Associates and Analysts supporting a Managing Director who serves as project manager. In a typical year, an Associate would work on between 10 and 20 projects and work with virtually every professional with the firm as a member of different project teams.

Discuss the lifestyle aspects of a career with your firm (i.e., average hours per week, amount of travel, flexibility to change offices, corporate culture, etc.).

One of Simmons & Company's enduring corporate goals is to offer a stimulating work environment for its professional staff and those who work with them. The work environment is fast-paced and engrossing, and domestic and international travel is involved; however, work hours and travel requirements do not preclude members of the firm from developing outside interests.

The Recruiting Process

Describe your recruiting process and the criteria by which you select candidates. Is prior experience necessary?

Simmons & Company seeks MBAs with two or more years of professional business experience, strong analytical ability, intellectual curiosity, an ability to work with others, a desire to keep on a fast learning curve, a sense of humor, and a commitment to excellence. A very important criterion for success is the *chemistry* fit with other members of the firm.

The firm's professionals come from remarkably diverse backgrounds. Prior exposure to the oil service industry is not required.

How many permanent associates and analysts do you hire in a typical year? How many summer interns to you expect to hire? If you have a formal summer program, please describe it. Please be sure to indicate whether the summer program is in place for all offices or just some.

Because Simmons & Company is, and plans to remain, a relatively small firm, recruiting for Associates is limited. Recently, two to three Associates have joined the firm each year. Simmons & Company also seeks one to two Associates for summer internships, which provides exposure to all of the firm's corporate finance activities.

Smith Barney Inc.

388 Greenwich Street
New York, NY 10013

MBA Recruiting Contact(s):
Investment Banking
Chip Rae, Senior Vice President
(212) 816-1764
Fax: (212) 816-2839

Anne Hitchcock, Assistant Vice President
(212) 816-1762
Fax: (212) 816-2839

Company Description

Describe your firm's business and the types of clients served by your finance group(s).

Smith Barney is a global securities firm that provides brokerage, investment banking, and asset management services to corporations, governments, and individuals. Our firm includes nearly 28,000 people in more than 500 locations worldwide. Smith Barney has offices throughout the United States, as well as in Amsterdam, Bahrain, Geneva, Hong Kong, London, Paris, Tokyo, Toronto, and Zurich. Strategic alliances with international organizations and our ownership of Atlanta-based Robinson-Humphrey, the nation's leading regional investment bank, expand Smith Barney's capabilities beyond our geographic locations.

We are active in all major sectors of finance and the second largest brokerage firm in the United States. Our core services include sales, research, and trading for individuals and institutions; underwriting, advisory, and specialty financing for corporations and government entities; mutual fund services; and futures and asset management. Smith Barney now manages over $112 billion in assets and oversees client accounts totaling more than $482 billion.

Describe your ownership structure.

Smith Barney's corporate foundations are strong. It is a wholly owned subsidiary of The Travelers Group with more than $151 billion in assets and $13 billion in equity capital. Travelers provides a full range of investment, insurance, and consumer finance services to individual, institutional, and government clients around the world.

How does your approach to finance differ from that of other firms, and what do you consider to be your strengths and distinctive capabilities?

In many ways, Smith Barney is a young company with old roots. We are well established in key markets, yet still in the process of building a unique franchise for the future. Our working environment is entrepreneurial. Individual effort is encouraged and recognized. Initiative is prized. The combination of our investment banking and trading capabilities with the power of our distribution network creates a broad and diversified revenue stream ensuring greater stability.

Our greatest strength is the ability of each business unit to work in close cooperation with the others. We have begun to create a culture that is unique on Wall Street, in which true integration and cooperation exists among investment banking, capital markets, research, asset management, and brokerage. It is a way of doing business that focuses the full force of our resources on the needs of every client, regardless of whether they are municipal governments, global corporations, large institutions, or enterprising individuals.

Discuss changes in your firm's revenues (both domestic and international) and professional staff over the past year; over the past five years.

Smith Barney's operating earnings for 1996 reached a record $889 million on net revenues of $6.3 billion in a year of surging securities markets, record-breaking volume levels, and historical highs in key market indices.

Among key 1996 performance measurements, the firm's after-tax return on equity was 34.5%, the highest of major firms in the securities industry. Pretax profit margins were 23.2%, up from 18.9% in 1995. Non-compensation expenses of 20.8% of net revenues were among the lowest levels in the industry.

The Investment Banking Division managed 707 domestic issues with a par value of $89 billion, and 254 common stock offerings, including 87 initial public offerings. It ranked #5 in the industry on common stock issues, #4 in initial public offerings, and #4 in preferred stock issuance. Equity transaction size averaged $162 million.

With a total of 103 completed merger and acquisition transactions in 1996, the firm ranked #4 in the industry in the number of completed deals. In 1996, the firm advised energy giant Enron Corp. in its acquisition of Portland General Electric Co., a $3.2 billion transaction selected as one of Institutional Investor's "Deals of the Year."

Since mid-1993, the Investment Banking Department has nearly doubled in terms of the number of professionals and now numbers about 400 worldwide. The increase is partly attributable to a targeted hiring program of experienced bankers, as well as an aggressive analyst and associate recruiting strategy.

Smith Barney has grown dramatically and is substantially a different firm from five years ago. Any comparison would not be meaningful.

The Finance MBA's Job Description

Describe the career path and corresponding responsibilities for an MBA at your firm.

Smith Barney's long-term success depends on the quality of individuals hired over time. In 1996–97, Investment Banking hired thirty associates and thirty-six summer associates.

Investment Banking associates initially receive offers to join the firm, with assignments to specific departments determined after acceptance of our offer. Each associate is given the opportunity to meet with a wide variety of departments prior to making a decision.

Associates in Smith Barney's Investment Banking Division are quickly expected to become active contributors to the firm's overall investment banking effort. The organization of the group is structured to offer rapid advancement and outstanding financial rewards to successful associates. Associates work directly with senior members of the Investment Banking Division as well as representatives of other divisions within the firm on a wide variety of transactions and financial projects. Transactions include domestic and international public offerings and private acquisitions, financial consulting projects, tender offers, and mergers and acquisitions. Financial consulting projects range from assisting corporate clients in formulating capitalization and dividend policies to evaluating acquisition or divestiture strategies. In addition, associates participate in the firm's ongoing business development activities.

All new associates start their career with four weeks of intensive classroom training beginning in August. The program focuses on a firmwide orientation, advanced accounting topics, investment banking products, financial statement analysis, financial modeling, taxation and valuation. Projects and case studies are also assigned giving new associates hands-on experience as well as the opportunity to work in teams. Our program also enables associates to take the Series 7 Exam. The training is conducted by Smith Barney professionals, business school professors, and industry experts.

Career paths and corresponding responsibilities vary depending on the business division. An MBA joining Investment Banking, for example, typically enters as an associate, responsible for the details of executing transactions and preparing proposals. After approximately four years, associates are eligible for promotion to vice president. Vice presidents manage the execution of transactions and identify new opportunities with clients.

About three years later, vice presidents become eligible for promotion to director, and several years later to the more senior title of managing director. Directors and managing directors are responsible for ongoing client relationships and identification of new business opportunities.

Describe the opportunities for professional mobility between the various departments in your firm.

First year associates join a specific industry or product group at the conclusion of the training program. Their success is often based on their ability to leverage the firm's resources and to develop contacts across the firm. As an individual's interests change, and as our businesses develop and evolve, new opportunities are often available.

The Recruiting Process

Describe your recruiting process and the criteria by which you select candidates. Is prior experience necessary?

Smith Barney participates in a wide range of campus recruiting events and on-campus interviews. Successful candidates are invited to New York for a final Super Saturday. The firm respects school policies in its recruiting practices.

We seek individuals with a record of achievement. Successful candidates display:

- Demonstrated leadership skills
- Relevant business experience
- Demonstrated work ethic
- Quantitative skills
- Client relationship ability
- Academic excellence
- Maturity and focus

Opportunities for associates also exist in Sales and Trading, Research, Public Finance, and Asset Management. Though these groups do not interview on campus, résumés sent to Anne Hitchcock will be forwarded to the appropriate area.

Stonebridge Associates, LLC

Ten Post Office Square
Suite 1330
Boston, MA 02109
(617) 357-1770
Fax: (617) 357-4933

MBA Recruiting Contact(s):
Patricia B. Davis, Vice President

Company Description

Describe your firm's business and the types of clients served by your finance group(s).

Stonebridge Associates, LLC is a private, Boston-based investment bank which specializes in providing a broad range of corporate finance services to middle market and emerging growth companies. Our primary areas of focus include mergers and acquisitions, divestitures, and private placements of debt and equity securities as well as related corporate advisory services such as fairness opinions, valuations, and restructurings and recapitalizations.

Describe your ownership structure.

Stonebridge has been organized as a limited liability company ("LLC"). An LLC is an unincorporated organization owned by "members" who hold equity "interests" in the organization.

How does your approach to finance differ from that of other firms, and what do you consider to be your strengths and distinctive capabilities?

Stonebridge Associates offers the creativity, technical skills, professional expertise, and global perspective typically found only in large Wall Street investment banking firms. At the same time, we are an investment bank that has consciously chosen to limit the range of its activities and services in order to provide our clients with a level of attention and responsiveness that distinguishes us from larger competitors. The company has not engaged, nor does it intend to engage, in any investment banking services which involve the underwriting or trading of securities. This focus and our capabilities, combined with our structuring and placement skills and broad industry experience, provide us with a distinct advantage in servicing the unique needs of middle market and emerging growth companies.

Stonebridge's emphasis on developing an in-depth understanding of each client's business needs and objectives, committing the resources necessary to provide solutions for complex transactions, providing senior-level attention, commitment, and focus for every transaction, has enabled the company to develop a reputation as a valued and trusted advisor.

The Finance MBA's Job Description

Describe the career path and corresponding responsibilities for an MBA at your firm.

For those candidates possessing capability, commitment, and exhibiting strong performance, there is an opportunity to gain broad and detailed experience in analyzing, structuring, and negotiating client engagements. A successful candidate should be prepared to operate effectively in a team setting within diverse business environments and to ultimately advance in both compensation and responsibility. Responsibilities allocated to staff members are highly challenging and involve a high degree of accountability. The associate participates in every aspect of a transaction from the initial engagement, to the preparation of offering materials, and marketing of the engagements. There is broad-based exposure to investment banking as well as the opportunity to work closely with senior management.

Describe the opportunities for professional mobility between the various departments in your firm.

Given the small size of the firm and the participating role in all tasks, there is both a high degree of mobility and an unprecedented opportunity for exposure to diverse responsibilities and development of investment banking skills and knowledge.

Discuss the lifestyle aspects of a career with your firm (i.e., average hours per week, amount of travel, flexibility to change offices, corporate culture, etc.).

Stonebridge Associates promotes a positive working environment where professionals share a dedication and purpose for doing the best job possible. From time to time, and dependent on deal flow, demands can be intensive; however, the firm encourages a balanced lifestyle. In as much as the firm has one office, transfer or office changes are not a consideration. Overall, there are reasonable travel requirements.

The Recruiting Process

Describe your recruiting process and the criteria by which you select candidates. Is prior experience necessary?

Our hiring needs and organizational structure are closely tied. We recruit through correspondence opportunities and on-campus interviews. We find the process of a successful recruiting program begins with a commitment to an annual recruiting effort. Our criteria by which we select candidates emphasizes proven written and oral communication skills, comfort and familiarity with quantitative analysis, emphasis on integrity, intelligence, interpersonal skills, willingness to work hard, and a teamwork orientation. Prior investment banking or consulting experience is essential and background in technology, engineering, or the healthcare/life science areas is preferred.

How many permanent associates and analysts do you hire in a typical year? How many summer interns do you expect to hire? If you have a formal summer program, please describe it. Please be sure to indicate whether the summer program is in place for all offices or just some.

In a typical year, one graduating MBA student is hired for the associate position and one pre-MBA financial analyst is recruited. We do not offer summer assignments.

Teachers Insurance and Annuity Association-College Retirement Equities Fund (TIAA-CREF)

730 Third Avenue
New York, NY 10017
(800) 842-2733
Web site: www.tiaa-cref.org

MBA Recruiting Contact(s):
Robert J. Burke, Staffing Specialist

Company Description

Describe your firm's business and the types of clients served by your finance group(s).

As the world's largest pension system, with over $165 billion in assets entirely managed internally, TIAA-CREF professionals skillfully invest in virtually every economic sector. TIAA assets are broadly diversified among private placements, publicly traded bonds, commercial mortgages, and real estate. CREF, the companion corporation, is a registered investment company.

Quality and yield are the bedrock of our investment activities. In fact, TIAA is a top performer in the insurance industry, and its strong balance sheets earn the highest possible ratings from Moody's, Standard & Poor's, Duff & Phelps, and A.M. Best.

TIAA-CREF originated a pension system of portable benefits in 1918 to help ensure the financial security of people employed in education and research. Today, over 1.8 million professors, research scientists, and other educators turn to TIAA-CREF for expert benefits counseling, affordable insurance protection, and retirement income that cannot be outlived.

Stable cash flows, innovative strategies, and years of experience make TIAA a leader in direct placement loans to private and public companies, as well as in publicly traded bonds. TIAA also invests in highly structured deals, including private securitized financings, hybrid credit/real estate deals, project financings, and secondary private placements.

The Finance MBA's Job Description

Describe the career path and corresponding responsibilities for an MBA at your firm.

Our steady stream of investment activity is ideal for MBAs who want to put their talent to work immediately, with financings in a broad range of industries. Individual responsibilities are balanced with teamwork at every level, enabling associates to gain broad industry knowledge and market experience.

Specifically, private placement associates monitor portfolios with investments in about 25 companies, valued at about a half-billion dollars. Associates analyze industry trends, make on-site evaluations of potential investments, negotiate new deals, and present recommendations to senior management.

Public market associates evaluate market trends, research bond offerings, develop trading strategies, and present recommendations to senior managers responsible for multibillion-dollar portfolios.

The Recruiting Process

Describe your recruiting process and the criteria by which you select candidates. Is prior experience necessary?

TIAA Investments seeks talented MBAs majoring in finance to join our Securities Division. Superior communications skills and prior credit training and analysis experience at a major financial institution are strongly preferred. Along with quality investing, we emphasize teamwork and a balanced work and personal lifestyle.

A successful screening interview will be followed by an opportunity to meet with Securities officers and associates at our New York City headquarters.

We believe cultural and ethnic diversity is the lifeblood of a successful corporation, and this is reflected in our hiring record, our tradition of promoting from within, and our career development activities.

Toronto Dominion Bank

TD Securities (USA) Inc.

31 West 52nd Street
New York, NY 10019-6101
(212) 468-0633
Fax: (212) 262-1922
Web site: www.tdbank.ca

MBA Recruiting Contact(s):
Reginald A. McQuay, Director
Human Resources

Company Description

Describe your firm's business and the types of clients served by your finance group(s).

Toronto Dominion Bank is a widely held, public corporation whose shares are listed on the Toronto, Montreal, Vancouver, Alberta, Winnipeg, International (London, England), New York, and Tokyo Stock Exchanges. Total assets, as of October 31, 1996, were Cdn. $126 billion. TD is the fifth largest Canadian bank in terms of total assets and on the basis of common shareholders' equity.

Formally titled The Toronto Dominion Bank, but usually referred to as TD Bank or simply TD, the bank was formed in 1955 through the merger of the Bank of Toronto (founded 1855) and the Dominion Bank (established 1869).

In Canada, TD serves individuals, businesses, financial institutions, and governments through a network of over 900 branches from coast to coast. The bank also offers complete trust and fiduciary services in both the personal and business fields.

Internationally, our staff offer a broad range of credit, non-credit, and financial advisory services to businesses, multinational corporations, governments, and correspondent banks through offices in the U.S. and in other financial capitals including Hong Kong, London, Mexico City, Mumbai (India), Santiago (Chile), Singapore, Taipei, Tokyo, and through our subsidiary bank in Australia. We also provide discount brokerage services in Canada, the United States, and Hong Kong. Worldwide, the bank employs over 32,000 people.

A major strength of TD is its financial position. TD maintains a position as one of the best capitalized banks in the world, with one of the highest credit ratings of all major North American banks. Financial strength is a major advantage in tough times; customers may be drawn to a bank offering financial stability that also has the capital to invest in service, to pursue new strategies, and to take advantage of opportunities that arise.

Another strength is that TD, unlike its major competitors, has built, rather than bought, its own securities operation and offers integrated corporate and investment banking services. This provides the bank with an edge in its ability to react innovatively to shifting customer needs and changing economic times.

Since its formal establishment in 1980, the U.S.A. Division of Toronto Dominion has successfully developed a solid Corporate Investment Banking business with noted strength in providing financing and advisory services to the communications, energy, health care, forest products, and public finance industries.

In recent years, TD has committed substantial resources to build a securities business in the U.S. Through the formation of TD Securities (USA) Inc., we continue to develop a broad array of products and services in areas where we can competitively add value to our focused industry niches. Since receiving approval to underwrite and deal in corporate debt and equity securities in the United States, we have built a thriving high yield debt business and a growing institutional equities presence. This has augmented our already strong capabilities in areas such as loan syndication, mergers & acquisitions, and merchant banking.

The Finance MBA's Job Description

Describe the career path and corresponding responsibilities for an MBA at your firm.

The Associate Development Program at TD Securities (USA) Inc., gives a broad understanding of our business strategy, organization, and values; fundamental product knowledge and skills; and the professional contacts and visibility that help integrate an individual into the firm. Following formal orientation, MBAs receive exposure to several areas of the firm which will enhance their skills and knowledge in preparation for the assignment to which they have been hired. After the program, associates typically work in a group charged with researching, structuring, and negotiating transactions. Most individuals will experience several groups during their career with the bank.

The Recruiting Process

Describe your recruiting process and the criteria by which you select candidates. Is prior experience necessary?

To excel as an associate at Toronto Dominion, one must be resourceful, flexible, and exhibit the desire and ability to work independently. While senior colleagues provide career direction, your path toward promotion and advancement is your own.

UBS Securities LLC

299 Park Avenue
New York, NY 10171
(212) 821-4000
Web site: www.ubs.com

MBA Recruiting Contact(s):
Erica Blechschmidt
(212) 821-4080
Fax: (212) 821-5271

Locations of Offices:
New York and San Francisco

Number of Professionals:
Approximately 2,200

Company Description

Describe your firm's business and the types of clients served by your finance group(s).

UBS is a premier resource for strategic advisory services, capital formation, and investment expertise throughout the Americas. At the center of our ability to create solutions with real value are our interdisciplinary client teams. We bring to our work specialized knowledge of leading industries and markets, noted skills in risk management, and access to the worldwide resources and capital strength of Union Bank of Switzerland. For the institutions, corporations, governments, and individuals that we serve, this distinctive combination of capabilities provides exceptional advantages in financial markets on a global scale. Our clients also value our dedication to service, high standards of professionalism, and commitment to building relationships that endure.

UBS offers specialized investment banking and investment management expertise that encompasses financial markets worldwide. Our growing recognition as an industry leader extends across key areas of service, including:

- Investment banking
- Debt and equity capital formation
- Sales, trading, and risk management
- Research
- Asset management/private banking

Describe your ownership structure.

UBS Securities LLC is a wholly owned subsidiary of the Union Bank of Switzerland.

The Finance MBA's Job Description

Describe the career path and corresponding responsibilities for an MBA at your firm.

Investment Banking
Associates in the Investment Banking Division should have the following qualifications: MBA, preferably in finance; superior academic credentials; 2 years' experience within a major financial services firm; excellent financial modeling abilities; strong written and verbal communications skills; high energy; team orientation; and self-motivation.

As members of the Investment Banking Division, Associates are responsible for the quantitative financial analysis as well as the qualitative document issues related to the execution of debt, equity, and merger and acquisition transactions on behalf of corporations, financial institutions, and government entities. Associates work closely with senior investment bankers in the marketing of UBS's services and client development. Assignments will provide exposure to a variety of specialized industry teams and capital market product groups within Investment Banking.

We offer competitive salaries. Investment Banking positions are available in New York, Europe, and Asia.

Trading and Sales Program
We also have a Trading & Sales Training Program. We look for these qualifications: MBA; excellent academic credentials; excellent communication skills; quantitative and analytical abilities; and entrepreneurship, team orientation, and self-motivation.

This program will introduce trainees to all aspects of a trading and sales environment. Trainees will receive a full overview of UBS's activities in North America, including debt and equities trading and capital markets. The remaining months of the sales and trading program will consist of academic sessions and practical rotations through each of the fixed income product areas such as corporate bonds, U.S. government bonds, and mortgage and asset-backed securities and derivatives.

Successful completion of the program will lead to an assignment in one of UBS's trading and sales groups in New York and the opportunity to develop a rewarding and challenging career. We offer a competitive salary.

The Recruiting Process

Describe your recruiting process and the criteria by which you select candidates. Is prior experience necessary?

The people of UBS do not fit any particular mold: we represent a variety of backgrounds, skills, and personalities. The only unifying factors here are intelligence, a strong ethical sense, and a commitment to UBS and its clients. We are looking for individuals who are bright, focused, and highly motivated. Investment banking draws upon a range of analytic and communication skills. Since you are likely to have frequent contact with UBS colleagues and clients abroad, knowledge of a foreign language can also be a benefit. In trading and sales, degree and major requirements vary. However, the nature of the work does require strong quantitative, analytic, and verbal skills, as well as a drive to succeed. Experience in the securities industry is preferred but not required. In a rapidly growing organization such as ours, people with the self-confidence to assert themselves are most likely to flourish. We want people with entrepreneurial drive who can get projects started and see them through to completion—people with fresh ideas and the courage to test them out in the real world.

United Airlines

P.O. Box 66100
Chicago, IL 60666
(708) 952-4000
Web site: www.ual.com

MBA Recruiting Contact(s):
Jim Rynott
College Relations

Company Description

Describe your firm's business and the types of clients served by your finance group(s).

United Airlines is one of the largest international airlines in the world, with annual revenues in excess of $12 billion, more than 76,000 employees, and a fleet of over 500 aircraft.

Headquartered in Chicago, United Airlines flies to 112 domestic and 40 international airports serving 32 countries on five continents. Our United Express partners fly to more than 180 destinations. Domestically, we maintain key hubs in Washington, D.C., Chicago, Denver, and San Francisco.

Independent industry sources rank United Airlines as one of the U.S. "big three" in terms of size and other operating criteria. Much of the airline's recent focus has been expansion into the European Community, South America, and Latin America and continued strengthening of our extensive route structure in the Pacific Basin. In June 1995 we introduced the B777 aircraft into our fleet of modern, spacious, quiet, and fuel-efficient aircraft.

Describe your ownership structure.

United Airlines is 55% employee owned with public shares being traded on the New York Stock Exchange, Midwest Stock Exchange, and the Pacific Stock Exchange under the symbol UAL. A copy of UAL Corporation's annual report to the Securities and Exchange Commission on form 10-K may be obtained from Investor Relations, UAL Corporation, (708) 952-7501.

The Finance MBA's Job Description

Describe the career path and corresponding responsibilities for an MBA at your firm.

MBA professionals who join United are initially assigned to positions in the Finance, Marketing, or Operations areas, providing a range of exposure to management issues. The continued emphasis is to utilize analytical tools to improve our competitiveness in both operations and financial markets. Our company has highly leveraged assets; thus, the goal is to maintain a balance sheet that gives management the freedom to pursue market opportunities competitively.

The Recruiting Process

Describe your recruiting process and the criteria by which you select candidates. Is prior experience necessary?

United Airlines seeks highly motivated individuals who have the ability to work in a team environment across functional organizations. Most MBAs enjoy our fast-paced, project-oriented environment. The majority have two to three years of work experience prior to attending graduate school. Progression is staff analyst, senior staff analyst, manager, and director and is based on a merit performance system.

Wasserstein Perella & Co. Inc.

31 West 52nd Street
New York, NY 10019
(212) 969-2700

MBA Recruiting Contact(s):
Frances A. Lyman, Recruiting Manager

Company Description

Describe your firm's business and the types of clients served by your finance group(s).

Wasserstein Perella Group, Inc. is a leading international investment banking firm active in three related lines of business: (1) advising a global base of clients on matters of corporate strategy, mergers, acquisitions, divestitures and restructurings, and corporate finance; (2) specialized sales, trading, and research of debt and equity securities; and (3) management of investment funds and products that seek superior risk-adjusted returns for investors.

Our firm is dedicated to providing superior client service and building long-term relationships. In pursuit of these goals, Wasserstein Perella has established an international presence through a network of offices in New York, London, Paris, Frankfurt, Tokyo, Chicago, Los Angeles, and Dallas. Our strategic alliance with The Nomura Securities Co., Ltd., the world's largest securities firm, which was formed in 1988, shortly after the firm's founding, gives Wasserstein Perella an unparalleled presence in and access to Japan and the Asian markets. Since its inception, Wasserstein Perella's professional staff has grown to number approximately 200 worldwide.

Wasserstein Perella has participated in many of the largest and most significant mergers and acquisitions in recent history and in some of the most innovative financings. The firm is equally proud of the many small divestitures and other transactions it has managed on behalf of its long-term clients and the numerous occasions when clients have been advised to forego transactions as a result of market or strategic factors. The firm has developed a strong high-yield origination effort targeting financial entrepreneurs and growth companies, and has served as a sounding board for larger clients with respect to various financing alternatives.

Wasserstein Perella's specialized sales, trading, and research activities are carried out through its wholly owned subsidiary, Wasserstein Perella Securities, Inc. ("WPS"). Within WPS, the Grantchester Securities Division is one of the leading dealers of high-yield debt securities. Grantchester traded more than $43 billion of high-yield securities over the last three years and has transacted business with 200 different institutions having varied investment profiles. The WPS Equity Division is a highly focused team that concentrates on the sales, trading, and research of selected equity securities. WPS's Emerging Markets Division provides investor and corporate finance services in the Latin American, Eastern European, African, and Asian markets.

Wasserstein Perella continues to build its asset management capabilities. The firm's focus is on equity and fixed income money management of U.S. securities, selected international products, and an array of higher return, higher risk private investment funds. The cornerstone of this effort to date is the firm's merchant banking fund.

Describe your ownership structure.

Wasserstein Perella is a privately owned corporation. Twenty percent of its equity is held by Nomura Securities, Ltd.

How does your approach to finance differ from that of other firms, and what do you consider to be your strengths and distinctive capabilities?

Wasserstein Perella offers custom-tailored mergers and acquisitions (M&A) and corporate finance solutions to meet clients' unique needs. The firm is known for its ability to solve complex financial and strategic problems. We are also viewed as an objective sounding board for financing decisions, and we are not prejudiced by a need to underwrite securities to cover the overhead of a large underwriting operation.

Discuss changes in your firm's revenues (both domestic and international) and professional staff over the past year; over the past five years.

We have had a gradual diversification of revenues away from domestic M&A toward high-yield and equity sales, trading and research, international M&A, privatizations, and asset management.

The Finance MBA's Job Description

Describe the career path and corresponding responsibilities for an MBA at your firm.

Financial associates at Wasserstein Perella & Co., Inc. are responsible for all aspects of analysis relating to mergers, acquisitions, restructuring, divestitures, and leveraged buyouts. After a relatively short "training" period, associates are expected to be proficient with the fundamental analytical principals of mergers and acquisitions and general corporate finance. Associates will participate in structuring and negotiating M&A transactions and financings and will gain increasing experience and responsibility as they develop expertise in these areas. In addition, associates will play a significant role in the firm's "new business" efforts and ongoing client relationships.

Associates are given responsibilities that are typically one year ahead of those at other investment banks. The typical time period between associate and vice president is three and a half years.

Describe the opportunities for professional mobility between the various departments in your firm.

Wasserstein Perella provides tremendous flexibility between departments and geographic locations.

Discuss the lifestyle aspects of a career with your firm (i.e., average hours per week, amount of travel, flexibility to change offices, corporate culture, etc.).

Lifestyle/culture is characterized as fun and entrepreneurial yet intense. Average hours per week are 60–70. Travel depends on the nature of projects. Associates usually travel 15–25% of their time.

The Recruiting Process

Describe your recruiting process and the criteria by which you select candidates. Is prior experience necessary?

We usually conduct two-on-one on-campus interviews, followed by one or two visits to our New York office. Decisions are usually made quickly. We look for smart, energetic self-starters. Grades and previous experience are important factors.

How many permanent associates and analysts do you hire in a typical year? How many summer interns do you expect to hire? If you have a formal summer program, please describe it. Please be sure to indicate whether the summer program is in place for all offices or just some.

Wasserstein Perella typically hires four to five associates domestically and one to two internationally. We also hire two to three summer associates.

Wessels, Arnold & Henderson

601 Second Avenue South
Suite 3100
Minneapolis, MN 55402
(612) 373-6100
(800) 955-0920
Web site: www.wessels.com

MBA Recruiting Contact(s):
Lisa Hoffmon

Location of Office:
Minneapolis, MN

No. of Professionals:
Approximately 70

Company Description

Describe your firm's business and the types of clients served by your finance group(s).

Wessels, Arnold & Henderson is a rapidly growing institutional investment banking firm based in Minneapolis that focuses on providing high-quality research, sales and trading, and investment banking services to growth companies in the technology, health care, and consumer sectors. Since its inception as a partnership in 1986, Wessels, Arnold & Henderson has focused on selectively building our firm through the hiring of highly motivated professionals. Our strength is our focus on very specific industry sectors and our commitment to building long-term relationships with our clients in order to provide them with the absolute highest level of service.

Wessels, Arnold & Henderson's Corporate Finance staff focuses on the management of public and private equity offerings, merger and acquisition advisory services, fairness opinions, and other financial services to companies in our selected industry sectors. Some of our recent clients include: Ascend Communications, Inc., Atria Software, Inc., CDW Computer Centers, Inc., Check Point Software Technologies, CIENA Corporation, EPIX Medical, Inc., Lonestar Steakhouse & Saloon, PCs Compleat, Inc., Powerwave Technologies, Inc., Rational Software Corporation, and Transition Systems, Inc. Corporate Finance associates work directly with senior investment bankers on these assignments.

The Finance MBA's Job Description

Describe the career path and corresponding responsibilities for an MBA at your firm.

Wessels, Arnold & Henderson seeks to hire MBAs that possess solid academic credentials, are highly competitive, are self-motivated, and have demonstrated the ability to work as part of a team. In return for displaying these attributes, associates will be rewarded with a highly challenging, well-compensated career in a competitive work environment. A typical career path varies depending on the business division. An MBA in corporate finance would typically enter our firm at the associate level and be responsible for the details of executing a transaction. When an associate displays an aptitude for identifying new business opportunities and maintaining client relationships, he or she would be eligible to become a managing director.

At the hub of our company is our Research Department, whose focus and ideas drive the Trading and Corporate Finance Departments. Our research effort is aimed at providing value to our institutional customers by providing a timely, focused product. Analysts identify market segments and companies that will provide investors with outstanding investment growth and also work closely with the Corporate Finance Department to guide the evolution and future focus of the firm. Associate research analysts are teamed with senior analysts and are expected to be the leading analysts in their sectors to the institutional marketplace.

Wessels, Arnold & Henderson's Sales and Trading operations are focused on providing deep and liquid markets in the stocks in which we are market makers. This is essential in order to provide efficient stock prices for growth companies. Historically, Wessels, Arnold & Henderson has always ranked highly in making liquid markets for our universe of stocks.

Weyerhaeuser Company

Tacoma, WA 98477
(206) 924-2367
Web site: www.weyerhaeuser.com

MBA Recruiting Contact(s):
Brian L. Haun, Director
Investment Evaluation Department

Company Description

Describe your firm's business and the types of clients served by your finance group(s).

Weyerhaeuser is the world's largest private owner of timber, a leader in commercial forest management, and one of North America's largest producers and exporters of forest products. Weyerhaeuser also has significant positions in U.S. real estate development and financial services operations.

Timber Growing and Harvesting

Weyerhaeuser Company owns about 5.8 million acres of timberland in the United States with a merchantable volume of over 8.6 billion cubic feet of timber, the largest of any private owner. In addition to company-owned lands in the United States, the company has long-term harvest licenses on approximately 12 million acres of productive forest land in the Canadian provinces of British Columbia, Alberta, and Saskatchewan. The company also grows about 300,000 seedlings a year in company-owned seed orchards, greenhouses, and nurseries. Weyerhaeuser supports the management of these resources with the largest private silvicultural and environmental research staff in the world.

Weyerhaeuser Company is unique in the quality of its timber resource and forest management programs. The company began growing timber as a crop in the 1930s. In 1941 the company publicly committed itself to sustainable yield forestry with the dedication of lands in southwestern Washington as a "Tree Farm," launching the national Tree Farm movement. A High Yield Forestry program was begun in 1966, which more than doubles annual growth per acre over unmanaged natural stands. These early decisions have provided a relatively stable raw material supply, making Weyerhaeuser less dependent on purchased timber and logs than other companies.

Wood Products Manufacturing

Weyerhaeuser is the world's largest producer of softwood lumber and the largest North American exporter of forest products. Weyerhaeuser manufactures a full range of wood products, including logs, lumber, chips, plywood, oriented strandboard, and composite products at 55 locations around the United States and Canada. The company markets and distributes these products through its own sales and distribution system to industrial, wholesale, and retail customers.

Pulp and Paper Manufacturing

Weyerhaeuser is a leading producer of pulp, newsprint, fine paper, containerboard and shipping containers, liquid packaging board, and chemicals with 63 manufacturing sites located throughout the United States and Canada. Weyerhaeuser's Pulp Division is the world's largest supplier of market pulp. The Newsprint Division is the largest foreign supplier of newsprint to Japan. Pulp and paper products are marketed through Weyerhaeuser's own sales and marketing organization, as well as through merchant distributors. The company also operates one of the nation's largest wastepaper recycling businesses. Weyerhaeuser's Recycling Division is almost 20 years old, and has grown rapidly to become one of the largest paper recyclers in the U.S. The company now recycles approximately 1.7 million tons of wastepaper in 20 facilities.

Real Estate Development and Financial Services

Weyerhaeuser Real Estate Company (WRECO), a wholly owned subsidiary of Weyerhaeuser Company, engages in real estate development, residential and commercial building construction, and venture capital projects. These activities are conducted through several operating companies in California, Florida, Maryland, New Jersey, North Carolina, Texas, and Washington. WRECO is one of the largest home builders in the United States. Weyerhaeuser Mortgage Company is one of the nation's largest residential mortgage bankers, with 40 retail branch offices nationwide.

The Finance MBA's Job Description

Describe the career path and corresponding responsibilities for an MBA at your firm.

The Investment Evaluation Department (IED) is the preferred entry point for high-potential MBAs. IED is responsible for providing strategic, financial, and analytical leadership in all acquisition, divestiture, merger, joint venture, and new business evaluations. The group is also responsible for analyzing and forming independent judgments on Weyerhaeuser's major capital investment opportunities. IED is a small group within Weyerhaeuser's finance organization. However, it deals substantially with the company's operating divisions, supporting major strategic and tactical decisions.

The analyst position is the traditional entry point for the department. Analysts typically spend two to three years in IED gaining a broad perspective on Weyerhaeuser's businesses and exposure to senior corporate and operating level managers. The Department's goal is to provide analysts with a good general understanding of Weyerhaeuser businesses as well as the opportunity to get to know many of the company's key managers in preparation for long-term careers in the company. The department project directors and manager provide guidance and advice as needed. Analysts tend to move into a business unit of their choice, gaining experience in their areas of interest (marketing, finance, operations management, etc.) to lead them into general management positions.

Weyerhaeuser evaluates many proposals to expand or reconfigure its business groups. They include acquisition and joint venture opportunities within existing businesses as well as in new business lines. They may also involve divestment or asset redeployment options aimed at upgrading Weyerhaeuser's existing portfolio of assets. The IED analyst is a key member of the team evaluating an opportunity, with primary responsibility for performing the economic analysis. In many instances analysts help develop the strategic framework for the opportunity. The analyst must also ensure that the presentation of the proposal provides senior management with the key information needed to make the decision. After a decision has been reached, analysts participate in the execution by drafting offering memorandums, working with investment bankers, coordinating buyers' due diligence, advising senior managers during negotiations, and evaluating alternative transaction structures.

Weyerhaeuser competes in highly capital-intensive industries and allocates significant capital resources to its existing businesses. IED brings conceptual and analytical leadership to the capital allocation effort. The analyst is primarily responsible for providing decision makers with independent, thorough, and timely economic analyses of diverse investment proposals. This is accomplished by working closely with business and operating groups, often on site. Some recent projects include the expansion of a joint venture newsprint operation with a Japanese partner, multi-stage modernizations and expansions at two Weyerhaeuser's largest pulp and paper complexes, and the reconfiguration of our Southern sawmill capacity to better align with available raw material and product markets.

The Recruiting Process

Describe your recruiting process and the criteria by which you select candidates. Is prior experience necessary?

IED is looking for MBAs who want to leverage their superior analytical ability, strong leadership, and interpersonal skills into a long-term general management career at Weyerhaeuser. New analysts should have significant prior work experience, good business judgment, and a sense of perspective. They should also be comfortable working independently in a relatively unstructured environment.

How many permanent associates and analysts do you hire in a typical year? If you have a summer program, please describe it.

IED hires one to three analysts a year, primarily through recruiting at top MBA schools around the United States. There is no summer program.

Wheat First Butcher Singer

901 East Byrd Street
Riverfront Plaza
Richmond, VA 23219
(804) 782-3516
Fax: (804) 782-3440
Web site: www.wheatfirst.com

MBA Recruiting Contact(s):
Jack Glover, Associate
Karen Hughes, Recruiting Coordinator

Company Description

Describe your firm's business and the types of clients served by your finance group(s).

Wheat First Butcher Singer is a 100% employee owned investment bank headquartered in Richmond, Virginia. Founded in 1934, the company provides a comprehensive range of financial services—including investment banking, securities brokerage, and asset management to individual and institutional investors worldwide. Wheat First employs more than 2,800 people, including 1,031 financial consultants located in 125 branch offices. Wheat First's retail branch system encompasses 17 states and the District of Columbia, and institutional sales offices are located in New York, Los Angeles, Palm Beach, and Richmond.

Wheat First is organized into three primary operating groups: Capital Markets, Private Client, and Investment Management. Capital Markets is comprised of Corporate Finance, Research, Sales and Trading, Taxable Fixed Income, and Municipal Finance. The Private Client Group includes Retail Branch Offices and Fully Disclosed Clearing. The Investment Management Group, which includes Mentor Investment Management, had over $10 billion in assets under management as of December 31, 1996.

Discuss changes in your firm's revenues (both domestic and international) and professional staff over the past year; over the past five years.

Wheat First has grown dramatically in the past five years from $194 million in revenues in fiscal 1991 to $420 million in fiscal 1996, achieving a compound annual growth rate of 16.4% over that period. In the first calendar quarter of 1997, Wheat First ranked 8th nationwide in IPO underwritings and 17th in equity underwritings.

Since 1992, Corporate Finance has completed 289 transactions valued at more than $25.7 billion, including 132 equity offerings totaling $8.7 billion and 72 strategic advisory engagements totaling $10.2 billion. The department focuses on six industry groups and one product group—Communications and Technology, Health Care, Financial Institutions, Furnishings, Textiles and Building Technologies, Retail and Consumer Products, Industrial Products and Services, and REITs—and is establishing itself as the industry leader in all of these areas.

The Finance MBA's Job Description

Describe the career path and corresponding responsibilities for an MBA at your firm.

Upon arriving at Wheat First, new associates in Corporate Finance begin a training program consisting primarily of on-the-job projects and classroom sessions covering various finance, accounting, and legal topics. The first 18 to 24 months are spent as a generalist working on a variety of transactions in several of the industry groups. Upon completion of the generalist program, associates join an industry or a product group working directly with a senior banker to further expand industry and product knowledge. The goal of the program is to expose associates to a rich variety of assignments and maximize the level of client responsibility.

Flat transaction teams allow associates to demonstrate their talents and, if capable, provide the opportunity for them to assume responsibility at an accelerated pace. Transaction teams generally consist of three professionals, including a financial analyst, an associate, and either a managing director or a vice president. Advancement is based on demonstrated ability; there are no predetermined time frames for promotion.

Corporate Finance seeks highly motivated individuals with a demonstrated record of achievement who have the ability to work effectively with clients and other professionals within the firm. Wheat First investment bankers have a diverse background, both with domestic and international experience. Common characteristics of Corporate Finance associates include strong initiative, team-oriented attitude, strong work ethic, and excellent analytical and communication skills. Corporate Finance associates typically have prior investment banking experience before coming to Wheat First.

The Recruiting Process

Describe your recruiting process and the criteria by which you select candidates.

In the fall, Wheat First begins recruiting at the top business schools in the country. Second and third round interviews are held in Richmond. Wheat First has one or two associate "Super Saturdays"—one in December and another in late January. Prospective associates interview one-on-one in half-hour sessions with associates and senior bankers of the department and selected department heads within Capital Markets.

How many permanent associates and analysts do you hire in a typical year? How many summer interns do you expect to hire? If you have a formal summer program, please describe it. Please be sure to indicate whether the summer program is in place for all offices or just some.

The number of associates hired each year depends on Wheat First's internal needs and the demands of the marketplace. Wheat First typically hires five to ten associates per year.

William Blair & Company

222 West Adams Street
Chicago, IL 60606
Web site: www.wmblair.com

MBA Recruiting Contact(s):
Brent Felitto
Corporate Finance
(312) 364-8013

Kent Brown
Debt Finance
(312) 364-8952

David Farina
Research
(312) 364-8918

Robert Newman
Investment Management
(312) 364-8783

Locations of Offices:
Chicago, San Francisco, London, Liechtenstein, and Zurich

Total Number of Professionals (U.S. and worldwide):
350

Company Description

Describe your firm's business and the types of clients served by your finance group(s).

William Blair & Company is a limited liability corporation offering a full range of investment banking and brokerage services to corporations, institutions, municipalities, and private investors across the United States and overseas. William Blair & Company is the largest full-service investment banking firm headquartered in Chicago with over 635 employees.

The firm was founded over 60 years ago to serve small and medium-sized companies and to participate in their growth through equity and debt financings; research, market making, trading, as well as other forms of aftermarket support; and financial advisory services such as merger and acquisition advice. To that end, the firm's Corporate Finance and Debt Finance Departments have continued to perform originating, structuring and distributing securities for middle-market companies while also assisting not-for-profit organizations and municipalities with their financing needs. William Blair's Mezzanine Debt Fund, Leveraged Capital Fund, and Venture Capital divisions also focus on providing capital for and making private equity investments in a variety of middle-market growth companies. The firm's Research Department is widely recognized as one of the industry's best in providing research coverage of small to mid-size growth companies in the United States, following approximately 250 companies and a number of specific industries. Finally, the firm's Investment Management Department currently manages approximately $8.0 billion for high-net-worth individuals, trusts, foundations, charitable and university endowments, pension and profit-sharing funds, and mutual funds.

Describe your ownership structure.

William Blair & Company is a limited liability corporation (LLC) registered to do business as a member of the New York Stock Exchange. As of December 31, 1995, the firm's capital position was stated at $85 million. There are currently 133 principals and 635 employees. The firm is entirely owned by the active principals.

How does your approach to finance differ from that of other firms, and what do you consider to be your strengths and distinctive capabilities?

Throughout the history of William Blair & Company, we have held fast to the objectives upon which the firm was founded: to identify moneymaking ideas for our investing clients and to provide superior execution for our corporate and public issuers. We have accomplished these goals by focusing on identifying high-quality long-term investment opportunities, by providing the highest standards of service, and by being conservative in the way we operate our business and advise our clients. Over the past six decades, we are proud to have helped our clients achieve superior investment returns and attractive financing in both good and bad markets.

Our long-term orientation permeates every aspect of our operations. Our ownership structure provides underlying stability and fosters longevity with the firm. Clients benefit from a continuity of performance and a personal familiarity with their needs that come only from long-standing relationships. Over time, the firm has expanded the scope of its investment banking and brokerage services to ensure our clients' enduring financial growth.

Today, William Blair strives to serve its clients as it has in the past: with prudent judgment, sound advice, and diligent follow-through. We appreciate the confidence our clients have in our abilities. Every day, in all aspects of our business, we work to preserve their trust.

Discuss changes in your firm's revenues (both domestic and international) and professional staff over the past year; over the past five years.

Despite the volatile nature of the securities industry and the downsizing of major Wall Street firms over the last several years, William Blair has continued to expand. In fact, all of the firm's departments have undergone considerable growth recently. Over the past five years, the Corporate Finance Department has increased from 15 to 30 banking professionals; the Fixed Income Department from 11 to 17 banking professionals; the Research Department has grown from 15 to 25 professionals; and the Investment Management Department has grown from 11 to 34 professionals. The growth in these departments is indicative of the growth of the entire firm.

William Blair & Company has also expanded its international presence both domestically and internationally by adding offices in San Francisco and Zurich.

The Finance MBA's Job Description

Describe the career path and corresponding responsibilities for an MBA at your firm.

William Blair & Company seeks qualified MBAs who desire to work with mid-sized companies, institutions, municipalities, and investors throughout the country. William Blair & Company recruits these individuals on a continual basis as the firm continues to grow. The firm feels the most effective "Training Program" it can offer is immediate exposure to the industry. New associates do not undergo any outside coursework but rather are assigned to live projects from the start.

Corporate Finance

Associates in Corporate Finance work in small project teams that typically include a principal, an associate, and an analyst. Associates work with multiple teams on a number of assignments simultaneously, including transactions such as equity offerings, mergers and acquisitions, private placements, as well as other financial advisory projects. From the time they are hired, associates act as "generalists," providing them with the flexibility to explore a broad array of industries, clients, and transactions. A decentralized, collegial and results-oriented management style creates an entrepreneurial atmosphere that both encourages and rewards a high degree of initiative. William Blair expects each MBA that it hires as an associate to become a principal of the firm.

Research

Research analysts typically cover up to fifteen companies in a sector such as health care, retail, technology, finance, and services. New hires select their own area of coverage, although most likely in an area that the MBA had prior work experience. William Blair & Company believes that the best training for a new MBA hire is "on the job" as new hires start researching companies from day one. New hires will have a senior analyst mentor as a guide. Nonetheless, the new hire will be responsible for choosing their own investment ideas and executing those ideas. Besides the researching of investment ideas, analysts are often involved in the underwriting process as well as the marketing of the ideas to institutional and retail customers. Roughly half of the analysts in the departments are principals.

Debt Finance

MBAs joining the Debt Finance Department enter as associates with responsibilities that include preparing proposals and marketing materials, assisting in marketing, working with clients on a daily basis, and overseeing details related to the execution of a transaction. Associates work in the fields of corporate debt, financing for not-for-profit institutions, hospitals and higher education entities, as well as for municipalities. This broad exposure provides a thorough understanding of the fixed income industry, the challenges of working on several financings at once, and the opportunity to be a "generalist" rather than an expert in only one facet of the industry. The day-to-day operations of the department and its team approach are similar in structure to the Corporate Finance Department.

Investment Management

The Investment Management Department at William Blair is composed of 34 investment professionals. The bulk of these are portfolio managers, about half of whom have research backgrounds and follow a number of stocks, in addition to their account responsibilities. The balance are full-time analysts. The research function in investment management is designed to complement and supplement the William Blair research product. This is done by following companies that have the following attributes: (1) they meet the William Blair criteria for high-quality growth companies; (2) they are desirable for the construction of well-diversified portfolios and; (3) for reasons having to do with either size or industry affiliation, they are not followed by the William Blair Research department. A new MBA would typically start out as an analyst and be responsible for developing a coverage list of stocks for the department to invest in, over an initial period of at least four to five years. Over the long term, both analytical and portfolio management career tracks are available, with both potentially leading to an invitation to become a principal in the firm. Currently, 16 members of the department are principals in the firm.

Describe the opportunities for professional mobility between the various departments in your firm.

Associates are hired to work within a specific department, although there is open communication between all departments of the firm. The firm addresses the needs of individuals who desire to change their focus and switch departments on an individual basis and after taking into consideration the needs of the firm.

Describe the lifestyle aspects of a career with your firm (i.e., average hours per week, amount of travel, flexibility to change offices, corporate culture, etc.).

A career at William Blair is exciting and rewarding and requires a significant commitment of time and energy. One's average hours and travel schedule will vary depending upon market conditions as well as the number and types of projects on which one is working. People who work at William Blair, however, generally seem to enjoy the lifestyle offered by a career with the firm and fostered by its location in Chicago. In addition, the relatively small size of the firm relative to Wall Street standards tends to encourage close relationships among co-workers, while the firm's long-term commitment to its employees and the broad partnership is representative of the firm's inclusive, not exclusive, culture.

The Recruiting Process

Describe your recruiting process and the criteria by which you select candidates. Is prior experience necessary?

William Blair's recruiting process varies across departments. While Corporate Finance and Research participate in on-campus interviewing, Debt Finance and Investment Management welcome on-site interviewing through correspondence opportunities. William Blair & Company adheres to school policies in its recruiting practices.

William Blair & Company hopes to attract highly motivated, quality individuals with strong quantitative, communicative, and interpersonal skills. In addition to demonstrating these skills, prior work experience, academic performance, and community service activities are considered in an applicant's evaluation.

How many permanent associates and analysts do you hire in a typical year? How many summer interns do you expect to hire? If you have a formal summer program, please describe it. Please be sure to indicate whether the summer program is in place for all offices or just some.

Hiring is based on the needs of each department. Typically, recruiting goals are set in the fall of the coming recruiting season; however, given the size and nature of the firm and our recruiting process, interviewing occurs on a continuous basis throughout the year. Summer associates are rare across divisions; however, opportunities sometimes present themselves depending on the staffing needs of each department.

The World Bank

The Young Professionals Program

1818 H Street, NW
Washington, DC 20433
(202) 473-0312
Web site: www.worldbank.org

MBA Recruiting Contact(s):
Young Professionals Program Administrator
Fax: (202) 522-3741
E-mail: Young Professionals Program@worldbank.org

Company Description

Describe your firm's business and the types of clients served by your finance group(s).

The World Bank, which consists of the International Bank for Reconstruction and Development (IBRD) and the International Development Association (IDA), promotes economic and social progress in developing nations by helping raise productivity so people may lead better and fuller lives. This is also the aim of the International Finance Corporation (IFC), which works closely with private investors from around the world in promoting commercial enterprises in developing countries. The principal objective of the Multilateral Investment Guarantee Agency (MIGA) is to encourage the flow of investments for productive purposes among member countries and in particular to developing member countries, thus supplementing the activities of the IBRD, IDA, and IFC.

The IBRD, IDA, IFC, and MIGA (collectively known as the World Bank Group) have three interrelated functions: to lend funds; to provide advice, consulting services, and investment promotion; and to serve as a catalyst to stimulate investments by others. The four institutions are closely associated, with IDA, IFC, and MIGA being affiliates of the IBRD. The same president serves all four institutions. The IBRD and IDA (which are jointly referred to as "the Bank") share the same operational staff, while the staff of IFC and MIGA is, for the most part, separate from that of the Bank.

The IBRD, IDA, and IFC differ in the types of financing that they provide for member developing countries. The IBRD makes loans at interest rates that reflect the Bank's cost of borrowing, while IDA provides concessionary financing for the poorest developing countries. Unlike the IBRD and IDA, IFC loans are not government-guaranteed. Rather, the corporation makes loans to private-sector companies at commercial interest rates. The IFC also takes equity positions in companies. MIGA, on the other hand, provides guarantees for non-commercial risks and also policy and advisory services to encourage the flow of capital to developing countries and to assist these countries in creating an attractive investment climate.

Describe your ownership structure.

The IBRD, established in 1945, is the oldest and largest of the institutions. It was conceived at the United Nations Monetary and Financial Conference held in Bretton Woods, New Hampshire (U.S.A.) in July 1944. The IFC was established in 1956, and IDA in 1960. MIGA began its operations in 1988.

The IBRD, IDA, IFC, and MIGA are owned by their member governments and controlled by their board of directors. To date, 178 countries have joined the IBRD. Membership in IDA is open to all members of the IBRD, and most countries have joined. The IFC has 165 member countries. As of July 1995, 152 countries had signed the MIGA Convention and 128 had completed the ratification process.

Most of the funds lent by the IBRD come from its borrowing in the world's capital markets. It also receives funds from the capital subscriptions of member countries, repayments on past loans, and sales of loans to other investors. Funding for IDA comes almost entirely from grants provided by its more affluent member countries and from contributions by the IBRD from its net income. The IFC obtains funds from its member governments and from borrowing, mainly from international financial markets. MIGA is financially and legally independent and obtains its funds from its member governments.

The Job Description

Describe the career path and corresponding responsibilities for an MBA at your firm. Describe the opportunities for professional mobility between the various departments in your firm. Discuss the lifestyle aspects of a career with your firm.

Young Professionals move across sectors and regions over the course of their careers. Their two rotational assignments in the program and first regular assignment often expose them to two or more Bank regions within the World Bank Group.

There is no typical career path for a Young Professional. Former Young Professionals work throughout the organization in a variety of staff and managerial positions. They usually start out as financial analysts/economists or investment officers.

Financial analysts and sector economists help identify, appraise, and work with clients in the implementation of projects. Many Young Professionals find themselves working on the appraisal and supervision of projects for, say, a country's financial sector development.

Investment officers in the finance complex manage specific portfolios, conduct risk analysis, experiment with innovative products, and monitor the returns on investments. They also coordinate the work of investment teams and develop investment strategies and support systems.

Operational staff travel three or four times a year to the countries they work on, with such missions generally lasting about three weeks.

The Recruiting Process

Describe your recruiting process and the criteria by which you select candidates. Is prior experience necessary?

The Young Professionals Program (YPP) was established in 1963 as a means of recruiting outstanding recent university graduates. Since then, over 1,000 young professionals (YPs) from over 100 different countries have joined the World Bank Group. The majority of all YPs recruited are still with the organization.

The YPP offers an exciting beginning to a career in the World Bank Group for people under 32 years of age as of January of the selection year, who have strong qualifications in finance, economics, or a related field. We encourage qualified candidates from all member countries to apply. As you consider whether or not to apply, please note the following information.

To apply to the program, candidates must have a master's degree (or equivalent) in finance, economics, or a technical field used in the group's operations, plus a minimum of two years of relevant work experience. The technical fields of particular interest to the Bank Group are education, public health, social sciences, urban planning, and civil engineering.

Fluency in English is required of candidates to the YPP. It is also beneficial that candidates have a speaking proficiency in one or more of the Bank's other most commonly used languages (i.e., Arabic, Chinese, French, Portuguese, and Spanish). Increasingly, proficiency in one or more languages of Eastern Europe and Central Asia is also being sought in YP candidates.

The YPP does not recruit individuals whose primary graduate-level training and work experience are in disciplines such as law, computer science, accounting, marketing, linguistics, etc. Candidates with specializations in those areas should contact the Staffing Division directly.

We are now reviewing applications for our upcoming selection (March of next year). Should you be selected to proceed to the second phase of the screening process, you will be required to complete a more detailed application package. For this reason, it is to your advantage to submit a detailed résumé prior to the annual recruitment visit in October, so that you could attend preliminary interviews. Any applications received after the final deadline will be held for review for the next selection.

How many permanent associates and analysts do you hire in a typical year? How many summer interns do you expect to hire? If you have a formal summer program, please describe it. Please be sure to indicate whether the summer program is in place for all offices or just some.

Competition for the YPP is high. Each year, about 30 YPs are selected from a pool of over 5,000 applicants from around the world. Therefore, many candidates whose qualifications exceed the minimum requirements of the program cannot be selected. In fact, in recent selections, successful candidates have generally exceeded the requirements for education and work experience. The average age for selected YPs has been 29. Those YPs with master's-level degrees (in finance, economics, or a technical field) had an average of five years of work experience in areas relevant to the operations of the World Bank Group. Most have gained familiarity with the issues facing developing countries, through work experience, focused study, or extended periods living and traveling in one or more developing countries.

The World Bank's Summer Employment Program is open to students who are nationals of the Bank's member countries, and attracts a large number of highly qualified candidates. The SEP hires approximately 150 summer interns each year. Candidates must have at least a bachelor's degree and be full-time degree-seeking graduate students in both Spring and Fall semesters. The program generally requires experience in business concentrations, such as economics, finance, accounting, and statistics. Computer skills, relevant work experience, and familiarity with one or more languages other than English would be useful. Needs also occur in other disciplines, such as agriculture, environment, information systems, and the social sciences. The Bank pays a monthly salary to all Summer Assistants and provides a travel allowance to contribute to travel expenses, where applicable. The Bank does not offer unpaid or volunteer positions. All summer positions are located in Washington, D.C. The SEP Office is open from December through June of each year. Applications must be received by January 31. Interested candidates may call (202) 473-0309, or send their inquiries to the attention of: The Summer Employment Program, The World Bank, 1818 H Street, N.W., Washington, DC 20433.

Glossary of Finance Terms

Excerpted from Doing Deals: Investment Banks at Work *by Robert G. Eccles and Dwight B. Crane (Boston: Harvard Business School Press, 1988). The following terms and definitions are intended to explain terms used in* Doing Deals *and do not necessarily cover all possible meanings of the terms.*

Arbitrage: occurs when there is an opportunity to buy one security and sell another security and make a riskless profit. An arbitrage opportunity exists when two securities are mispriced relative to each other, so that it is possible to buy one and sell the other and make a risk-free profit. In the investment banking context, the term *arbitrage* is often used to refer to an activity when an acquisition is announced at a higher price than the current stock price of the target firm. The risk arbitrage department of an investment bank then decides whether to buy the stock to take advantage of the higher offer price.

Asset-Backed Securities: a security backed by a pool of assets, such as automobile loans. The cash flow from the pool of assets is used to make interest and principal payments on the securities.

Asset Valuations: usually refers to the valuation of assets in a merger and acquisition transaction. An investment bank is asked to estimate the value of the various parts of the firm that might be acquired.

Block Trading: trading of a large quantity of securities. The New York Stock Exchange considers a block trade to be equal to ten thousand or more shares.

Bond: see **Debt.**

Bought Deal: in securities underwriting, a firm commitment to purchase an entire issue outright from the issuing company. In recent years this term has been used to mean a firm commitment by one or a small number of investment banking firms.

Boutique: a small, specialized securities firm that deals with a limited clientele and offers a limited product line . . . [e.g.,] with advisory services for issuers.

Bridge Loan: a short-term loan made by an investment bank to facilitate a transaction. It is made in anticipation of a security issue that would repay the loan.

Call Date: the date on which issuers have the right to call in or redeem outstanding bonds before their scheduled maturity.

Capital Markets Desk: a group of investment bankers who typically sit on the trading floor. They provide a direct link between issuing customers and the market.

Collaterized Mortgage Obligation (CMO): a security backed by mortgage bonds. The cash flows from the mortgage bonds are typically separated into different portions (e.g., they can be separated into short-, intermediate-, and long-term portions of the mortgages). Each class is paid a fixed rate of interest at regular intervals.

Co-Manager: works with a lead manager and often a group of other co-managers to manage a security underwriting.

Commercial Paper: a short-term debt with maturities ranging from 2 to 270 days, issued by corporations and other short-term borrowers.

Common Stock: a security representing ownership in a public corporation. Owners are entitled to vote on the selection of directors and other corporate matters. They typically receive dividends on their holdings, but corporations are not required to pay dividends. In the event that a corporation is liquidated, the claims of creditors and preferred stockholders take precedence over the claims of those who own common stock.

Convertible Bond: a bond that can be exchanged for a specified number of shares of common stock.

Credit Rating: typically refers to bond and commercial paper ratings assigned by Standard & Poor's, Moody's, or other credit-rating agencies.

Debt: a security that indicates a legal obligation to a borrower to repay principal and interest on specified dates. It is a general name for bonds, notes, mortgages, and other forms of credit obligations.

Distribution: the sale of a new security issue to investors.

Divestiture: the sale of a corporate asset such as a division.

Due Diligence: a process investment banks undertake to assure that information provided in a security offering is accurate.

Earnings per Share (EPS): the net income of a corporation divided by the number of shares outstanding.

Equity: represents ownership in a public corporation as evidenced by holding of common stock or preferred stock.

Eurobond: bond denominated in U.S. dollars or other currencies and sold to investors outside the country whose currency is used (e.g., a U.S. corporation could issue U.S. dollar-denominated securities to European investors).

Fixed-Income Security: a security that pays a fixed rate of return, such as a fixed rate of interest on a corporate bond.

Floating-Rate Debt: a security with interest payments that vary or "float" in response to prevailing interest rates, such as U.S. Treasuries.

Full-Service Firm: an investment bank that offers a wide range of financial services. The term is also used to refer to securities firms that have both extensive retail brokerage and investment banking services for large institutions.

Hedge: an investment strategy used to reduce risk. It typically involves the purchase or sale of contracts designed to offset the change in value of another security.

Hostile Takeover: an acquisition that takes place against the wishes of the management and board of directors of the target company.

Initial Public Offering (IPO): a corporation's first offering of common stock to the public.

Institutional Investor: an organization that holds and trades large volumes of securities such as pension funds, life insurance companies, and mutual funds.

International Bond: a bond issued outside the home country of the borrowing entity. International bonds can be subdivided into Eurobonds and foreign bonds. Foreign bonds are bonds sold primarily in the country of the currency of the issue.

Investment-Grade Bonds: typically regarded as a bond with a credit rating of A or better.

Junk Bond: see **Noninvestment-Grade Bond.**

Lead Manager: works with a group of co-managers to form a syndicate to underwrite a security issue. A lead manager normally "runs the books" (manages the underwriting and determines distribution allocation) and is usually the investment bank that originated the deal.

League Table Rankings: published in various trade magazines that rank security underwriters by the volume of securities underwritten.

Lease: a contract granting use of real estate, equipment, or other fixed assets for a specified period of time in exchange for a series of payments.

Leveraged Buyout (LBO): the purchase of a company, or part of a company, using borrowed funds. The target company's assets frequently serve as security for the loans taken out by the acquiring firm. These loans are then repaid out of the acquired company's cash flow.

Make a Market: trading a security in order to provide liquidity and market prices to investors.

Master Limited Partnership: a limited partnership comprises a general partner, who manages a project and limited partners, who invest money but have limited liability. Frequently, limited partnerships are found in real estate and in oil and gas. A master limited partnership is a limited partnership that is publicly traded to give the investors liquidity.

Merchant Banking: in the context of U.S. investment banking, *merchant banking* refers to activities in which the firm commits its own capital to a transaction, as it does with bridge loans or when it makes equity investments in a company.

Mergers and Acquisitions (M&A): a general term that refers to various combinations of companies. A merger occurs when two or more companies combine; an acquisition occurs when one company takes over a controlling interest in another. M&A groups in investment banks work on these transactions, and they also advise on other kinds of related transactions, such as divestitures and repurchase of significant amounts of corporate stock.

Money-Market Paper: a short-term instrument such as commercial paper that is purchased by corporations and institutions that hold short-term liquid investment portfolios.

Money-Market Preferred Stock: a preferred stock instrument that has been structured to appeal to short-term investors such as investors that purchase regular money-market paper. The preferred stock is repriced every forty-nine days so that it trades like an instrument with a forty-nine-day maturity. From the point of view of the buyer, the advantage of preferred stock is that corporate holders of preferred and other stock only pay income tax on 15% of the dividend.

Mortgage-Backed Security: a security backed by a pool of mortgages. The cash flow from the pool of mortgages is used to make interest and principal payments on the security.

Noninvestment-Grade Bonds: technically, bonds with credit ratings of less than A. They are typically issued by companies without a long track record of sales and earnings or by companies that have experienced difficulty and have questionable credit strength. These securities are often used as a means to finance takeovers.

Origination: obtaining a mandate from an issuer to manage the underwriting and distribution of a new security issue.

Preferred Stock: a class of security that lies somewhere between bonds and common stock. Like interest on debt, dividends are paid on preferred stock at a specified rate, and holders of preferred stock take precedence over holders of common stock in the payment of dividends and liquidation of assets. Creditors, however, are ahead of preferred stockholders in the event of liquidation, and the company does not have a legal obligation to pay preferred stock dividends. Most preferred stock is cumulative, so that if the dividends are not paid for any reason, they accumulate and must be paid before dividends are paid to common stockholders.

Preliminary Prospectus: the first document released by an underwriter describing a new issue to prospective investors. It offers financial details about the issue but does not contain all of the information that will appear in the final prospectus. Portions of the cover page of the preliminary prospectus are printed in red ink, so it is popularly called a red herring.

Primary Market: the first time a security is sold to investors.

Private Placement: securities that are directly placed with an institutional investor, such as an insurance company, rather than sold through a public issue. Private placements do not have to be registered with the Securities and Exchange Commission, so these placements can occur more rapidly and with less information made available to the public.

Recapitalization: a change in a corporation's capital structure such as when the corporation exchanges bonds for outstanding stock. Some companies have been recapitalized in this fashion to make them less attractive targets for takeover.

Refinancing: when outstanding bonds are retired by using proceeds from the issuance of new securities. Refinancings are undertaken to reduce the interest rate or to otherwise improve the terms of the outstanding debt.

Restrictive Covenants: terms in a debt agreement that are designed to protect the creditor's interests. Covenants normally cover such matters as minimum amounts of working capital, maximum debt-equity ratios, and limits on dividend payments.

Retail Distribution: the capability of a securities firm to distribute securities to individual investors through retail brokers.

Secondary Trading: trading of securities which have already been issued in the primary marketplace. Thus, proceeds of secondary-market sales accrue to selling dealers and investors, not to the companies that originally issued the securities.

Securities and Exchange Commission (SEC): the federal agency created by the Securities Exchange Act of 1934 to administer that act and the Securities Act of 1933. The SEC is made up of five commissioners, appointed by the president. The statutes they administer are designed to promote full public disclosure and protect the investing public against malpractice in the securities markets. All issues of securities in the United States must be registered with the SEC.

Shelf Registration (Rule 415): a rule adopted by the SEC in 1982 that allows a corporation to preregister a public offering of securities. That is, they can preregister for up to two years prior to a public offering of securities. Once the security has been registered it is "on the shelf" and the company can go to market with the security as conditions become favorable.

Special Bracket Firm: an investment banking firm that leads the bulk of securities underwritten in the United States. The six special bracket firms [in 1987] are First Boston; Goldman, Sachs; Merrill Lynch; Morgan Stanley; Salomon Brothers; and Shearson Lehman Brothers.

Swap: has two meanings in the context of the securities markets. First, *swap* refers to the act of swapping from one type of security to another, such as an investor who swaps out of bonds into equities. Second, in a more recent use of the word, *swap* refers to debt obligations that are swapped between two borrowers (e.g., a borrower with floating-rate debt may swap its interest payment obligations with a borrower of fixed-rate debt; thus, the floating-rate debt issuer converts its debt into a fixed-rate obligation).

Syndicate: a group of investment banks that agree to purchase a new issue of securities from an issuer for resale to the investment public. These investment banks agree to underwrite the securities. That is, they guarantee to purchase the securities. This group of banking firms is normally part of the selling group that distributes the security to the ultimate investors.

Syndicate Desk: coordinates the underwriting function of an investment bank. It helps price the security, works with the other members of the syndicate, and determines the allocation between retail and institutional investors.

Tax-Exempt Bond: a bond whose interest is exempt from taxation by federal, state, or local authorities. It is frequently called a municipal bond even though it may have been issued by a state government or agency or by an entity that is not a municipality. General obligation bonds are backed by the full faith and credit of the issuing entity. These bonds may be underwritten by commercial banks as well as by investment banks. Revenue bonds are backed by the anticipated revenues of the issuing authority. Under present legislation, commercial banks may not underwrite revenue bonds.

Tender Offer: an offer to buy shares of a corporation for cash or securities, or both, often with the objective of taking control of a target company. The Securities and Exchange Commission requires a corporate investor accumulating 5% or more of a target company to disclose the investment.

Thrift Institution: the major forms of thrift institutions are savings and loans and savings banks. These and other organizations receive consumer savings deposits and invest most of their assets in residential mortgages.

Tombstone: an advertisement placed in newspapers and magazines by investment bankers to announce an offering of securities. It gives basic details about the issue and lists the underwriting group members in a manner that indicates the relative size of their participation.

Underwrite: securities firms underwrite a securities issue by assuming the risk of buying the issue and then reselling the securities to the public either directly or through dealers.

U.S. Treasuries: securities issued by the federal government to borrow money.

Wirehouse: a national or international brokerage firm that has a large retail network of branch offices.

Finance Career Resources

Carol J. Elsen, Corporate Reports/Business Information Librarian
Sue Marsh, Director of Information Services
Baker Library
Harvard Business School

For those MBAs expanding their job search to companies not included in this book, the following bibliography provides additional job search resources. Directories provide additional companies and company information, rank companies, track industry trends and statistics, and often provide background information on the industry. The journals cited are important for understanding and keeping abreast of recent trends and activities. The Internet addresses provide additional ways to find information on careers in finance, job openings, and current industry, company, and market information.

Directories

America's Corporate Finance Directory. New Providence, NJ: National Register Publishing Company. Focuses on public and private U.S. companies with revenue income and/or pension assets over $100 million per year. Large subsidiaries of foreign companies are also included. The listing for each firm includes financial data, key executives, outside service firms, description of business, personnel, and area of responsibility. Indexes include financial responsibility, company, SIC code, geography, who's where, private companies, and an integrated company index. Annual companion to the *Corporate Finance Sourcebook.*

British Venture Capital Association. *Membership Directory.* London: British Venture Capital Association. Includes a list of full members and lists of associate members by type (financial organizations, professional advisors, academic and honorary). Company profiles include address, telephone and fax numbers, type of organization, funds managed, investment preferences, portfolio size, and contact names. Annual.

Corporate Finance Sourcebook. New Providence, NJ: National Register Publishing Company. Nineteen types of capital funding and management firms, including venture capitalists, major private lenders, commercial financiers and factors, lessors, commercial and investment banks and bankers, intermediaries, pension managers, cash managers, corporate and real estate services, business insurance brokers, and CPAs. Data concerning firms vary according to types of activity. Over 3,700 firms are covered. Also included is a three-year financing retrospective listing all corporate public offerings. Annual companion to *America's Corporate Finance Directory.*

Directory of Buyout Financing Sources. New York: Securities Data Publishing. Detailed profiles of more than 600 firms worldwide that provide debt and equity financing for buyouts. Arranged alphabetically within U.S. and foreign sections, information includes addresses, principals, services offered, and the types of transactions. Indexes include a list of leveraged buyout professionals, industry preferences, international activities, and companies. Emphasis is on U.S. firms. Annual companion to the *Directory of M&A Intermediaries.*

Directory of M&A Intermediaries. New York: Securities Data Publishing. Over 770 investment banks, business brokers, law firms, and their intermediaries throughout the world. Contains articles on mergers and acquisitions and leveraged buyouts. The U.S. listings are by state; foreign firms are listed alphabetically. Entries include name and title, type of firm, affiliation, services offered, percentage of intermediary work and other financial services, transaction, geographic and industry preferences, and types of principal clients. Indexes are by industry preference, professionals, areas of international activities, and type of firm. Annual companion to the *Directory of Buyout Financing Sources.*

Directory of Private Equity Investors. New York: Securities Data Publishing. This directory provides profiles of 450 capital sources in the field of private equity. There are articles on private equity and detailed profiles of the larger investors. There are several sections of short directory listings for investment advisors, public pension plans, corporate pension plans, endowments and foundations, insurance companies, and financial corporations. There are indexes by company name, personnel, location (U.S. state), investment interest, and assets under management. Annual.

EVCA Yearbook. London: Ernst & Young; European Venture Capital Association. This is a comprehensive survey of the European private equity and venture capital industry. Statistics on European private equity are listed overall and by country. There is also a directory of the members of the European Venture Capital Association, listed by country. Annual.

Financial Yellow Book. New York: Leadership Directories. Over 1,100 public and private U.S. financial institutions, 41,000 executives and board members, and 4,100 subsidiaries are covered in this directory. Profiles for each company include name, address, e-mail address, officers, subsidiaries, divisions, affiliates, and board of directors. Indexes by type of organization, geography, and personal name. Semiannual.

Fitzroy Dearborn International Directory of Venture Capital Funds. Chicago: Fitzroy Dearborn. This directory covers over 1,000 funds and is arranged in five sections: General Companies; High Technology/Medical Funds; Minority and Socially-Useful Funds; Strategic Partners; and Venture Capital Funds outside the U.S. Entries include address, phone, e-mail, year founded, average and minimum investment, industry group preferences, and portfolio companies. There are alphabetical, geographic, personnel, and category (investment preference) indexes. Annual.

Guide to Venture Capital in Asia. Hong Kong: AVCJ Holdings Limited. Sections include a history and prospective of venture capital in seventeen countries in the Asia Pacific region, details of the industry by country, and profiles of 490 venture capital firms operating in Asia. Company name, location, fund, and name indexes are included. There is a geographical index as well as a listing of venture capital associations in Asia. Charts and graphs. Annual.

Major Financial Institutions of Europe. London: Graham & Trotman. Countries covered: Austria, Belgium, Denmark, Eire, Finland, France, Germany, Greece, Italy, Luxembourg, the Netherlands, Norway, Portugal, Spain, Sweden, Switzerland, and the United Kingdom. Arranged by country, information varies. Listings include directors, board members, principal activities, principal shareholders, number of employees, parent companies, and subsidiaries. Alphabetical index to all companies. Annual.

Money Market Directory of Pension Funds and Their Investment Managers. Charlottesville, VA: Money Market Directories. This directory covers 48,000 organizations managing $4.3 trillion in assets. There are sections for funds and investment managers and indexes by geography as well as rankings by assets and by tax-exempt funds under management. Investment managers are listed by type of activity (e.g., global custodians, international investment services, 401K/defined contribution service providers, investment manager consultants, etc.). Annual.

Nelson's Directory of Investment Managers. Port Chester, NY: Nelson Publications. Two thousand investment management firms profiled, including key executives, organizational overviews, affiliations, specialties, asset and location, clients, decision-making process, fees, and holdings. Indexes by geography, total assets managed, investment managers by organization, type of investment, specialties, and products offered. Additional index by minority- and woman-owned investment managers. Annual.

Nelson's World's Best Money Managers. Port Chester, NY: Nelson Publications. Comprehensive survey of institutional money managers. Rankings include the top ten, twenty, forty managers in all areas of financial management including U.S. and international equity, growth, small cap, large cap, fixed income, etc. Ratings based on results of the Performance Presentation Standards of the Association for Investment Management and Research. Annual.

Pratt's Guide to Venture Capital Sources. New York: Securities Data Publishing, Inc. Signed articles on the background of venture capital, how to raise venture capital, and sources of financing and business development. Profiles of U.S. venture capital firms are listed by state and include contact names, type of firm, type of financing, annual sales, geographic location, industry, and project preferences. There is a separate section of foreign firms, reflecting the growing globalization of venture capital. Indexes by company, personal name, industry preference, and stage preference. Annual.

REIT Handbook: The Complete Guide to the Real Estate Investment Trust Industry. Washington, DC: National Association of Real Estate Investment Trusts, Inc. Alphabetical listing of member profiles includes officers, stock exchange information, trustees and directors, description of business investments, assets, most recent public offerings and private placement of debt and equity, liabilities and shareholder equity, and investment research companies. Industry statistics included. Annual.

Securities Industry Yearbook. New York: Securities Industry Association. Ranking of 700+ Securities Industry Association members by capital, number of offices, employees, and registered representatives. The major section is alphabetical by firm and includes parent companies, major subsidiaries, number of offices, employees, customer accounts, registered representatives, year founded, form of ownership, senior management and department heads, and capital position. Industry trends and statistics. Annual.

Standard & Poor's Security Dealers of North America. New York: Standard & Poor's Corporation. Brokers, distributors, dealers, and underwriters listed geographically and alphabetically. Data include officers, exchange and association membership, type of business, employer's industry number, and number of employees. There is a separate listing for foreign offices and representatives, new addresses, and discontinued firms. Semiannual.

The Venture Report Guide to Venture Capital In The UK & Europe: How and Where to Raise Risk Capital. Henley on Thames, Oxon: Venture Capital Report. Introductory sections include detailed information on preparing business plans and personal experience of entrepreneurs.

Profiles of UK venture capital firms include firm history, sources of funds, fees, decision-making process, key management, and profiles of investments. There are indexes of investees, people, and investors. Annual.

Periodicals

The Asian Venture Capital Journal. Hong Kong: AVCJ. Monthly.

Buyouts. New York, NY: Securities Data Pub. Twenty-five issues/year.

European Venture Capital Journal. New York, NY: Securities Data Publishing, Inc. Bimonthly.

Financial World. NY: Financial World Partners. Eighteen issues/year. [Also available on the Internet: http://www.financialworld.com/]

Futures: The Magazine of Commodities and Options. Cedar Falls, IA.: Commodities Magazine. Fifteen issues/year.

Going Public: The IPO Reporter. Philadelphia: Howard & Co. Weekly.

Institutional Investor. NY: Institutional Investor. Monthly.

Investment Dealers' Digest. NY: IDD. Weekly.

Investor's Business Daily. [Also available on the Internet: http://www.investors.com/]

Mergers and Acquisitions. NY: IDD. Bimonthly.

NASBIC News. Washington: National Association of Small Business Investment Companies. Biweekly. [Sample issue available on the Internet: http://www.envista.com/nasbic/pubs.html#NEWS1]

Pensions & Investments. Chicago: Crain Communication. Biweekly.

Private Equity Analyst. West Newton, MA: Asset Alternatives, Inc. Monthly.

Red Herring. San Francisco: Flipside Communications. Monthly. [Also available on the Internet: http://www.herring.com/home.html]

Start-Up. Belgium: European Seed Capital Fund Network. Quarterly.

Upside. Foster City, CA.: Upside Pub. Co. Monthly. [Also available on the Internet: http://www.upside.com/]

Venture Capital Journal. NY: Venture Capital Journal. Monthly.

Finance Sites on the Web

The following categories are not intended to be exclusive. Many of the sites listed cover more than one topical area. Annotations are provided to give an idea of the information and links contained in these sites.

Associations

Association for Investment Management and Research
[http://www.aimr.com/]
The Association for Investment Management and Research is an international, nonprofit organization of investment professionals and educators with 27,000 members. It is the certifying organization for Chartered Financial Analysts. Information about and publications of the association are included.

The American Risk and Insurance Association
[http://www.riskweb.com/jri.htm]
The Web site for this association covers articles on risk and insurance theory and issues. Abstracts from 1986-present are searchable by keyword.

Financial Executives Institute
[http://www.fei.org/]
FEI is an organization of 14,000 CFOs, controllers, treasurers, and finance VPs for U.S. and Canadian companies. Information is provided on association conferences, technical issues, publications, career services, and legislative/regulatory issues.

National Association of Real Estate Investment Trusts
[http://www.nareit.com/]
This site provides information on the performance of the REIT industry as well as articles on the industry and information on conferences and activities of the association.

National Association of Securities Dealers, Inc.
[http://www.nasd.com/]
NASD is the largest securities-industry self-regulatory organization in the United States. The Web site has sections on individual investor services, public policy, academic research, market data and research, and services.

Securities Industry Association
[http://www.sia.com/]
SIA is a trade association for North American securities firms. There is a list of members with links to their home pages, articles, and issue briefs.

Banking/Investment Banking/Brokers

Brokers and Brokerage Firms
[http://www.moneypages.com/syndicate/finance/broker.html]
The Syndicate's list of links to dozens of brokerage firms.

Wall Street Net
[http://www.netresource.com/wsn/]
Wall Street Net offers up-to-date information on corporate debt and equity financing. Includes sections on featured financings, done deals, deals in registration, international data, mergers & acquisitions, league tables, banks, accounting firms, and stock exchanges. Much of the information on deals is searchable by: investment bank, instrument type, industry category, and company name.

Career Information

Bloomberg Financial Markets
[http://www.bloomberg.com/fun/jobs.html]
Bloomberg's Web site provides job listings in the field of finance as well as a sampling of information found in its full on-line version.

Business Job Finder. Ohio State University.
[http://www.cob.ohio-state.edu/dept/fin/osujobs.html]
This comprehensive site for information about finance jobs is a good starting place. Covers accounting, finance, and consulting. Information is provided about job descriptions, salaries, print resources, future outlook, and leading employers. Areas covered include: accounting, commercial banking, corporate finance, insurance and risk management, management consulting, management and financial planning, and real estate.

CareerMosaic
[http://www.careermosaic.com/]
The job listings on CareerMosaic are searchable by city, state, and country as well as by company, position, and description (it sometimes helps to put "MBA" in the description field).

CareerPath
[http://www.careerpath.com]
CareerPath has classified job listings from the *Boston Globe, Chicago Tribune, Los Angeles Times, Philadelphia Enquirer, San Jose Mercury News, South Florida Sun-Sentinel, and Washington Post* and many other newspapers. Listings are searchable by individual newspaper, keyword, and job category.

Monster Board
[http://www.monster.com/home.html]
The career search section of the Monster Board allows you to search job postings by state, industry, company, and job title.

National Association of Colleges and Employers
[http://www.jobweb.org/]
The National Association of Colleges and Employers JobWeb has links to employment centers, colleges and universities, jobs, job search and industry information, and career planning information.

Whalebone MBA Search
[http://www.mbasearch.com/]
This site is geared specifically toward MBAs. Jobs can be searched by job function, region, or city. There is also a resume posting service.

Company Information - General

Fortune 500
[http://pathfinder.com/@@fCP9fgYAypTBZx7n/fortune/1996/specials/f500/f500.html]
The full Fortune 500 listings are available and can be downloaded into spreadsheet format.

Fortune Global 500
[http://pathfinder.com/@@TmriWwYAy5RR3Ume/fortune/1996/specials/g500/intro.html]
The full Fortune 500 Global listings are available and can be downloaded into spreadsheet format.

Hoover's Online
[http://www.hoovers.com/]
Search Hoover's database for brief company profiles. From the company profile, link to financial statements, news, and quotes for the selected company.

NETworth Equities Center
[www.networth.galt.com/www/home/equity/irr/]
NETworth Equities Center has links to all public companies with home pages and also offers a quote service.

U.S. Securities and Exchange Commission EDGAR Database
[http://www.sec.gov/edgarhp.htm]
Full-text SEC filings for public companies are available through the EDGAR database. The EDGAR archives cover from 1994 to the present for all documents that are filed electronically with the SEC.

Yahoo's Business and Economy
[http://www.yahoo.com/Business_and_Economy/Companies/]
Yahoo, the Internet search engine, also has links to companies in over 100 industry categories in its companies page.

Finance and Economics - General

Corporate Finance Network (CorpFiNet)
[http://www.corpfinet.com/welcome.html]
CorpFiNet is a comprehensive source for locating corporate and commercial finance sources on the Internet. There are articles and features as well as links by subject category.

Finance and Insurance
[http://www.lib.lsu.edu/bus/finance.html]
Louisiana State University has a wealth of links to many areas of finance. Some of the more unique categories are banking, bankruptcy, economic and corporate research reports, U.S. and international financial directories, bonds/treasuries, currency exchange rates, initial public offerings, insurance, journals and scholarly publications, U.S. and international stock markets, and the Uniform Commercial Code.

FINWeb: a financial economics www server
[http://www.finweb.com/]
FINWeb is a financial economics Web site whose primary objective is to list Internet resources providing substantive information on economics and finance-related topics. Some of the areas covered are: journals, working papers, financial databases, and other finance and World Wide Web servers.

Institute of Finance and Banking at the University of Göttingen
[http://www.wiso.gwdg.de/ifbg/ifbghome.html]
There are links to international business sources on the Web, including financial markets, financial management, financial services, education in finance, banking and banks of the world (includes country-by-country links to banks).

The Syndicate Finance Pages
[http://www.moneypages.com/syndicate/finance/index.html]
This investment-related Web site is designed to help investors find information. This section of the Web site has the Syndicate's top picks for categories such as accounting and taxes, bonds, brokerage firms and brokers, economics, foreign, newsletters, personal finance, and stock research and forecasts.

General Business Information

Baker Library Home Page
[http://library.hbs.edu/]
Baker Library's home page has links to many business and financial internet resources.

Government - Finance

Federal Reserve Board
[http://www.bog.frb.fed.us/]
The Board of Governors of the Federal Reserve System's Web site has links to all Federal Reserve Bank home and some foreign central banks. There are articles from the *Federal Reserve Bulletin* and many other publications and research papers.

FinanceNet
[http://www.financenet.gov/]
This site is associated with Vice President Gore's office of the National Performance Review in Washington, D.C. FinanceNet provides links and information for public and private sector financial management professionals in federal, state, and local government, academia and industry on issues of fiscal management and responsibility. There are also listings of government asset sales, news, and links to government jobs, federal CFOs, BudgetNet, electronic commerce, and more.

U.S. Department of the Treasury
[http://www.ustreas.gov/]
The Treasury Department has sections for each of its bureaus (Public Debt, IRS, Financial Management Service, U.S. Mint, etc.).

Market Information

American Stock Exchange
[http://www.amex.com/]
The American Stock Exchange provides market summaries, news, links to listed companies, and information on options & derivatives.

Bloomberg Financial Markets
[http://www.bloomberg.com/]
Bloomberg's Web site provides job listings in the field of finance as well as a sampling of information found in its full on-line version.

Chicago Board of Trade
[http://www.cbot.com/]
The Board of Trade has a chart watch, trend analysis, and a live broadcast of the latest monthly crop report. There are also many links to market information sites and news and commentary sites for commodities.

Chicago Mercantile Exchange
[http://www.cme.com/]
Information from the CME News Center and sections on Products and Prices, About the Exchange, Educational Resources, and CME Member Firms.

Nasdaq
[www.nasdaq.com]
Nasdaq has a quote service, Nasdaq index activity and information, and market news as well as sections on Nasdaq listing standards and shareholders' survey.

New York Stock Exchange
[http://www.nyse.com/]
The New York Stock Exchange Web site provides news, links to listed companies, glossary, and daily market summary.

PCQuote
[http://www.pcquote.com/]
PCQuote's MarketSmart Real-Time is the first investor Web site to offer free unlimited interactive access to real-time stock, option, and commodity quotes.

Quote.com
[www.quote.com/]
In addition to real-time quotes, there are links to earnings estimates, mutual fund reports by Morningstar, and news.

Security APL Quote Server
[http://www.secapl.com/cgi-bin/qs]
This Web site provides stock quotes (15 minute delay) as well as a market watch (Nasdaq, S&P and others).

Stockmaster
[http://www.stockmaster.com/]
Stockmaster offers free comprehensive quotes and charts on U.S. stocks and mutual funds.

World-Wide Web OnLine Market Data
[http://www.nd.edu/~keating/marketdata/market.html]
This page from the Department of Finance and Business Economics at the University of Notre Dame has a wealth of links for financial exchanges (including quotes), news services, commercial financial markets sources, and government financial market sources.

Mutual Funds

NETworth Mutual Fund Market Manager
[http://networth.galt.com/www/home/mutual/]
NETworth provides Morningstar Mutual Fund profiles and current mutual fund quotes as well as mutual fund related news. Mutual funds are searchable by investment and return criteria.

News

Corporate News on the Net
[http://www.businesswire.com/]
Current news for Business Wire member companies.

CNNfn: the financial network
[http://www.cnnfn.com/]
Cable News Network Financial News has daily news articles and briefs on business, finance, and the economy.

Financial Times
[http://www.usa.ft.com/]
The Financial Times Web site has the day's leading stories as well international market quotes and index reports.

Investor's Business Daily
[http://www.investors.com/]
Investor's Business Daily provides news analysis and information on companies, industries, the economy, and national issues. Full-text articles are available in the web version and previous issues are searchable by keyword.

PR Newswire
[www.prnewswire.com/]
PR Newswire offers the latest press releases on companies, industries, and executives. Releases are from participating PR Newswire members.

RCM Financial Group LLC
[http://www.rcmfinancial.com/fin_news.htm]
There are numerous links to financial and business news sites, including audio news, U.S. regional news, and international news. Also included are several search options from within the site.

Wall Street Journal Interactive
[http://www.wsj.com/]
Up-to-date coverage of the top stories in business and finance. News and information from *The Wall Street Journal, The Asian Wall Street Journal,* and *The Wall Street Journal Europe.* Also includes information on investing, taxes, college financing, retirement planning, and other

personal finance topics. Available by subscription, free during a trial period.

Venture Capital

Capital Venture
[http://www.capitalventure.com/]
Capital Venture, a "trade association" for venture capital and related professionals, provides links to venture capital firms on the web. Also included are Capital Venture happenings, private equity 101 (an overview of venture capital), private equity jobs listings, and information on how to get a job in venture capital.

FinanceHub
[http://www.FinanceHub.com/welcomec.html]
FinanceHub is a site for entrepreneurs and investors that has links to venture capital sites on the Web, banks, and stock market among other categories.

Kauffman Fellows
[http://www.emkf.org/fellows/index.html]
The Kauffman Fellows program is a venture capital fellowship designed to immerse fellows in the venture capital process. The program is conducted by venture capitalists, entrepreneurs, and scholars, and sponsored by the Ewing Marion Kauffman Foundation.

Mailing List

This is a mailing list of the firms profiled in this book. Entries are arranged alphabetically by firm and contain the name of the MBA recruiting contact, firm, address, and phone number. Some entries contain alternate contacts. Please refer to the company profile to see if another contact would be more appropriate for you. Before sending letters to the firms on the list, always call to verify the address and the name of the recruiting contact.

Barbara H. Boyle
A.G. Edwards & Sons, Inc.
One North Jefferson
St. Louis, MO 63103
(314) 955-3691

Anne Ford
Alex. Brown & Sons, Inc.
135 East Baltimore Street
Baltimore, MD 21202
(800) 638-2596

Rachel Goldgrob
Banco Pactual S.A.
Av. Rep. do Chile, 230/29° andar
Rio de Janeiro-RJ, 20.031-170
Brazil
(55-21) 272-1300

Debbie Barry
Bankers Trust
130 Liberty Street
New York, NY 10006

Jennifer Rolnick
Bear, Stearns & Co. Inc.
245 Park Avenue
New York, NY 10167
(212) 272-7749

Matthew B. Salisbury
Bowles Hollowell Conner & Co.
227 West Trade Street
Charlotte, NC 28202
(704) 348-1015

Bonnie Frankel
Broadview Associates, LLC
One Bridge Plaza
Fort Lee, NJ 07024
(201) 346-9000

Donna Freet
BT Wolfensohn
599 Lexington Avenue
New York, NY 10022
(212) 909-0878

Jessica Dwerryhouse
BZW
5 The North Colonnade
Canary Wharf
London E14 4BB
England
(44) 171-623-2323

Annette Cuffley
The Chase Manhattan Corporation
270 Park Avenue
New York, NY 10017
(212) 270-7072

Donald Paiva
Chevron Corporation
575 Market Street
Suite 3438
San Francisco, CA 94105
(415) 894-2752

Sheila Cull
Credit Suisse First Boston
11 Madison Avenue
New York, NY 10010
(212) 325-7758

Charles A. Kennedy
Dain Bosworth Incorporated
60 South Sixth Street
Minneapolis, MN 55402
(612) 371-2863

Sarah Seaman
Deutsche Morgan Grenfell
31 West 52nd Street
New York, NY 10019
(212) 469-8459

J. Morton Davis
D.H. Blair Investment Banking Corp.
44 Wall Street
New York, NY 10005
(212) 495-5000

Elizabeth Derby
Donaldson, Lufkin & Jenrette
277 Park Avenue
New York, NY 10172
(212) 892-7217

Cindy Shiffler
Enron
1400 Smith Street
Houston, TX 77002
(713) 853-6402

Mark Knakowski
First Marathon Securities Limited
The Exchange Tower
2 First Canadian Place
Suite 3200, Box 21
Toronto, Ontario M5X 1J9
Canada
(416) 869-3707

FMC College Relations
FMC Corporation
200 East Randolph Drive
Chicago, IL 60601
(312) 861-6000

Malcolm Macdonald
Ford Motor Company
World Headquarters Building
11th Floor—East Wing
The American Road
Dearborn, MI 48121
(313) 323-0850

Diane Kopyscianski
Furman Selz LLP
230 Park Avenue
New York, NY 10169
(212) 309-8653

Niharika Tasker
General Motors Corporation
GM Building
767 Fifth Avenue
New York, NY 10153
(212) 418-6193

Jide J. Zeitlin
Goldman, Sachs & Co.
85 Broad Street
New York, NY 10004
(212) 902-1000

Laurence H. Lebowitz
HBK Investments L.P.
777 Main Street, Suite 2750
Fort Worth, TX 76102
(817) 870-6100

Employment Response Center
Hewlett-Packard Company
3000 Hanover Street/MS: 20APP
Palo Alto, CA 94304
(415) 852-8473

IBM Staffing Services
IBM Corporation
3808 Six Forks Road
Raleigh, NC 27609
(800) 964-4473

Cornelis de Kievit
The International Finance Corporation
2121 Pennsylvania Avenue, NW
Room 11K-290
Washington, DC 20433
(202) 473-7972

Andrea Beldecos
J.P. Morgan & Co. Incorporated
60 Wall Street
New York, NY 10260
(212) 483-2323

Rita Haring
Lehman Brothers
Three World Financial Center
New York, NY 10285
(212) 526-4162

Roslyn N. Dickerson
Merrill Lynch & Co., Inc.
World Financial Center
250 Vesey Street
New York, NY 10281
(212) 449-8790

Maggie Woodward
Montgomery Securities
600 Montgomery Street
San Francisco, CA 94111
(415) 627-2314

Bruce Cohen
Morgan Stanley & Co. Incorporated
1585 Broadway
New York, NY 10036
(212) 761-4000

Stanley Merriwether
NationsBank
100 N. Tryon Street
NC1007-21-10
Charlotte, NC 28255
(704) 386-4258

Jeff Watchorn
Nesbitt Burns Inc.
1 First Canadian Place
4th Floor
P.O. Box 150
Toronto, Ontario M5X 1H3
Canada
(416) 359-4000

Human Resources Department
Nomura Securities International, Inc.
2 World Financial Center
Building B
New York, NY 10281

Kelly A. Decker
PaineWebber Incorporated
1285 Avenue of the Americas
New York, NY 10019
(212) 713-3406

Diane Coffey
Peter J. Solomon Company
767 Fifth Avenue, 26th Floor
New York, NY 10153
(212) 508-1600

Jennifer Piehl
Piper Jaffray Inc.
222 South Ninth Street
Minneapolis, MN 55402
(612) 342-6000

Gerald K. Hwasta
Raymond James & Associates, Inc.
880 Carillon Parkway
St. Petersburg, FL 33716

H. Martin Kent
RBC Dominion Securities Inc.
P.O. Box 50
Royal Bank Plaza, South Tower
Toronto, Ontario M5J 2W7
Canada
(416) 842-7588

Pam Smith
The Robinson-Humphrey Company, Inc.
Atlanta Financial Center
3333 Peachtree Road, NE
Atlanta, GA 30326
(404) 266-6919

Stephen L. Shapiro
Rothschild Canada Limited
1 First Canadian Place
Suite 3800
P.O. Box 77
Toronto, Ontario M5X 1B1
Canada
(416) 369-9600

Maureen Horan
Salomon Brothers Inc.
Seven World Trade Center
New York, NY 10048
(212) 783-5924

Basil Bliss
Schroder Wertheim & Co. Incorporated
787 Seventh Avenue
New York, NY 10019
(212) 492-6290

Matthew R. Simmons
Simmons & Company International
700 Louisiana, Suite 5000
Houston, TX 77002
(713) 236-9999

Chip Rae
Smith Barney Inc.
388 Greenwich Street
New York, NY 10013
(212) 816-1764

Patricia B. Davis
Stonebridge Associates, LLC
Ten Post Office Square
Suite 1330
Boston, MA 02109
(617) 357-1770

Robert J. Burke
Teachers Insurance and Annuity Association-College Retirement Equities Fund (TIAA-CREF)
730 Third Avenue
New York, NY 10017
(800) 842-2733

Reginald A. McQuay
Toronto Dominion Bank
31 West 52nd Street
New York, NY 10019-6101
(212) 468-0633

Erica Blechschmidt
UBS Securities LLC
299 Park Avenue
New York, NY 10171
(212) 821-4080

Jim Rynott
United Airlines
P.O. Box 66100
Chicago, IL 60666
(708) 952-4000

Frances A. Lyman
Wasserstein Perella & Co. Inc.
31 West 52nd Street
New York, NY 10019
(212) 969-2700

Lisa Hoffmann
Wessels, Arnold & Henderson
601 Second Avenue South
Suite 3100
Minneapolis, MN 55402
(612) 373-6100

Brian L. Haun
Weyerhaeuser Company
Tacoma, WA 98477
(206) 924-2367

Jack Glover
Wheat First Butcher Singer
901 East Byrd Street
Riverfront Plaza
Richmond, VA 23219
(804) 782-3516

Brent Felitto
William Blair & Company
222 West Adams Street
Chicago, IL 60606
(312) 364-8013

Young Professionals Program Administrator
The World Bank
1818 H Street, NW
Washington, DC 20433
(202) 473-0312

Industry Index